LESSONS FROM THE VIETNAM WAR

Truths the Media Never Told You

Leonard M. Scruggs

Warren Publishing, Inc.

Disclaimer: This book contains true case histories. In order to preserve the privacy of the people involved, we have made changes in locales, names, and certain aspects of the personal stories so they are not identifiable. Any resemblance to any persons, living or dead is strictly coincidental.

Published by Warren Publishing, Inc.
www.warrenpublishing.net

ISBN: 9781886057951

Library of Congress Catalog Number:
2009930881

Printed in the United States of America

DEDICATION

This book is dedicated to all those who have served their people in the defense of truth, justice, liberty, honor, and the common good. May their posterity take up their cause with tenacious determination and courage and may the Author of these sacred principles vindicate their suffering, toil, and blood.

CONTENTS

CHAPTERS

APPENDIX CHAPTERS

LESSONS FROM THE VIETNAM WAR

Truths the Media Never Told You

FOREWORD

The Battle for Historical Perspective

The late Harry G. Summers, Jr., Colonel of Infantry and distinguished faculty member of the Army War College, often called people's attention to the fact that considerable differences in the treatment of the Vietnam War can be seen in the literature published in academia and that published by the veterans who served during the war. Summers also called attention to the fact that the perspective of veterans differs considerably among themselves with respect to the time frame of their involvement. U.S. involvement in the war started in a counterinsurgency role, but we were soon involved in trying to hurl back major North Vietnamese Army (NVA) offenses, starting with Ia Drang in 1965 and ending with the NVA's heavily mechanized Easter Offensive in 1972. Only a handful of Americans were in South Vietnam during the early 1975 NVA offensive that finally crushed a South Vietnamese Army in desperate need of ammunition and equipment. Their perspective also differs according to their operational exposure—whether they were slugging the war out in the infantry or artillery, off-loading cargo at Cam Ran Bay, flying off aircraft carriers to hit targets in North Vietnam, making strafing runs on enemy trucks along the Ho Chi Minh Trail, or dropping 30,000 pound loads of explosives on railroad marshalling yards near Hanoi.

Besides academics and soldiers, journalists and politicians have also made their contribution to understanding or misunderstanding the war. Michael Lind, though a self-described liberal, has also observed the ideological bias of academic writers, noting academia's still strong connection to the anti-war mythologies of the 1960s.

"For the most part, the academics, journalists, editors, and producers who opposed the Vietnam War came from the core constituencies of the post-sixties Democratic Party. As a result, the consensus story that the liberal left told about the Vietnam War in particular and the Cold War in general combined themes from both the *(secularized)* northern Protestant progressive tradition and the radical leftist mythology." [1]

(The italicized parenthetic insertion describing the northern Protestant progressive tradition as *secularized* is mine, but in other paragraphs Lind indicates his agreement with this assessment.)

The modern intellectual straight-jacket of political correctness has tended to strengthen the pervasiveness of anti-war folklore in American academia and much of the media. Though it is largely disinformation, it has unfortunately had considerable impact on the conventional wisdom about the Vietnam War. Most books on Vietnam, whether by solders, journalists, academics, or politicians, tend to fall on either side of a realist-conservative worldview or an idealist-liberal worldview. Lind manages to straddle that divide in many areas and so is a refreshing break from the chains of political correctness.

President Richard Nixon, in his 1985 book, *No More Vietnams,* devotes a substantial portion of his book to exploding the mythology of the anti-war left on Vietnam. Summers also addresses many of these issues, as do the writings of Admiral U.S. Grant Sharp, Army Lt. Gen. Dave Palmer, Army Maj. Gen. Thomas Lane, and former Army intelligence officer, Louis A. Fanning.

Some of the more easily recognized articles of misguided academic faith about the Vietnam War are:

- The war in Vietnam was immoral.
- The war in Vietnam was unwinnable.
- Diplomacy without force is an effective strategy for peace.
- We were on the wrong side of history in Vietnam.
- The Vietnam War was a Civil War.
- Ho Chi Minh was a popular nationalist first and a Communist second.
- The National Liberation Front and Viet Cong were independent from North Vietnam.
- Airpower was an ineffective and inappropriate weapon to defeat the Communist threat to South Vietnam.
- It was the calculated policy of the U.S. to bomb civilian targets.
- U.S. and South Vietnamese incursions into Cambodian and Laotian sanctuaries were a needless expansion of the war.
- The 1954 Geneva Declaration bound South Vietnam and the U.S. to unify the two halves of Vietnam by elections.
- The Buddhist protests against the Diem regime in 1962 and 1963 resulted from religious suppression of Buddhists.
- The United States lost the war militarily.
- Anti-war demonstrations had no connections to Communist front organizations or radical New Left organizers.
- The domino theory that the security of Southeast Asia would be threatened by the fall of South Vietnam was false.
- Conventional Army and Marine fire-power was not effective against guerilla insurgents.
- The Vietnam War was from first to last a guerilla war.

- There were no significant consequences to U.S. withdrawal and Communist victory to the people of South Vietnam, Cambodia, and Laos.
- There were no significant international consequences to Communist takeover of Indochina.
- Communism is a harmless ideology.
- The South Vietnamese Army remained ineffective and unmotivated to resist the Communist threat throughout the war.
- The South Vietnamese people were largely indifferent to whether Hanoi or Saigon ruled them.
- Corruption in the South Vietnamese government was so prevalent that it precluded sustained military and political resistance to North Vietnam.

None of these common academic and media assertions about the Vietnam War are true, but they are still widely believed. None of them have a substantive factual or historical basis. Many of them are ideological preconceptions. Some are rationalizations. Some are based on twisted half-truths. Some are outright propaganda designed to deceive the American people.

Fanning's 1976 book, *Betrayal in Vietnam*, makes a unique contribution by tracing and documenting some of the connections of the anti-war movement to their Communist and radical left origins. My contention is not that every anti-war demonstrator or sympathizer had such connections, but that the left was very active in organizing and influencing the direction of the anti-war movement. Judging from internet sources, there is a scarcity of reliable information available on the organizations involved, many of which were of a changing or fleeting nature. Hence there is much confusion on organizations, leaders, and objectives.

Robert McNamara's 1995 book, *In Retrospect: The Tragedy and Lessons of Vietnam*, makes clear his dovish inclinations and influence on President Johnson from the very beginning of the war. On military matters, he was the personification of un-teachable academic bias. Hence his relationships became strained with the Joint Chiefs and especially Admiral Sharp, the supreme Pacific Area Commander (CINCPAC) from 1964 to 1968. I came into the Air Force as an intelligence officer in 1961, just nine months following Kennedy's inauguration and McNamara's appointment as Secretary of Defense. Even many junior officers came to think of McNamara as devoted to mindless quantitative decision making. He seemed oblivious of human nature and the accumulated experience and wisdom of generations of American soldiers. This was true in everything from personnel policy to force deployment and strategy. McNamara consistently resisted anything more than the tactical use of air power in South Vietnam. His limited and restrained bombing of North Vietnam was designed to signal Hanoi's leaders that it was time to negotiate. But his policy of only gradually expanding target priorities and the intensity of air strikes sent a different message to Hanoi. What such restraint really signaled to the North Vietnamese was a lack of American resolve. Johnson's sixteen bombing halts added to that impression.

Following his removal as Defense Secretary, McNamara became an outright critic of the war, but I believe this was where his heart was all along. In his book, McNamara indicated that he did not believe political stability in South Vietnam was possible or that the South Vietnamese, even with our training and logistical support, were capable of defending themselves. Unremarkably, many of his lessons from the Vietnam War conformed to the academic mindset and many of the anti-war myths, especially that the war was unwinnable—a self-fulfilling prophesy under his administration as Defense Secretary.

A serious shortcoming of many books on the Vietnam War, especially among academics and journalists, but also among some military authors, is confusion about the effectiveness of airpower in the war. There is a common assertion that airpower was proven ineffective based on the great cost and tonnage of explosives expended without corresponding results. This, however, confuses the Johnson-McNamara misuse of airpower in Operation Rolling Thunder with the forceful and decisive use of airpower consistently advocated by Admiral Sharp and the JCS and finally implemented by Nixon in 1972. Operation Rolling Thunder wasted a large part of our fighter-bomber force in highly restricted and restrained attacks on heavily defended secondary targets. Admiral Sharp referred to this as a "powder-puff" use of our most potent means of warfare.[2] Air Force General Momyer complained that it was a good way to maximize our cost and not the enemy's. When in 1972, Nixon finally used Navy and USAF airpower to mine enemy ports and devastate strategic targets in North Vietnam, Hanoi's leaders were brought to their knees and sought to negotiate in earnest. We were in a position to demand unconditional surrender, but our great victory was not fully grasped by a Congressional majority. It was finally thrown away when Congress abandoned South Vietnam and Cambodia to the Communists in 1975.

The clearest picture of military frustration over McNamara's policy of timid gradualism in air warfare can be found in Admiral Sharp's 1978 book, *Strategy for Defeat.*

Nixon's spectacular victory over North Vietnam was the result of Operation Linebacker I from May through October 1972 and then the climactic B-52 knock-out punch of Linebacker II in December 1972. The most complete work on Linebacker II is Marshall Michel's 2002 book, *The Eleven Days of Christmas: America's Last Vietnam Battle.*

4

Lt. Gen. Dave Palmer's 1978 book, *Summons of the Trumpet; U.S.— Vietnam in Perspective*, is a very useful narrative of the key events of the war from the history of Indochina to the fall of South Vietnam and Cambodia and beyond. It is written with a keen insight for major issues, major turning points, and both tactical and strategic operations. It is the quickest way to get a sound overall understanding of the war.

The 1968 Tet Offensive was a critical political turning point in the war and deserves special attention. Don Oberdorfer, formerly with the *Washington Post*, gives a dramatic and gripping account of Tet and many interesting and significant details of its impact on Johnson's closest advisors. The most useful research and analysis to me, however, was found in James H. Willbanks' more recent concise history, *The Tet Offensive*, published in 2007. Willbanks is Director of the Department of Military History at the Army Command and General Staff College. Willbanks had the advantage of having the most recent translations of North Vietnamese documents on Tet. He also gives a concise treatment of various views of both the military and political aspects of the Tet Offensive.

H. R. McMaster's 1997 book, *Dereliction of Duty*, dwells upon the alleged failure of the JCS to dissuade Johnson and McNamara from their disastrous policies and strategy. Many junior officers in all the services frequently asked among themselves why their generals and admirals stood for what surely seemed like a "strategy for defeat." However, I believe McMaster, who did not graduate from West Point until more than ten years after the war was over, overstates his case against the JCS. Admiral Sharp was persistent in his attempts to persuade McNamara to dispense with timid gradualism. The JCS supported Sharp, not McNamara.[3] The conservative Senate Armed Forces Committee recognized the conflict between the JCS and McNamara and rebuked McNamara who was soon sent packing to minimize Johnson's political embarrassment. Many high-ranking officers were frustrated or even appalled by McNamara's policies, but they did not feel the country would be well served by falling on their swords and allowing McNamara to replace them with officers more sympathetic to his aberrant thinking.

The account of the My Lai massacre is covered extensively in the appendix. One of the unfortunate results of the My Lai investigation is that it became a battle ground of ideological conflict with the left trying to exploit it for anti-war propaganda, and many well-meaning people on the right trying to deny or excuse it. For the gruesome details of the massacre and many details about the personnel involved, *Four Hours in My Lai*, by Michael Bilton and Kevin Sim is a good reference. It also covers the heroism of Warrant Officer Hugh Thompson and others in opposing the massacre as it progressed. For understanding the legal challenge of the trials, Michael Belknap's *The Vietnam*

War on Trial is an excellent reference, but assumes the truth of many of the anti-war myths in its general background narrative. Reading the 1970 Peers Commission Report is essential. Very helpful in understanding the causes of My Lai is *Facing My Lai: Moving beyond the Massacre*, a 1998 book edited by David Anderson. Its most impressive contributor is Vietnam author and military strategist, Col. Harry G. Summers.

On the Prisoner of War issues, I cannot recommend more highly the Naval Institute's *Honor Bound* by Stuart Rochester and Frederick Kiley.

One of the most important but little known facts about the Vietnam war, was the terrible slaughter of South Vietnamese and Cambodian civilians following the Communist victory. Civilian deaths are often difficult to estimate, and there are incentives either to exaggerate or to minimize the numbers. An excellent evaluative reference on civilian casualties in war and the murderous records of totalitarian regimes is R. J Rummel's 1994 book, *Death by Government*.

Diplomacy and negotiations, although not often visible to the public, played a huge role in the Vietnam War. Approaches varied from a naive and almost frantic eagerness to negotiate in the Johnson years to increasingly tough-minded negotiations under Nixon.

Nixon, however, had an increasingly anti-war Congress pressuring him to get the U.S. out of the war in a hurry. This forced him to make some serious compromises in negotiating the January 1973 peace accord. These ultimately contributed to the fall of South Vietnam and its tragic aftermath. Two of Henry Kissinger's books, *The White House Years* (1979) and *Years of Renewal* (1999), written with the perspective he developed as National Security Advisor and Secretary of State under Nixon, are riveting accounts of the role that diplomacy and negotiations played in the war.

The most indispensable book on understanding the Vietnam War, in my opinion, is Harry G. Summers' 1982 book: *On Strategy: A Critical Analysis of the Vietnam War*. Summers also wrote two equally indispensable reference books: an almanac on the war in 1985 and a historical atlas of the war in 1995. Before his death in 1999, Summers was recognized by most high-ranking military officers as one the most influential military thinkers that America has ever produced. When he retired from the Army in 1985, he held the Douglas MacArthur Chair of Military Research at the Army War College and was in wide demand as a speaker and writer. He was instrumental in the Army's rediscovery of Carl von Clausewitz's *Principles of War*. Summers was not a West Pointer. He enlisted in the Army at the age of fifteen. In 1950, Corporal Summers, still less than nineteen-years-old, was a machine-gunner assigned to the badly under equipped and outnumbered 24th Infantry Division, facing an invading North Korean Army. He had ten years of service before he was commissioned in 1957. Before being assigned to the Army War College, Summers managed to get two degrees and numerous medals for valor in combat, including the Silver Star. He was on the last helicopter to leave the roof of the American Embassy when Saigon fell to the North Vietnamese Army on April 30, 1975. During the First Iraq War in 1990 and 1991, Summers became a frequent commentator and familiar face on nightly TV news coverage the war. He was dedicated to his country and the truth.

In addition to the three works by Summers cited above, essential reading in understanding the Vietnam War would include: Richard Nixon's 1985 book, *No More Vietnams;* Admiral U.S. Grant Sharp's 1978 book *Strategy for Defeat;* Lt. Gen. Dave Palmer's 1978 book, *Summons of the Trumpet*; Dr. Louis Fanning's 1976 book, *Betrayal in Vietnam; and* though I do not agree with all of it, Michael Lind's 1999 book, *Vietnam: the Necessary War,* and finally James H. Willbanks' 2004 book, *Abandoning Vietnam.*

I believe that, next to the so-called "Civil War" of 1861-65, the Vietnam War is the most misunderstood war in American history. My motivation for writing this book was not only to contribute my own experience to its understanding, but to set the broader historical record straight where it has been obscured or distorted.

Leonard M. Scruggs

GLOSSARY

AA	Antiaircraft
AAA	Antiaircraft Artillery
AFB	Air Force Base
Air Commandos	USAF units engaged in special air warfare including: counterinsurgency, night armed reconnaissance, and close ground support. Typical aircraft used were the A-1E, A-26/B-26, AC-47, AC-119, AC-130, C-47, C-123, O-1, and O-2.
Americal Division	Nickname for U.S. Army 23rd Infantry Division
ARVN	Army of the Republic of Vietnam (South Vietnamese Army).
Chaff	A radar countermeasure to confuse radar controlled SAM and antiaircraft batteries, generally consisting of a cloud of tiny pieces aluminum or metalized fibers released by electronic countermeasures aircraft.
Chinese Nung People	An ethnic Chinese minority in Vietnam going back over 2,000 years. They speak the Cantonese language of Southern China and are largely urban. They were especially concentrated around Saigon and dominated many commercial interests. Over 250,000 were forced out of or fled the country after the Communist takeover in 1975.
CIA	Central Intelligence Agency
CID	Army Criminal Investigation Division
CIDG	Civilian Irregular Defense Group. Local South Vietnamese defense forces organized in minority ethnic regions of the country by U.S. Army Special Forces teams (Green Berets). These were especially important in the predominantly Montagnard Central Highlands. Over 40,000 Montagnard villagers served in CIDG units. Most of these were converted into South Vietnamese Army Ranger units in 1970.
CINCPAC	Commander-in-Chief, Pacific Area Command

CO	Commanding Officer
CPUSA	Communist Party in the United States.
Dolphins	Nickname for troop-carrying helicopters, typically UH-1 liftships carrying 9-12 combat troops.
DMZ	Demilitarized Zone—a narrow zone along the 17th Parallel that divided North and South Vietnam in the 1954 Treaty.
ECM	Electronic Countermeasures
ELINT	Electronic intelligence.
EW	Electronic Warfare
EWO	Electronic Warfare Officer-a specialized Navigator
FAC	Forward Air Control from air or ground
FWMF	Free World Military Forces. In addition to American troops, nearly 70,000 other Allied troops assisted South Vietnam. South Korea furnished 49,000; Thailand, 11,500; Australia, 7500 and New Zealand, nearly 600, in a joint Task Force; and the Philippines, nearly 2,000.
Gradualism	Also called **Graduated Escalation, Measured Escalation,** and **"the slow squeeze."** A controversial and unsuccessful doctrine of air warfare espoused by Robert McNamara.
GCA	Ground Controlled Approach for guiding aircraft as they land.
Green Berets	U.S. Army Special Forces teams. See also CIDG.
Hainan	A Chinese island not to be confused with the North Vietnamese cities of Hanoi and Haiphong.
Haiphong	The principal port of North Vietnam and the main initial entry point for Soviet and Chinese logistical support for the war. The approximate population in 2007 was 1,900,000.
Hanoi	The capital city of North Vietnam. The population in 2007 was 3,400,000.
Huey	Nickname for UH-1 Army helicopter.
IG	Inspector General
Indochina	The collective name for Vietnam, Cambodia, and Laos.

JAG	Judge Advocate General, the military legal organization.
JCS	Joint Chiefs of Staff
Jolly Green Giants	Nickname for the large HH-3 and HH-53 rescue helicopters.
KIA	Killed in action.
Khmer Rouge	Communist Cambodian forces
Lamplighter	Call sign for C-130 flare ships illuminating the Ho Chi Minh Trail during night armed reconnaissance missions.
Linebacker I	An extensive USAF and Navy bombing campaign against North Vietnam and an invading NVA force in South Vietnam from May 9 to October 23, 1972. Measures included mining Haiphong harbor for the first time. See Navy Operation Pocket Money.
Linebacker II	An extensive USAF and Navy bombing campaign against North Vietnam in December 1972 using massive B-52 Bomber attacks and devastating North Vietnam's military and economy. As a result, North Vietnam was forced to negotiate a cease-fire and peace agreement effective in January 1973, temporarily ending their major aggressive actions against South Vietnam.
LZ	Landing Zone, particularly for helicopters and paratroopers.
MACV	Military Assistance Command Vietnam (U.S. military headquarters for South Vietnam)
MIA	Missing in Action
MiG	Mikoyan and Gurevich, designers of Soviet fighter aircraft.
MiG-21	The most advanced Soviet fighter aircraft flown by the North Vietnamese Air Force during the war.
MOBE, Mobe	National Mobilization Committee to End the War in Vietnam, established May 1967. Responsible for many anti-war demonstrations including those at the 1968 Democratic Convention in Chicago. See also New Mobe.

Montagnard	A French name meaning "from the Mountains" for the Degar people or tribes native to South Vietnam's Central Highlands, where they formed the great majority of the population until the Communist victory in 1975. More than 70 percent of them were Christian (50 percent Protestant and 20 percent Catholic). Hence they tended to be helpful and friendly to American forces. Many fled following the Communist victory, and the one million remaining constitute only 25 percent of the present population of the Central Highlands. Several thousand were relocated to the United States where they are concentrated in Greensboro, Raleigh, and Charlotte, North Carolina. See also CIDG.
My Lai	A group of hamlets in the Son Mai District of Quang Ngai Province in South Vietnam, associated with the massacre of civilians in March 1968 by a U.S. Army task force.
NCO	Non-commissioned officer, corporals and sergeants.
New Left	An umbrella term for the many left-wing political activist organizations that took root in the 1960's. They became increasingly radical during the Vietnam War and became very influential in the anti-war movement. They differed from the Old Left in their tendency to adopt the counterculture of the 1960s and to concentrate their efforts more on social issues than economic issues. See MOBE, New Mobe, and SDS.
New Mobe	New National Mobilization Committee to End the War in Vietnam, established July 1969 to succeed Mobe. New Mobe wanted to broaden the agenda and appeal of the anti-war movement by relating it to other economic and social issues like poverty and racism.
Nimrod	Call sign of A-26 Air Commando squadron
Nung	See Chinese Nung people.

NLF	National Liberation Front, the Communist political front in South Vietnam associated with the Viet Cong.
NVA	North Vietnamese Army
OCS	Officer Candidate School
Pathet Lao	Communist Laotians
Peers Commission	A special commission headed by Army Lt. Gen. W. R. Peers in November 1969 to investigate the My Lai (Son My) Massacre in March 1968
PDR	People's Democratic Republic (of North Vietnam)
Pocket Money	The U.S. Navy operation that mined North Vietnam's ports in May 1972 and again in December 1972.
POL	Petroleum, oil, and lubricants. Petroleum products and fuels.
POW	Prisoner of War
PRC	People's Republic of China
ROK	Republic of Korea, (South Korea/Korean)
Rolling Thunder	Code name for bombing North Vietnam under the Johnson Administration—governed by Robert McNamara's controversial **Gradualism doctrine** of air warfare. A total of 922 U.S. aircraft were lost over North Vietnam alone.
RVNAF	Republic of (South) Vietnam Armed Forces. See SVNAF.
SA-2	Soviet built surface-to-air missile system used for antiaircraft defenses.
SAC	Strategic Air Command, home command of B-52s.
Saigon	The capital city of South Vietnam, now called Ho Chi Minh City. The population in 2007 was 6,650,000.
SAM	Surface-to-air missile
SDS	Students for a Democratic Society. A radical student and political activist organization prominent in the anti-war movement.
SEA	Southeast Asia

SEAD	Suppression of Enemy Air Defenses. See Wild Weasel.
SEATO	Southeast Asia Treaty Organization. A treaty originally established in 1954 to prevent the spread of Communism in Southeast Asia. Members included the U.S., Great Britain, France, New Zealand, Australia, the Philippines, Thailand and Pakistan. Protected observer members included South Vietnam, Cambodia, and Laos.
Sharks	A nickname for UH-1 helicopter gunships.
Son My	Administrative district of Quang Ngai Province containing the hamlets designated as **My Lai** on U.S. Army maps.
SVNAF	South Vietnamese Armed Forces, consisting of the Army (ARVN), Navy (VNN), Air Force (VNAF), and Marines (VNMC). In addition to these regular units there was a lightly armed Territorial Force consisting of Regional Force (RF) companies and local Popular Force (PF) platoons.
Task Force 77	Task Force 77 is the aircraft carrier battle/strike force of the U.S. Navy Seventh Fleet, a component of the U.S. Pacific Fleet. During the Vietnam War it operated from the Gulf of Tonkin and the South China Sea. It was sometimes known informally as the "Tonkin Gulf Yacht Club."
Tet	The Vietnamese lunar New Year—the main holiday in both North and South Vietnam—which occurs in late January or early February. Celebrations last about a week.
Tet-68	The coordinated general offensive against South Vietnam by North Vietnamese and Viet Cong troops beginning January 30 and lasting about one month. Lesser NVA attacks extended through July.
USAF	United States Air Force
USMC	United States Marine Corp
USN	United States Navy
USSR	Union of Soviet Socialist Republics

VC Viet Cong, South Vietnamese Communist military and para-military organization. Main Force VC units were organized into companies, battalions, regiments, and even divisions. The paramilitary units usually numbered under 30 men. The initial VC cadre were predominantly North Vietnamese who had infiltrated into South Vietnam following the Viet Minh defeat of the French in 1954. South Vietnamese were probably less than 60 percent of the VC prior to the 1968 Tet offensive. Thereafter, the VC were predominantly and increasingly North Vietnamese. The VC were never independent of Hanoi.

Viet Minh Communist political party and forces headed by Ho Chi Minh, opposing French Colonial rule during the First Indochina War.

Vietnam Also spelled Viet-Nam and Viet Nam.

Vietnamization Nixon plan to gradually replace American troops in Vietnam as the South Vietnamese Armed Forces could be increased in strength and properly trained and equipped to deter North Vietnamese aggression on their own.

VNAF (South) Vietnamese Air Force.

WIA Wounded in action.

Wild Weasels F-105G and F-4G aircraft equipped with special radar identification and jamming equipment. Frequently used to locate, identify, and destroy enemy SAM and antiaircraft batteries. See **SEAD.**

WO **Warrant Officer.** Four ranks (WO1 to WO4) between NCOs and officers, typically specialists, including many Army helicopter and observer pilots.

WSO Weapons Systems Officer-a specialized Navigator.

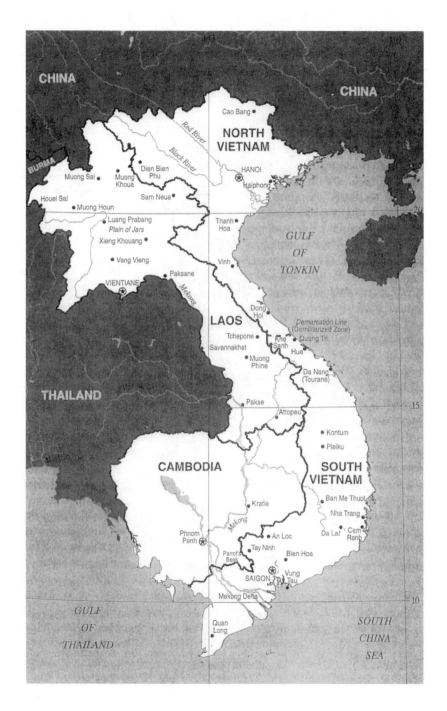

Southeast Asia/Indochina

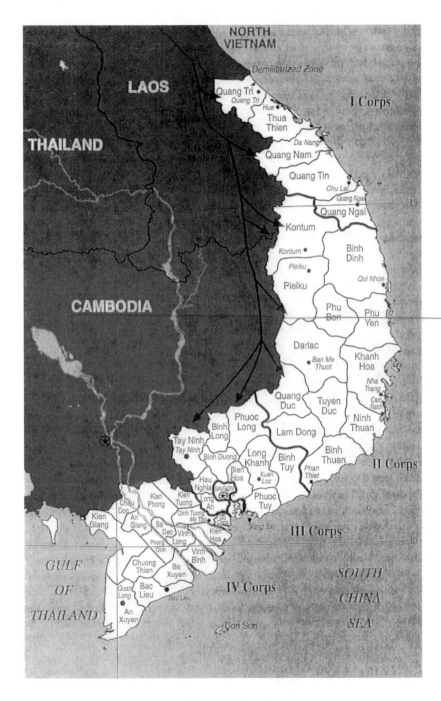

South Vietnam Provinces

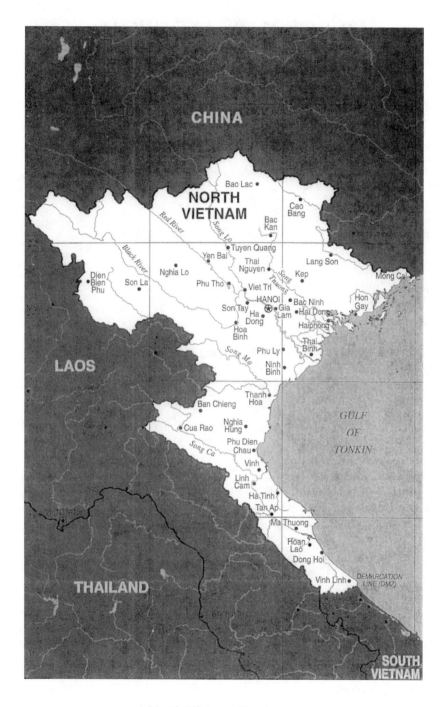

North Vietnam Provinces

LIST OF MAPS AND PHOTOS

MAPS

LIST OF AIRCRAFT PHOTOS BY CHAPTER

Chapter 7 The Great Logistics Race to Ia Drang
US Army UH-1 Huey deplaning troops
US Army UH-1 Gunship
US Army UH-1 Huey deplaning troops on hill

Chapter 10 The 1968 Tet Offensive
USAF AC-47D Spooky
(Puff the Magic Dragon)

Chapter 16 Operation Linebacker I
Navy A-7 Corsair on USS Ranger
USAF B-52D Stratofortress
Navy F-8 Crusader on USS Midway
USAF F-4C Phantom

Chapter 17 Operation Linebacker II
USAF B-52D   Stratofortress
USAF F-111 Aardvark used for SEAD
USAF   F-105F Wild Weasel
Navy A-6 Intruder

Appendix 3 Missing in Action
USAF C-130 Hercules
USAF C-123 Provider

PHOTOGRAPHS OF PERSONS BY CHAPTER

Chapter 1
John F. Kennedy
Nikita Khrushchev
Ho Chi Minh

Chapter 2
Ngo Dinh Diem

Chapter 6
President Lyndon B. Johnson
Sec. of Defense Robert McNamara
Admiral U.S. Grant Sharp, CINCPAC

Gen. Maxwell Taylor
Gen. Earle Wheeler, Chairman JCS

Chapter 7
Gen William C. Westmoreland, Commanding General MACV

Chapter 9
NV Gen. Vo Nguyen Giap
Le Duan, NV Politburo

Chapter 13
President Richard M. Nixon
Admiral Thomas H. Moorer, Chairman JCS

Chapter 17
Henry Kissinger, National Security Advisor and Secretary of State.

Chapter 20
SVN President Nguyen Van Thieu
 President Gerald R. Ford

Chapter 21
Pol Pot (Cambodian Communist leader)

Appendix 1
1Lt William Calley
Lt. Gen. William R. Peers
WO1 Hugh Thompson

Appendix 2
Jeremiah Denton

ACKNOWLEDGEMENTS

I owe thanks to many friends and readers for encouraging me to write this book, which first appeared in a series of articles on the Vietnam War in the *Asheville Tribune* and the *Hendersonville Tribune* in North Carolina and the *Times Examiner* in Greenville, South Carolina. A special thanks goes to the editors and publishers of those papers: David and Katrina Morgan, Bill Fishburne, Mark White, and Bob Dill.

I also owe a special thanks to those who at one time or another toiled in the tedious and sometimes frustrating work of editing my writing and who made many helpful comments: Ken Bachand, Jan Kral, Ben Moon, Judy Malphurs Pair, and Amy Shook.

In addition, I have greatly appreciated the many readers and friends that encouraged me with emails, phone calls, and letters. They often enhanced my knowledge and understanding of the Vietnam War by sharing their personal experiences and recommending important reference materials.

Finally, I would like to thank the authors of the many books and articles I used as references. Though I never met them, some became like close and familiar friends. In particular, I salute the late Harry G. Summers, Jr., Colonel of Infantry and faculty member of the Army War College.

Soli Deo Gloria

June 1, 2009
Hendersonville, North Carolina

Leonard M. Scruggs

INTRODUCTION

The Vietnam War is one of the least understood wars in American history. Indeed, one of the problems of the Vietnam War was that in its early years our political leaders did not fully grasp Communist strategy. This led to one of the most persistent myths about the war. It is still widely believed among the public, academia, and the media that Vietnam was predominantly a guerilla war against lightly armed and untrained peasants in black pajamas, which the U.S. inappropriately fought by massive applications of firepower on the ground and from the air. It *was* largely a guerilla war until late 1964, when heavily equipped North Vietnamese Army forces began to invade South Vietnam. In 1964, even the Viet Cong guerillas were equipped with considerably more firepower than the South Vietnamese Army.[4]

As the North Vietnamese escalated their strategy to conquer not only South Vietnam but also Cambodia and Laos, the latest Soviet tanks, artillery, antiaircraft guns, rocket launchers, and small arms poured into North Vietnam and then into Laos, Cambodia, and South Vietnam. In reality, the war quickly became like the Korean War, in which North Korean guerillas were first sent south to weaken South Korea's political and economic infrastructure and were then followed by fully equipped North Korean divisions. The North Vietnamese strategy continued to use Viet Cong guerilla units for diversionary purposes and as supplemental forces.

The Vietnam War was essentially a proxy war between the Soviet Union and the United States. At stake were all of Southeast Asia and Soviet versus American influence in the world. The People's Republic of China joined the Soviets in supplying North Vietnam with weapons and supplies, but it was primarily the Soviet Union that advised and funded North Vietnam's strategy.[5] Moreover, beneath the surface of Sino-Soviet cooperation, the relationship between the world's two giant Communist powers was competitive and often uneasy. The Chinese acted more out of a spirit of ambition than cooperation. The Chinese once dominated Vietnam for more than a thousand years. Consequently, Hanoi's leaders always feared Chinese help might lead to Chinese control.

It is still widely believed in academia that Ho Chi Minh and other North Vietnamese leaders were primarily nationalists rather than Communists. However, Ho Chi Minh ruthlessly eliminated his nationalist competition, and his Stalinist-leaning Communist ideology was impeccable in its pitiless practice.[6]

As American involvement in Vietnam was prolonged, strong opposition to American policies and continued support for South Vietnam developed in the media and academia. Their anti-war legacy lives on in the form of many false impressions about the war. Much of it is the warmed-over propaganda of the anti-war movement. Many of these false impressions have risen to mythical status and, unfortunately, persist most strongly in academia where today's politically correct climate insists on a left-leaning worldview. In addition, many of the politicians, political activists, academics, and journalists who were involved in the ultimate betrayal of South Vietnam have a vested interest in perpetuating the myths and misinformation that influenced them.

Contrary to popular opinion, Vietnam is not a small country. In population, it is the thirteenth largest country in the world with a population of 86 million in 2008. This is slightly larger than Germany, which ranks fourteenth, and larger than France or the United Kingdom. In area, it is only slightly smaller than Germany. Contrary also to media impressions, Vietnam has not prospered under communism. Its annual gross domestic product per person, adjusted for purchasing power parity (PPP), was only $2,800 in 2008, barely 27 percent of the world average and a mere 6 percent of the U.S. average. Things are better in Vietnam, however, than in North Korea, where the PPP adjusted gross domestic product per person is only $1,700, less than seven percent of that of South Korea. Both Vietnam and North Korea are conspicuous examples of the abysmal failure of the Communist economic system.[7]

Approximately 87 percent of the people of what is now the Socialist Republic of Vietnam are ethnic Vietnamese, who are largely a coastal people. Even among the ethnic Vietnamese, the cultural difference between northern and southern Vietnam is great. Vietnam is also the home of several major and many smaller ethnic groups. Most of these make their homes in the highlands or in the Mekong Delta. The population of South Vietnam's Central Highlands was almost exclusively Montagnard until after the war. However, the Montagnards, who were 70 percent Christian and especially friendly with American Special Forces troops, have been largely displaced. Many fled after the fall of South Vietnam. They are now only about 25 percent of the population of the Central Highlands. The Socialist Republic of Vietnam continues to be one of the world's most severe persecutors of Christianity. The Nung Chinese, another large ethnic minority, were notably successful in commercial endeavors in South Vietnam, especially around Saigon. Several hundred thousand Chinese ethnics fled Vietnam after the Communist take-over in 1975. A substantial number of these were of the Nung ethnic group. The United States has accepted 830,000 Vietnamese refugees since the war. The total Vietnamese diaspora around the globe is now believed to be approximately two million.[8, 9]

Operation World estimates that Vietnam is about 54 percent Buddhist. Another 6 percent belong to culturally related religious sects. Some estimates of

Buddhist identity range as high as 85 percent, but most Buddhism in Vietnam is nominal and cultural rather than intensely religious and often overlaps with Confucianism and other traditions. Christians make up about 8 percent of the population, most of whom are Roman Catholic.

Vietnam was dominated by the Chinese for a thousand years until 938, when the province of Tonkin (the northern part of North Vietnam) gained its independence. There followed a long process of wars and political intrigues before the southern provinces of Annam and Cochin China were completely consolidated into Vietnam in 1788. By 1857, the French had already begun consolidating Vietnam, Cambodia, and Laos into their colonial empire. The French consolidation of its Indochina colony was complete by 1884. The French remained in control until Indochina was occupied by Japanese troops during World War II.

Following the war and French reoccupation, the Communist Viet Minh, who had come to dominate the northern half of Vietnam, began to agitate for independence. This led to eight years of war, ending with the French defeat at Dien Bien Phu in 1954 and resulting in the Geneva Conferences that partitioned Vietnam at the 17th Parallel. The partition was theoretically temporary, but the United States and its free allies knew that elections in the Communist northern half of the country would be impossible. Because of Communist domination in the North, the U.S. and its allies never supported the unification of North and South Vietnam. Two countries emerged from the arrangement: the Communist People's Democratic Republic of Vietnam in the north and the Republic of Vietnam to the south.

Until 1955, the South Vietnamese Army was advised by the French. Because of French preoccupation with war in its Algerian colony and the resulting domestic political turmoil, the United States assumed the primary advisory and training role for South Vietnam's armed forces.

In January 1959, the Central Executive Committee of Communist North Vietnam issued Resolution 15, changing its policy toward South Vietnam from "political struggle" to "armed struggle." By late 1959, U.S. and allied intelligence agencies had unequivocally established that North Vietnam's aggressive posture toward South Vietnam was being supported, advised, and approved, step by step, by Moscow.[10]

Following his inauguration in January 1961, President John F. Kennedy viewed North Vietnamese insurgency into South Vietnam with increasing alarm. Consequently, he began to increase U.S. counterinsurgency capabilities and strength there. Hence the number of U.S. advisors in South Vietnam increased from 900 to 3,200. At least one contingent of USAF advisors were part of a covert Air Commando operation called "Farm Gate," designated the 4400th Combat Crew Training Squadron. This squadron expanded its advisory and training role to flying combat missions in unmarked B-26, T-28, C-47, and T-10 aircraft in support of South Vietnamese Army and Air Force operations.

Kennedy made two serious mistakes. First, in July 1962, he had unwisely agreed to a Geneva Accord that essentially forfeited our ability to oppose North Vietnamese occupation of much of Laos. Second, in 1963, by meddling in a domestic South Vietnamese political crisis over alleged discrimination against Buddhists, he caused the overthrow of South Vietnamese President Ngo Dinh Diem. The South Vietnamese generals who led this coup decided to execute Diem in the process. This threw the South Vietnamese government and military leadership into chaos for two years and made direct U.S. military intervention necessary to save South Vietnam.

Following Kennedy's assassination, his successor, Lyndon Johnson, continued to increase our advisory commitment to South Vietnam. By December 1964, there were over 23,000 American military personnel in South Vietnam. The first combat troops arrived in March 1965. U.S. military presence peaked at over 543,000 in April 1969. This huge reliance on American ground forces was primarily due to Lyndon Johnson's aversion to using the full capabilities of U.S. airpower. This is a major theme of this book that is often overlooked by academic authors.

President Johnson pursued a strategy of "graduated escalation" that hamstrung the use of Air Force and Naval airpower and necessitated a massive U.S. troop buildup in South Vietnam to prevent a Communist takeover. Meanwhile, he wasted a considerable part of our Air Force in highly restricted attacks against largely secondary targets in North Vietnam. He also committed the U.S. to years of fruitless negotiations with Communist diplomats who consistently used negotiations and bombing halts to further Communist military objectives. Despite a substantial victory by South Vietnamese and American troops over North Vietnamese and Viet Cong troops during the Tet holiday early in 1968, the American media portrayed the Communist Tet offensive as a major Communist victory. Johnson withdrew his name from the Democratic Presidential Primary in March, and by late 1968 had halted all bombing of North Vietnamese targets and placed his hopes on a negotiated peace despite the Communist record of insincerity and deception.

Coming into office in January 1969, Nixon was left holding an unpromising hand of cards for saving South Vietnam and bringing our troops home. The American people were growing weary of a war with no victory in sight, and support for abandoning South Vietnam and all of Indochina was growing strong in Congress.

Yet Nixon, by a combination of actions—strategic bombing of major North Vietnamese military and logistic centers, mining the major entry ports for Soviet and Chinese war materials, denying the North Vietnamese sanctuaries in

Cambodia and Laos, building and training the South Vietnamese Army to formidable levels, and a no-nonsense attitude at the negotiating table—was able to bring Hanoi's leaders to their knees in December 1972. The war had essentially been won, and the resulting 1973 peace treaty should have brought a workable peace for South Vietnam.

A persistent myth about Vietnam is that the war was unwinnable. Most airpower advocates believe it could have been won easily in early 1965, before the Soviets had time to build the most impressive antiaircraft defenses in history for North Vietnam. It could probably have been won with the proper use of airpower in late 1967, when General Westmoreland's war of attrition—despite Johnson-McNamara policies allowing enemy sanctuaries in Cambodia and Laos and severely restricting strategic use of airpower—was taking an irreplaceable toll on North Vietnamese manpower and materials.[11] It certainly could have been won with a proper application of airpower after the devastating defeat the North Vietnamese and Viet Cong suffered during the 1968 Tet offensive. It essentially *was* won when the Navy mined North Vietnamese harbors and massive B-52 strikes devastated military and transportation targets around Hanoi and Haiphong in late 1972.

However, this victory and peace were undermined and thrown away by Congress, resulting in the fall of both South Vietnam and Cambodia in early 1975. The terrible consequence of Communist victory was that millions of once free people were enslaved to ruthless Communist despots, and more than 3.5 million Cambodian and South Vietnamese civilians were murdered, starved to death, or drowned in the South China Sea. These horrendous facts are generally left out of the standard left-liberal accounts of the war. This political and human tragedy should not be buried or covered with political whitewash. Truth is a necessary foundation for avoiding future moral and political errors.[12, 13, 14]

I served in the U.S. Air Force from 1961 to 1969 and had occasion to view the war first as an intelligence officer in the Strategic Air Command and later as a crew member on transport, combat, and air rescue aircraft either directly involved in or supporting operations in South Vietnam and Laos. I left the Air Force in 1969 to attend graduate studies at Stanford University in California. There I witnessed first-hand the activities of the anti-war movement and their impact on domestic politics. It was a gut-wrenching experience for me and many of my fellow Vietnam veterans in the MBA program at Stanford. We had come home to much criticism and protest—both sincere and opportunistic—in the press, on college campuses, and by politicians over American involvement in Vietnam. The same misinformation and anti-war propaganda that I heard on campus then is still prevalent today.

Several years ago, looking for a book on a completely different historical subject (Napoleon's generals), I inadvertently spotted a book at a local book store entitled *Air Commando*, by Philip Chinnery, published in 1998. Since I had served with the Air Commandos in 1966 and 1967, I immediately opened it up. To my surprise, my name was mentioned in regard to the loss of two A-26s on February 22, 1967. (The A-26 was an Onmark Corporation update of the old Douglas B-26 Invader). After I had explained a little of this incident to my wife and two sons at the dinner table later that evening, my youngest son asked, "Dad, were you in World War I or II?" My brother, Randy, is also a Vietnam veteran, having served there as a sergeant in the U.S. Army from late 1970 to the fall of 1971. He is presently teaching in North Carolina public schools and recently lamented to me that the vast majority of his students have only a hazy impression of the Vietnam War and are uncertain of its historical time frame. Not only is the Vietnam War still badly misunderstood, the latest generations scarcely have any knowledge of it at all. Public ignorance and persistent misinformation on the war expose the present and future generations of voters, soldiers, and politicians to the same tragic political mistakes of the Vietnam era.

There are dozens of misconceptions about the nature and conduct of the war that persist as part of the left-liberal worldview about Vietnam. These misconceptions must be corrected for the sake of truth and intelligent national security policy. Persisting in the left-liberal worldview of the war and its many accompanying myths could severely impact the development of sound national security policies in the future. Basing national security and foreign policy on ideologically based myths could have a devastating cost to future generations of Americans. They would be better served by the truth. There are valuable lessons to be learned from the Vietnam War. We made some serious mistakes. We should not make them again. It is for this purpose that this book is written.

I am proud to have served my country in the Vietnam War and to identify myself with the brotherhood of men and women who have served their country in peace and war. I believed then, and still believe today, that defending the nations of Southeast Asia from Communist aggression and murderous occupation was a worthy cause. Not all the political strategies, not all the military strategies and tactics, and not all the restrictions imposed on our armed forces were wise, but the cause was just.

CHAPTER 1

Let the Word Go Forth

On January 20, 1961, a white blanket of snow covered the nation's capital as a young and vigorous new president, John F. Kennedy, delivered a stirring inaugural address. A thrill hung in the air as he declared, "Let the word go forth . . . to friend and foe alike, that the torch has been passed to a new generation of Americans . . . unwilling to witness or permit the slow undoing of those human rights to which this nation has always been committed, and to which we are committed today at home and around the world."

Then he boldly asserted, "Let every nation know, whether it wishes us well or ill, that we shall pay any price, bear any burden, meet any hardship, support any friend, oppose any foe to assure the survival and success of liberty."[15]

Kennedy was not speaking in a rhetorical vacuum. In Moscow, less than a week earlier, Soviet Premier Nikita Khrushchev had boldly pledged the power of the Soviet Union to support "wars of national liberation." Conceding American nuclear superiority for the time, he reminded the Communist world of a doctrinal Marxist strategy for worldwide domination. He called for Communists everywhere to foment and support insurgency warfare against all capitalist governments and declared such conflicts to be just wars of liberation.

Ominously, Khrushchev announced to the world that the prototype for such warfare would be the "liberation" of South Vietnam. At the same time, Radio Hanoi announced the formation of a new "National Liberation Front" of Marxist political organizers and armed insurgents. Thus began the long struggle between the United States and the Communist Bloc for South Vietnam. In its broader reality it was a proxy war between the United States and the Soviet Union with the People's Republic of China aligning with the Soviets to assist North Vietnam in its aggression against South Vietnam.[16]

An Overview of the Vietnam Tragedy

Kennedy made two serious errors in his decisions on Indochina policy that would create immense problems for his successors, Johnson and Nixon. First, in April 1961, he agreed to the idea of a neutral Laos, which was finalized in Geneva in July 1962. However, as could have been expected, North Vietnam did not honor the treaty, and North Vietnamese troops occupied eastern Laos and then eastern Cambodia. Kennedy compounded his error by failing to contest North Vietnam's aggressive violation of the treaty immediately. Thus the North Vietnamese Army (NVA) was able to use south-eastern Laos and eastern Cambodia as a huge sanctuary with networks of heavily defended supply routes threatening South Vietnam. This became known as the Ho Chi Minh Trail, in honor of North Vietnam's famed and powerful Communist dictator. This put the South Vietnamese Army in the untenable position of having to defend a 640-mile frontier rather than a narrow 40-mile frontier at the Demilitarized Zone (DMZ) separating the two Vietnams.

Second, beginning in May of 1963, President Kennedy and many of his advisors began to be uncomfortable with South Vietnamese President Ngo Dinh Diem's handling of Buddhist political demonstrations in Saigon and Hue. Diem already had enough problems dealing with Communist terrorism and acted quickly to suppress the Buddhist demonstrations. In June, however, militant Buddhists dramatized their protest against Diem when a young monk doused himself with gasoline and set himself on fire. The photo of the burning monk accompanied by anti-Diem propaganda inflamed the liberal media around the world. This led Kennedy and several of his closest advisors to decide that a regime change was needed in South Vietnam. Using both diplomatic and intelligence channels, the Kennedy Administration aided and abetted an overthrow of the Diem government by a group of South Vietnamese generals.

The coup occurred on November 1, and Kennedy, acting through Ambassador Henry Cabot Lodge, promised safe passage to the U.S. for Diem and his family, but unfortunately some of the plotting generals had different ideas, and the next day Diem and his brother Nhu (his chief political advisor) were murdered. President Kennedy himself was assassinated less than three weeks later. The overthrow of Diem, who had been a stabilizing influence in South Vietnam since his ascendancy to the presidency in 1955, threw the country into a political and military leadership crisis for two years. The North Vietnamese were quick to take advantage of the situation and escalated their invasion of South Vietnam.

The United States acted largely in an advisory capacity to South Vietnam from 1961 to August 1964. The 20,000 U.S. troops there saw occasional action, but they were mainly engaged in training the South Vietnamese Army in counter-insurgency warfare. Our initial focus on the guerilla war, however, was a misreading of the full scope of Ho Chi Minh's plan. Ho used the guerilla war to divert our attention from his preparations for a full scale conventional invasion of South Vietnam and to soften South Vietnamese defenses in preparation for that invasion. Many academics still write about the Vietnam War as if it were a guerilla war that the U.S. tried to fight with conventional weapons. But it was much like the Korean War which was preceded by a guerilla insurgency stage followed by a full scale conventional invasion.

Because of the chaos resulting from the overthrow of Diem, President Johnson was forced to rely on a massive increase in U.S. troops to save South Vietnam from a North Vietnamese invasion and Communist takeover.

In June 1964, North Vietnam began to filter heavily armed regular army units into South Vietnam. In August, two U.S. Navy destroyers, the *Maddox* and the *Turner Joy*, were attacked by North Vietnamese torpedo boats in the Gulf of Tonkin. Congress then passed the Tonkin Gulf Resolution permitting President Lyndon Johnson, without a formal declaration of war, to take whatever steps were necessary to defend the nations of the Southeast Asia Treaty Organization from Communist aggression.

On April 20, 1965, Secretary of Defense Robert McNamara announced that U.S. airpower would not be used for strategic bombing of North Vietnam. Its principal use would be to support U.S. ground troops. The bombing of North Vietnam under Operation Rolling Thunder would generally be restricted to sub-strategic targets at modest levels to avoid threatening the Soviet Union and China. This was, according to Pacific Area Commander Admiral U.S. Grant Sharp, a decision that ultimately lost the war.[17] The Vietnam War became a land war in which 550,000 U.S. troops were engaged by 1969.[18]

Until Nixon became president in 1969, the war was micromanaged by Johnson, McNamara, and his civilian advisors in the Defense Department. The Joint Chiefs of Staff (JCS) continually urged President Johnson and Secretary McNamara to bomb strategic targets in North Vietnam and mine the harbor at Haiphong, but their advice was consistently ignored until Nixon finally made full use of Air Force and Navy airpower in 1972. By that time, Nixon's policy of Vietnamization had built the South Vietnamese Armed forces to a well-trained force of over one million men, allowing U.S. troop strength to be reduced to 20,000. Both Johnson and Nixon had engaged in years of fruitless negotiations with the North Vietnamese until Nixon implemented the JCS plans for mining Haiphong harbor and extensive bombing of strategic targets in North Vietnam. These plans, called Linebacker I and II, brought the leaders of Hanoi to their knees.

According to Admiral Sharp and most other senior naval and military commanders, the war could have been easily won in early 1965, before the Johnson-McNamara policy of "gradual response" or "graduated escalation" allowed North Vietnam, with extensive Soviet and Chinese assistance, to create the greatest anti-aircraft network in history. It could have been won in late 1967, though with heavier air casualties, when increased sub-strategic bombing in North Vietnam was wreaking growing devastation on Hanoi's ability to man and supply North Vietnamese Army (NVA) units in the field.[18] Following the crushing defeat of NVA and Viet Cong (VC) forces during their Tet offensive in January and February 1968, the leaders of Hanoi were ready to throw in the towel. Strategic bombing of North Vietnam could have easily finished them off, but Tet was portrayed by the U.S. press as a shocking reversal in the war. Anti-war demonstrators and nervous U.S. Congressmen intimidated Johnson into halting the bombing of North Vietnam altogether, thus letting a tremendous opportunity for complete victory slip away.

Nixon's Linebacker I and II essentially won the war. A peace treaty was signed in Paris in January 1973, and Hanoi returned its 591 American prisoners or war. But as soon as the Americans were gone, the Communists ignored the ceasefire and began to prepare for a new invasion of South Vietnam. Because of an anti-war majority in Congress, Nixon was unable to contest these violations of the peace treaty. In August 1974, Nixon was forced to resign because of the Watergate scandal. This also resulted in a tremendous Democratic victory in the November 1974 Congressional elections. As a consequence of a greater anti-war majority in Congress, military aid to South Vietnam was cut drastically. When North Vietnam launched another invasion of South Vietnam in December 1974, Congress refused to meet its obligations to enforce the Paris treaty and provide South Vietnam with the arms and logistics needed to defend itself. Both Cambodia and South Vietnam fell in April 1975, resulting in several million civilian deaths at the hands of their Communist liberators.[19] The remainder of Laos fell to the Communist Pathet Lao in December 1975. Nearly 57,000 Americans and more than 250,000 South Vietnamese and allied servicemen were killed in the Vietnam War, but still, the freedom of millions in Indochina was lost to the brutal and despotic tyranny of Communism.[20]

John F. Kennedy

Nikita Khrushchev

Ho Chi Minh

Leonard M. Scruggs

CHAPTER 2

The Biggest Mistake of the War
The Overthrow and Death of Ngo Dinh Diem

On November 1, 1963, the Kennedy Administration encouraged and abetted a military overthrow of South Vietnamese President Ngo Dinh Diem. As a consequence, Diem and his brother and chief political advisor, Ngo Dinh Nhu, were killed the next day. This led to more than two years of unstable government in South Vietnam, which was fully exploited by North Vietnam's Communist leaders and led to more extensive commitments of American manpower to save South Vietnam.[21] President Johnson, who succeeded to the presidency after Kennedy's own assassination on November 22, later called the overthrow of Diem the biggest mistake of the Vietnam War.[22] President Nixon, writing in 1985, pointed it out as one of the three greatest mistakes of the war.

In May 1963, Viet Cong insurgency incidents had dropped fifty percent from their previous peak in early 1962. President Diem's Strategic Hamlet Program seemed to be working, and with American advice and equipment the South Vietnamese Army held the upper hand over the North Vietnamese-backed insurgents. New public schools, bridges, and foreign investments were springing up around the country, and land reform was giving farmers a stake in their future. Rice production reached its highest level ever. Both North Vietnam's leaders in Hanoi and Communist insurgents in South Vietnam were discouraged with their political and military progress.[23] But their hopes and morale would soon be revitalized.

Beginning in May of 1963, President John F. Kennedy and many of his advisors began to be uncomfortable with South Vietnamese President Ngo Dinh Diem's handling of Buddhist political demonstrations on the streets of Hue and Saigon. The protests began on Buddha's birthday—May 8 in 1963—over a ban on flying religious flags higher than the national flag. But the focus was soon broadened to alleged discrimination against Buddhists by the staunchly Roman Catholic Diem and his Administration. The protests were organized by a highly political Buddhist group led by 39-year-old Thich Tri Quang. Following an incident where eight protestors were killed in Hue, the protest organizers carefully contrived a protest that would get international attention.

On June 11, Thich Quang Duc, a Buddhist monk, clothed in saffron-yellow robes and sitting in the Buddhist posture of prayer, was doused with gasoline and set himself on fire. Thousands of pre-mimeographed copies of his thoughts were distributed by the militant Buddhist cadre who had recruited him.

A small group of Tri Quang's allies in the American press had been tipped off to the event, and the dramatic photograph and critical commentary were soon seen on the front pages of thousands of newspapers and magazines around the world. In addition, Diem's sister-in-law, the beautiful, colorful, and sharp-tongued Madam Nhu (essentially the first lady of the Diem regime and sometimes referred to as "the Dragon Lady") joked in an American interview that these "flaming barbeques" were only eliminating her husband's enemies.[24] Consequently, Diem's popularity in the United States plummeted, and American media criticism of the U.S. advisory role in South Vietnam, led by the very influential *New York Times*, escalated.[25] Meanwhile, in August, 17,000 Buddhists demonstrated against Diem in Saigon.

On August 21, the government raided the twelve Buddhist pagodas associated with Tri Quang—out of a total of 4,776 in the country. No one was killed, but that was no barrier to the press reporting widespread government murder of Buddhists monks, who were invariably depicted as an "oppressed holy people" without any political agenda but peace and justice.[26]

Although Diem had been President of South Vietnam since 1955 and had brought considerable stability to its government, Kennedy and a majority of his closest advisors decided that they would welcome a regime change in Saigon. In arriving at this decision, Kennedy placed his trust in the biased, sensationalist reports in the U.S. media and misinformed public opinion rather than the more balanced reporting of former South Vietnamese Ambassador Frederick Nolting and the CIA. Any action to remove Diem was also strongly opposed by Vice President Johnson, CIA Director John McCone, and General Maxwell Taylor.[27] Nevertheless, on August 24, Kennedy and his like-minded anti-Diem advisors acted through Henry Cabot Lodge, the newly appointed Ambassador in Saigon, to convey their sympathy for replacing Diem to a group of ambitious South Vietnamese generals who were already plotting his overthrow because of disagreements over military policy. Meanwhile, acting through Lodge, Kennedy demanded that Diem fire his chief political advisor and younger brother, Ngo Dinh Nhu—an action which would be untenable to Diem and serve as a pretext for severing American support for him when he refused. Against American advice, Diem continued to act with the firmness and independence that had characterized his leadership successes in the past.

At this point, the Communists made a concerted effort to retake Ben Tuong, the original strategic hamlet. This surprise attack was successful in both capturing Ben Tuong and throwing a shadow over the success of Diem's highly touted Strategic Hamlet Program.

On November 1, the forces of the plotters—generals Duong Van "Big" Minh, Tran Van Don, and Le Van Kim—surrounded the government palace and began to exchange fire with Diem loyalists. Diem and his brother Nhu, however, escaped through a secret tunnel to a Catholic church in Cholon, the Chinese district of Saigon. From there they telephoned Lodge who had, of course, been in contact with the rebel generals. Lodge offered no American help but urged Diem to resign and go into exile. He offered the brothers safe conduct if they resigned. They reluctantly agreed and within minutes a caravan of armored vehicles was on its way to the church to carry them to Ton Son Nhut airfield and a flight to exile and safety.

However, the generals knew that Diem had extraordinary influence in the United States and other Western countries, especially in the Roman Catholic Church. If he should ever return to power in South Vietnam, they were dead ducks. Big Minh—so called because his six-foot-200-pound size was uncommon in Vietnam—ordered his aide, Captain Nguyen Van Nhung, a former counterintelligence officer and trained assassin, to kill Diem. According to the most reliable sources, when Diem and Nhu entered an M-113 armored vehicle, Captain Nhung had their hands bound behind them and then blew their brains out with a pistol.

President Kennedy and his advisors were shocked when they heard that Diem and Nhu had been murdered by the military junta. The North Vietnamese and Viet Cong Communists, however, could not believe their good fortune. Nguyen Huu Tho, a National Liberation Front Leader, said, "Americans have managed to do what we could not in nine years. It is a gift from heaven."[28] South Vietnam had needed a strong leader rather than a popular celebrity. Now South Vietnam was in chaos and for two years would lack firm anti-Communist leadership. It was thus seriously threatened with Communist takeover. North Vietnam was encouraged enough to send 12,000 troops into South Vietnam in 1964, followed by 36,000 in 1965, 92,000 in 1966, and 101,000 in 1967. Viet Cong ranks expanded from 10,000 to 30,000 in 1964, and their paramilitary auxiliaries expanded from 30,000 to 80,000.[29]

Duong Van Minh was elected President of South Vietnam by the Military Revolutionary Council but proved a lethargic leader. He was himself overthrown by General Nguyen Khanh on January 30, 1964, less than three months after taking office. Big Minh was exiled for three years, and his bodyguard, Captain Nhung, was executed just three months after his killing of Diem and Nhu.

The presidency of South Vietnam became a revolving door. There were ten changes in government within two years and even more changes in military leadership until civilian leaders appointed Vietnamese Air Force General Nguyen Cao Ky to the position of Prime Minister, with full powers of state in December 1965. Ky was a strong leader and became Vice President when Nguyen Van Thieu was elected President on September 3, 1967. Thieu also proved to be a strong leader.

There is no doubt that Diem had an authoritarian style of leadership, with which most Americans would not be comfortable. But Diem understood that the first task of government is to establish order. While serving as Eisenhower's Vice-President in 1956, Richard Nixon visited Diem in Saigon. Diem defended his autocratic leadership style by pointing out that he was dealing with Communist terrorism, assassinations, and armed insurrections, and that ordinary peacetime rules of conduct would lead to Communist victory. "We are at war," he said, "and in war it is necessary to use wartime measures."[30] But by 1960, when Diem had completed his assault on the Communist underground, there were at most 300 political prisoners in South Vietnamese prisons.[31] This was quite low by third-world standards. When Ho Chi Minh took over North Vietnam in 1954, he had 50,000 nationalist opponents executed and placed another 100,000 in forced-labor camps.[32] Unlike Ho, Diem was an authentic nationalist whom the French feared but respected. Ho was primarily a power-seeking doctrinaire Communist who used the French to help eliminate his nationalist adversaries.

The true facts of the Buddhist crisis of 1963 have been largely buried and distorted by the same anti-Diem journalists who reported from Saigon in those days. They were the same *New York Times, Time* magazine, and Associated Press reporters who became the core disseminators of distorted anti-war propaganda right through the fall of Cambodia and South Vietnam in 1975 and continue to this day to defend a left-liberal interpretation of the Vietnam War. Marguerite Higgins, who had won a Pulitzer Prize for her Korean War writing, frequently clashed with these younger male reporters in Vietnam. She derided them as "typewriter strategists who were seldom at scenes of battle" and alleged that they "would like to see us lose the war to prove that they're right." Whatever their motives, their left-liberal spin on Diem and objections to U.S. involvement in defending South Vietnam from Communist takeover resulted in tragedy. They must take some responsibility for aiding a Communist takeover of Indochina that resulted in the death of at least 3.5 million civilians and crushed the hopes of freedom for millions more.[33]

Many of these anti-Diem reporters distorted public understanding by leaving out important facts. For example, Diem first cracked down on Catholics who were flying Vatican flags in a celebration during the first week of May 1963.[34] Two days before Buddha's birthday on May 8, he wisely ordered that the rules be suspended, knowing that there had not been enough time for people to take his recent invocation of an old law into account.

The eight people killed at a Buddhist protest in Hue—where Tri Quang had demanded his anti-Diem speech be read over the radio—were not killed by gunfire. They were the victims of a plastic bomb of the same type used by Viet Cong terrorists.[35] Tri Quanq had probably picked Hue because one of Diem's brothers was the Mayor of Hue. Tear gas was used at Hue and its outdated age caused burns on some of the protestors, but none of them had acid poured on their heads as was claimed by several journalists and believed by some of Kennedy's advisors.

The issue of religious repression was largely a political fabrication. Of the eighteen ministers in Diem's cabinet, only five were Catholic. Five were Confucianist, and eight were Buddhist. Of the thirty-eight provincial governors, twelve were Catholic, and twenty-six were either Confucianist or Buddhist. Of the nineteen top generals, only three were Catholic, and the rest were Taoist, Confucianist, or Buddhist. Buddhists were exempt from mandatory military service. No Buddhist was ever arrested for practicing his religion.[36] Diem was quick to put down any protests, but to preserve order, not to suppress non-Catholic religions. Approximately seven percent of the population of South Vietnam was Roman Catholic in 1963.[37] That included 600,000 Catholic refugees from North Vietnam fleeing Ho Chi Minh's repression of all freedoms. The fact that over one million refugees in all fled North Vietnam in 1954 says something about where the oppression was taking place in Indochina.[38]

According to a CIA report shortly after the ouster of Diem, Tri Quang was not a Communist. He told the CIA he was for a theocracy. However, since the CIA was involved in the liaison between Lodge and the rebel generals, this damages the reliability of the report. Tri Quang was arrested twice by the French in conjunction with his working associations with the (Communist) National Liberation Front. Diem actually acquiesced to some of Tri Quang's reasonable demands, but then the Buddhist leader confronted Diem with unreasonable demands, showing that what he wanted was conflict rather than peace. Nixon's take on Tri Quang was that he wanted Diem out of the way so the Communists, with whom he was on friendlier terms, could take over the government. [39]In fact, Tri Quang was a disciple of Thich Tri Do, leader of the Communist-dominated Buddhist church in North Vietnam, and believed that Communism was completely compatible with Buddhism.[40] During Diem's crackdown on Tri Quang's followers, Ambassador Lodge gave him refuge in the U.S. Embassy.

John F. Kennedy was strongly anti-Communist, but his overly strong desire to curry favor with the liberal media caused him to be misled by Tri Quang, the junta generals, and journalists with strong anti-Diem and anti-war agendas. Surely, promoting a regime change in an allied nation is an appalling violation of the principle of national sovereignty, which only the most drastic circumstances would warrant. It should not be taken lightly that, when Diem fell, South Vietnam's Constitution also fell. Kennedy's decision to dump Diem was ill-advised and ill-considered. It is easy to agree with both Presidents Johnson and Nixon that it was a huge, costly, and disastrous mistake.

Ngo Dinh Diem

CHAPTER 3

An Airman's Perspective

My perspective on the Vietnam War comes from nearly eight years in the Air Force, where I served from 1961 to 1969, first as an intelligence officer and later as a crew member of transport, fighter-bomber, and air-rescue aircraft.

From early 1962 to early 1964, as an intelligence officer at Strategic Air Command (SAC) Headquarters, near Omaha, Nebraska, I was head of a team of photo-analysts with responsibility for identifying Soviet and Chinese intercontinental and medium range missiles, long range bombers, surface-to-air missiles (SAMs), nuclear weapons production, and missile and attack submarines and their support ships. In October 1962, our intelligence team was among those who first identified medium range, potentially nuclear armed missiles in Cuba. The result was the unnerving Cuban Missile Crisis. My geographic area of responsibility later became the Far East, which included most of Russian Siberia and all of China and Southeast Asia. Because I was involved in the first identification of certain nuclear facilities, I was sometimes consulted on nuclear weapons production regardless of location. I was later assigned responsibility for coordinating identification of all Soviet or Chinese nuclear missile and attack submarines and their support ships, wherever located, with Naval Intelligence. During those days I was sometimes privileged to give a morning briefing on highlights of overnight intelligence developments. Late in 1963 was the first time I remember summarizing strategic news about significant Chinese and Soviet arms shipments flowing into North Vietnam and the shadow it cast on the Republic of South Vietnam.

In March 1965, I was assigned as a navigator with the 3rd Air Transport Squadron at Charleston AFB in South Carolina. From then until late 1966 I flew at least a dozen combat support missions into South Vietnam on C-124 and C-141 aircraft. Trips from Charleston to South Vietnam and back were long and grueling, but the return trips made the most lasting impression on me. We sometimes carried back cargos of aluminum coffins. It was depressing, but before we took off, I always inspected the cargo section of the aircraft and paid my respects to these Americans whose patriotic devotion often went unheralded. I read and contemplated as many of the names as I could. They were mostly U.S. Army and Marines. A disproportionate number were battalion-grade officers (lieutenants, captains, majors and lieutenant colonels) and sergeants of all grades, evidence that Army and Marine officers and NCOs from squad leaders to battalion commanders were heavily and personally involved in frontline combat leadership. But there was no scarcity of young corporals and privates who had given the ultimate sacrifice for their country. I could not help wondering about their last moments and their families at home. I knew they were headed home, not to the herald of brass bands, but to tears and weeping. I also could not help recalling the World War I poem, "In Flanders Fields," written by Canadian Army Surgeon, Lt. Col. John McCrae just before his death in 1918. McCrae's poem is also relevant to World War II, Korea, and Vietnam, and we should be especially mindful of its relevance to Iraq and Afghanistan.

In Flanders Fields the poppies blow
Between the crosses row on row,
That mark our place; and in the sky
The larks, still bravely singing, fly
Scarce heard amid the guns below.

We are the Dead. Short days ago
We lived, felt dawn, saw sunset glow,
Loved and were loved, and now we lie
In Flanders Fields.

Take up our quarrel with the foe:
To you from falling hands we throw
The torch; be yours to hold it high.
If ye break faith with us who die
We shall not sleep, though poppies grow
In Flanders Fields.

I flew thirty-five combat missions as a navigator in the A-26K fighter-bomber during the Vietnam War. The A-26K Counterinvader, also called the B-26K, was a modernized version of the twin-prop World War II and Korean War B-26. Its two Pratt-Whitney engines reflected the latest technology in propeller-driven power, but it was still much slower than jet aircraft. Yet it could stay on station much longer than a jet, and its slower speed and shorter turning radius around a target made its strafing, bombing, and rocketing much more accurate. Our most accurate weapons were eight machine guns in the nose. These fired a deadly stream of .50 caliber incendiary shells and were so powerful that we normally loaded only six of them. Even with only six guns loaded, we could knock a large North Vietnamese transport truck for a flip, if we hit it broadside.

Although we sometimes flew infantry or rescue support sorties, our primary mission was night armed reconnaissance. Using the call sign, *Nimrod*, we hunted and destroyed enemy trucks making their way down the Ho Chi Minh Trail from North Vietnamese ports into South Vietnam. The Nimrods were by far the most successful truck killer in the war up until 1969, when they were replaced with the phenomenally destructive C-130 Specter gunships. Sadly, however, about one-third of the Nimrod crews were killed in action during the three years of their use until 1969. I was myself shot down on February 22, 1967, and hospitalized for five months.

On January 26, 1967, in a letter to my parents, I indicated my frustration with our strategy in Vietnam: "We're not winning the war here, only harassing them a bit. It looks like the war will last indefinitely. It will last as long as the American people stand for our *no win* policy."

On February 5, I wrote my younger brother, Randy, elaborating on the frustration that I and most other Air Force and Naval aircrews were feeling:

> . . . A considerable source of frustration is our conduct of the war. We are not winning. We are restrained from dealing the enemy any really devastating or lethal blows. I am not for hitting population centers. We don't have to. We are not hitting the heart of their military, industrial, and logistic centers. Of course, we wouldn't want to offend Ho Chi Minh or Mao. Ho Chi Minh must be laughing up his sleeve at us. At present status the war will go on indefinitely. Ho Chi is no fool. He is fighting a war we're too polite to make uncomfortable to him. What has he to lose? Aggression is quite appealing to him, as long as he knows he won't have to suffer any vast consequence. He may not win, but with our present conduct of the war, he hardly risks losing.
>
> Every time we are shot at I remember that the gun, the ammo, and the trucks could have been eliminated at their source. I'd like to have some of the State Department officials and politicians who make the policies ride with us in the jump seat for a few missions. Like Brer Bear, I think they would soon dispense with polite, limited war theories and go far "knocking their heads clean off." That way I can come home. All of us can come home.

Secretary of Defense Robert McNamara's Vietnam War strategy was called "graduated escalation." McNamara believed the United States could *slowly* ratchet up the intensity of U.S. military activity until the North

Vietnamese and their Viet Cong subsidiary realized their aggressive insurgency against the Republic of South Vietnam was too costly. McNamara and President Lyndon Johnson especially wanted to avoid any direct confrontation with the Soviet Union and China over Vietnam. As a result, the Johnson Administration's "graduated escalation" strategy was not only slow but overly cautious. Johnson and McNamara's extreme caution in using airpower in Vietnam virtually telegraphed timidity to the Soviets and Chinese, resulting in their being able to play a no-risk game of nuclear bluff at the expense of the U.S. and the free world. In addition, Johnson embraced a completely unwarranted delusion that hardened North Vietnamese Communists negotiate in good faith.

Operation Rolling Thunder, which began on March 2, 1965, and lasted through 1968, is a tragic example of the misuse of airpower under Johnson and McNamara's "graduated escalation" or "gradualism" doctrine of warfare. The targets, timing, and details for the first attack on North Vietnam were all decided in Washington. Squadrons of USAF and Navy aircraft were sent to bomb two minor targets just north of the Demilitarized Zone. Similar futility continued for forty-six months of highly restricted but costly use of airpower. By the end of 1968, a catastrophic 922 American aircraft had been lost over North Vietnam alone, including 354 F-105s, nearly half the 833 ever built.[41,42] But such restricted air warfare proved an impotent deterrent to North Vietnamese aggression.

There were several gaping flaws in the McNamara strategy. First of all, our slow escalation of military, naval, and airpower allowed North Vietnam a luxurious amount of time to build up their own forces and defenses. Meanwhile, the Soviets and Chinese poured weapons, supplies, and especially anti-aircraft guns and SAMs into North Vietnamese ports as fast as the limits to their resources and logistical systems would allow.

Since the U.S. was very cautious about hitting targets too near the North Vietnamese capital of Hanoi or its large seaport at Haiphong, American interdiction of enemy supplies was spread out over a large area of roads and jungle trails. Interdiction targets were at best truck convoys rather than principal rail lines and ports. The generous time and force gradients of American escalation allowed the North Vietnamese to build up formidable modern anti-aircraft defenses around important military and logistical facilities long before they might be targeted by Johnson and McNamara. In addition to Johnson's own naïve faith in negotiating with hardened Communist dictators, Congressional doves put considerable pressure on him to halt American bombing in hopes of a negotiated peace. Johnson never got a single concession during the many bombing halts he declared in the interest of "possible negotiation breakthroughs." The Soviets, Chinese, and North Vietnamese, however, used the bombing halts to make maximum efforts to transport weapons, supplies, and new anti-aircraft guns to the South. After every bombing halt American aircrews encountered substantial increases in anti-aircraft fire. USAF and Navy airpower was confined to hitting at best secondary targets in a rapidly escalating environment of sophisticated enemy anti-aircraft weapons.

In December 1972, President Richard Nixon approved Operation Linebacker II, which allowed Air Force B-52s and supporting Air Force and Navy aircraft to pound formerly restricted North Vietnamese targets into oblivion. This brought Hanoi to the negotiating table. But the victory was thrown away by Congress.

USAF C-124 Globemaster "Old Shakey"

USAF C-141 Starlifter

USAF A-26 K

CHAPTER 4

Air Commando

On January 7, 1967, the last of a flight of six twin-prop A-26s started on its final landing approach to Nakhon Phanom (NKP), a Royal Thai airbase on the border of northeastern Thailand and Laos. Once the first five aircraft had landed safely, the runway was cleared and fire trucks and ambulances lined the taxiway. The flaps of the last aircraft were stuck in the up position. It would have to come in at a high speed and would need every inch of NKP's 6000-foot pierced steel planking runway.

Captain James L. McCleskey and I set our camouflaged fighter-bomber down on the runway smoothly and brought the aircraft to a gentle stop without incident—to the cheers of the fire and ambulance crews on the taxiway. Our successful landing completed a sometimes perilous journey of ten days from our training base in Louisiana. The new A-26 crews joined six other A-26 crews of the 606th Air Commando Squadron who had already been at NKP several months. The 606th was part of an Air Commando Wing stationed at NKP that consisted of several squadrons with a wide variety of propeller-driven aircraft used for special missions.

The next day, I wrote my parents in a letter: "We arrived yesterday at Nakhon Phanom (NKP), Thailand. Everything is neatly military, but still the overwhelming impression is hot, dusty-brown, and isolated. The area seems impoverished in both economy and vegetation. So far my pilot, Jim McCleskey, and I have been living in a big open barracks. Most of our missions will be at night, and it is hot, humid, and altogether too miserable to get much sleep during the day. But we hope to get better quarters in a week. We fly our first combat mission tonight. NKP is in northeastern Thailand near the Mekong River. The time here is exactly 12 hours opposite EST. . ."

The USAF 606th Air Commando Squadron was equipped with A-26K attack-bombers. The A-26K was a revamped model of the old World War II and Korean War B-26 Invader. This one and only squadron of A-26s, never having more than a dozen aircraft, proved to be the most effective enemy truck destroyer in the U.S. weapons inventory from 1966 to 1969.[43] One-third of the squadron's aircrews, however, were killed or reported missing in action during that period. In 1969, the A-26s were replaced by the extraordinarily effective and less vulnerable AC-130 Specter gunships.

As a twin-prop attack-bomber, the A-26 was used principally for night armed reconnaissance during the Vietnam War. The primary objective was to

51

intercept and destroy enemy trucks transporting munitions and supplies from North Vietnam through Laos along the Ho Chi Minh Trail to South Vietnam. In addition, the aircraft was frequently used for the support of ground forces and for combat support roles in air rescue missions.

Although old and relatively slow, the remodeled A-26 had the advantage of being able to stay on station much longer than jet aircraft and was considerably more accurate in its bombing and strafing, especially at night. The aircraft had eight .50-caliber machine guns in the nose, but to reduce exhaust fumes in the cockpit, normally only six were loaded. This still delivered enough impact to send a large transport truck cartwheeling. We also had eight weapon stations on the wings and a bomb bay that could carry a bomb-load of 2,000 pounds.

We did fly our first night armed-reconnaissance mission under the squadron call sign of "Nimrod" that evening, and we flew almost every night thereafter. The call sign for the A-26s, "Nimrod," was a biblical reference to an ancient Mesopotamian king described as "a mighty hunter" (Genesis 10:9).

For our missions, we generally carried only two crew members, a pilot and a navigator. The navigator was seated to the pilot's right in the co-pilot seat. As the navigator, I performed many co-pilot, radio, and armament functions as well as navigation and map reading. For some special missions we carried a third crewmember. The A-26K did not have an ejection system like most modern combat aircraft, so we picked up parachutes as well as radios, personal pistols, and other equipment on reporting to operations before a mission. Unlike most regular Air Force units, the Air Commandos allowed crewmembers some deviation from the standard weapons issue, and I carried a light-weight .38-caliber Colt revolver and a Bowie knife. A few in the squadron carried sub-machine guns with folding stocks. Our assigned missions were generally dangerous, and aircraft frequently returned with battle damage. Many never returned.

The night of January 15 was the first time we were fired at by enemy antiaircraft guns. We were flying alone in an area of Laos just southeast of NKP to investigate intelligence reports of enemy trucking. We did not have a C-130 flare ship or a sister Nimrod with us, so we dropped flares and patrolled in a heavily forested area between two ridges. Nothing could be seen at night. I remember having an uneasy feeling as we dropped flares and flew down the valley trying to see any signs of a road or trucks.

Suddenly the sky lit up with streams of white tracers from .50-caliber enemy antiaircraft guns shooting down at us from the ridges on both our left and right. We seemed to fly through a hail of enemy fire, yet miraculously were not hit. My right knee began to quiver involuntarily as a result of this frightening close encounter with death. It was a few moments before it quit. You have to concentrate on what you are doing and get your nerves under control in that kind of situation. I knew from first-hand experience that steeling your nerves when under fire is not as easy as it sounds. I also knew the exhilaration that Churchill spoke of in the Boer War—of being shot at and missed. However, the experience took much of the adventurous spirit out of me. I now knew this was not an adventure; it was deadly serious business. Anybody that liked this kind of business did not understand probability.

January 18 was our first mission to the area we called "Barrel Roll" in northern Laos. We flew alone, as was the usual practice for such missions. Barrel Roll was a mountainous area, heavily forested, but with an occasional dirt road along the ridges or valleys. Reconnaissance in such a mountainous area was not ideal for the A-26. If we lost an engine in the black of night, we would not be able to climb out of the mountains. There were no lights on the ground, so we would have to pick our way through dark mountain passes by map reading and dead reckoning.

We never saw much activity in Barrel Roll. Later in 1967 the squadron lost at least one plane there. The area was close enough to North Vietnam so that Soviet-built jet fighters (MiGs) sometimes ventured out to kill some poor little prop plane for sport or target practice. We usually stayed on station alone for about four hours. The Meo tribesmen inhabiting this area were friendly, but because the area is near the North Vietnamese border, there were plenty of unwelcome insurgents. On these missions I just kept watching the clock hoping the four hours would pass uneventfully. It was an eerie, vulnerable feeling. I never liked Barrel Roll missions for that reason.

On January 26, we departed NKP alone and flew almost due East into Laos for about thirty minutes until reaching our target search area. It was early evening and still light when we arrived. On a dirt road there was a single large truck trying to make it across a clearing into better jungle cover for the night. We made a strafing run on the truck with six of the eight .50-caliber machine guns in the nose of our A-26. This was our most accurate and most frequently used weapon. Our guns were usually loaded with incendiary tracer rounds for setting enemy vehicles on fire. We only got credit for a truck if it caught fire. In this case, the truck stopped but failed to burn. We made another strafing run, hitting the truck on its left side and knocking it for a flip, proving the power of six .50-caliber guns on a well placed hit. Finally, the truck began to burn. McCleskey looked down as we made an inspection pass and said, "Burn, baby, burn!" Then he looked up to heaven and said something like, "God forgive me for using such pagan language." I was happy to get credit for the truck but was on the lookout for a possible lightning strike from the Almighty.

On February 7, we took off in late afternoon on a mission to provide close combat support for a rescue mission. About a week before, one of the O-1 observer aircraft from the USAF Wing at NKP was hit by ground fire in the heavily defended Mu Ghia Pass between North Vietnam and Laos. The pilot, an acquaintance of ours, was an easy-going Captain probably ten to fifteen years older than McCleskey and I. His six-foot-three, broad-shouldered frame hardly seemed appropriate to the small single engine O-1 aircraft. Yet he was able to bail out of his severely damaged plane and signal his position to another USAF aircraft.

Because he had not been heard from for several days, many feared he had been captured or killed. However, early in the morning of February 7, he had again been in radio contact with a USAF aircraft, and plans were made for his rescue. We were one of two A-26s and two A-1E Skyraiders (rather large WWII Navy, single-prop fighters) from NKP to fly this "Rescap" Mission. It was our job to provide close-in combat support for two Jolly Green Giant rescue helicopters coming from Udorn Air Base in northern Thailand. In the meantime, both USAF and Navy jet fighters were working over Mu Ghia Pass to suppress enemy resistance.

We could not see much of what was going on. We listened intently to our radio as the mission proceeded. The first Jolly Green reached the area within a few minutes and reported, "We have him on board. We're lifting off." Then came the report: "We're getting a lot of ground fire." Speaking directly to the pilot of the second Jolly Green, following about 150 yards behind them, the pilot said, "We're hit!" A moment later, in a very tense voice: "We're going in! Get down here quick, Chuck! Get down here quick!" Then there was silence, as the first Jolly Green hit a steep mountainside and exploded into flames. Then came a determined voice from the second Jolly Green: "We're going in to see if there are any survivors." At this point the second chopper was also experiencing a hail of ground fire. Having seen the crash and explosion, the second Jolly Green crew was astounded that there was a survivor.

A young rescue paramedic had been thrown clear as his helicopter hit the mountainside. He had just secured the 0-1 pilot in the helicopter and was not completely on board himself as the aircraft hit and exploded. Fortunately, the explosion threw him clear of the burning inferno. He stood there on the steep mountainside, waving at them. Despite their own mortal danger, the second Jolly Green, still under intense fire and taking hits, moved in, picked him up, and lifted off. The two A1-Es then engaged the enemy with a ferocious display of firepower, but we were held in reserve. Very shortly thereafter, more Air Force and Navy jets were taking an awesome vengeance on the North Vietnamese.

In the meantime, the second Jolly Green, carrying the young paramedic survivor from the first crew and still under fire, headed due west into Laos. Within minutes, they had to crash-land their heavily battle-damaged helicopter in the middle of Laos. They were not picked up until the next morning by a third Jolly Green. This time they made it back to home base in Udorn, Thailand.

The next day, I wrote my parents a brief letter: "I just spent a bad four hours. We just flew escort for a rescue mission that ended in disaster. One of our O-1E pilots was downed just inside North Vietnam. He and three helicopter crewmembers were killed in the attempt to lift him out. One young paramedic miraculously survived. I thank God at least for that. I am tired of dallying around in this war. If we want to end the war, we're going to have to make the North Vietnamese suffer the consequences of war. We're not really doing that now."

I did not write my parents the last words of the Jolly Green chopper pilot to his backup, but the words are etched forever in my mind: "We're going in! Get down here quick, Chuck! Get down here quick!"

I was destined to meet the young paramedic who was rescued from that flaming hillside again. He was Sgt. Duane Hackney, who later received the Air Force Cross for his heroism on February 7 and became one of the most highly decorated Air Force enlisted men in the Vietnam War. I don't know who the crew members of the second Jolly Green were or what decorations they received, but they certainly number among the bravest and noblest of American servicemen anywhere, anytime.

The very next night we flew a solitary truck-hunting mission in a heavily forested area south of the Ho Chi Minh trail. After dropping a few flares and making a few strafing runs on a suspected target, we suddenly came under intense fire by at least one .50-caliber antiaircraft machine gun and a .37mm antiaircraft flak gun. In order to avoid the flak and machine gun fire near the target, McCleskey flew right down to treetop level. While we were still only a few feet above the trees, which we could see by a dim moonlight, two flak bursts went off just above and to the left of us. We could hear the bursts and the metal hitting the plane. It was so close we both instinctively ducked, and McCleskey seemed to slump over the steering column. When he did not sit back up immediately, I thought he was wounded or dead. I also saw a large tree coming up right in front of us. I pulled back on the wheel to lift us above the looming trees, but McCleskey, with his head still down to duck any additional flak, said, "Get your damn hands off the wheel!" Happy that McCleskey was alive and alert, I was delighted to oblige.

We barely missed the treetops but got out of range of the antiaircraft guns. Needless to say, getting hit by flak and antiaircraft machine guns at such a low level and narrowly missing a huge treetop while trying to escape in the dim moonlight made a harrowing experience. As the navigator, I was perfectly happy to miss out on the experience of flying a battle-damaged aircraft out of a gauntlet of antiaircraft guns at night. When we landed at NKP, there were plenty of shrapnel souvenirs in the fuselage, the left wing, and especially the tail of the aircraft.

We flew again on the night of February 10. When we returned to NKP, the ground crew reported several shrapnel hits. We didn't even know the enemy had been shooting at us!

On February 13, we flew a daylight mission in the early evening. Intelligence had reported a Pathet Lao battalion in an area only about forty miles east of NKP in Laos. The Pathet Lao, or Communist Laotians, had a reputation for ruthless intimidation and murder of their own people and also for grotesque and inhumane torture of downed USAF and Navy flyers. The target was an area of thick jungle near a dirt road. We could see nothing, but we strafed and bombed the area as requested. Several days later friendly intelligence reported about 150 Pathet Lao killed in the area. It could have been our doing, but other aircraft also bombed and strafed the area over a few days.

The next week was more routine and without incident. We flew four hours each night scouting for some sign of enemy trucks or activity, but found none. Soon things would change dramatically.

USAF O-1 Bird Dog

USAF A-1E Skyraider

USAF A-26K Counterinvader

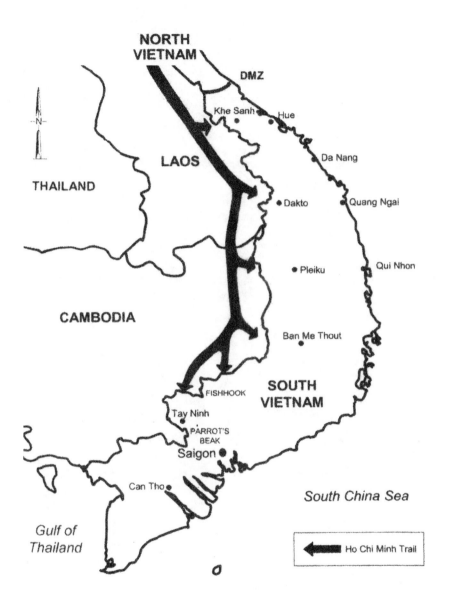

Ho Chi Minh Trail

CHAPTER 5

Fire in the Night Sky

On the evening of February 22, McCleskey and I reported for duty on what would be my 35th combat mission in the A-26.[44] On two previous missions we had received some battle damage. As usual, we were carrying flares on the outside weapon stations, anti-personnel bombs on the inner stations, and rockets on the four middle positions. In the bomb bay we carried two monstrous one-thousand-pound bombs.

This particular night we were to follow, by about thirty minutes, another A-26 that had been designated Nimrod 36. We were designated Nimrod 37. The crewmembers of Nimrod 36 were Captain Dwight Campbell, pilot, and Captain Bob Scholl, navigator, both good friends of ours. The Ho Chi Minh Trail on the eastern border of Laos was only about thirty-five minutes away at our normal cruising speed of 200 knots. We had been forced to change aircraft because of an oil leak, and when we caught up with Nimrod 36, it was working with a C-130 flare ship with the call sign Lamplighter. They had located a large convoy of enemy trucks several miles south of the Ban Karai Pass bordering North Vietnam and Laos. Nimrod 36 had set fire to six of them and was continuing to work the area along the road with its six .50-caliber machine guns. However, they were under fire from at least four antiaircraft guns that we could spot.

It became our task to suppress the guns while Nimrod 36 continued to work over the trucks. We spotted a Soviet-made ZPU-4, identifiable by its red tracers, two 37mm flak guns, and a .50-caliber antiaircraft machine gun near the trucks. We decided the ZPU-4 was far enough to the west that we could avoid its area of effective fire and still work the trucks. As Nimrod 36 went in for a strafing run on the trucks, we made a rocket attack on the nearest 37mm gun. Diving at approximately a 40° angle, we fired rockets simultaneously from each wing. Both rockets seemed to make direct hits, but, within a few minutes, the gun recovered and resumed firing at Nimrod 36. We made another steep dive at the gun, this time delivering a thousand-pound bomb from the bomb bay. As we pulled off target and up from the dive, the tremendous blast of our bomb shook us even though we were now several thousand feet away. No more was heard from that antiaircraft gun.

We then went after the second 37mm gun, again firing rockets from the wing positions. Again, both seemed to be direct hits, but, as before, the gun resumed firing within a few minutes. By now we were disgusted with the rockets but confident of the power of the thousand-pound bombs.

Consequently, we made a steep dive on the gun and released our second and last thousand-pound bomb. We felt the now familiar jolt of the blast as we pulled off target. No more was heard from that gun either.

The .50-caliber antiaircraft machine gun was positioned to make strafing runs on the truck convoy especially dangerous. When we spotted the white tracers following Nimrod 36 as it made another strafing run on the trucks, we made a low-angle strafing run on the gun using our six .50-caliber machine guns in the nose. We managed to get several long bursts of strafing on target. For several minutes the gun was not heard from, so we began to strafe the trucks along with Nimrod 36. By this time, there were several more burning trucks along the road. I am not sure anyone ever got an exact count, but we had inflicted severe damage on the enemy truck convoy.

Several minutes later, however, the .50-caliber antiaircraft gun was back in action and firing at us. This time we made a very low, shallow strafing run, firing several long bursts of three to five seconds at the gun, and pulled up from the target no more than fifty feet from the ground. As we climbed off target, I could see the tell-tale white tracers of a .50-caliber antiaircraft gun going up just in front of and behind our right wing. Then there was a shattering clank and thud, and I knew we had been hit. I immediately called to McCleskey's attention that the fuel gauge for the right engine indicated we were rapidly losing fuel in the right main tank. The engine also began to smoke and behave erratically, so after a few more seconds of climbing away from the gun, we feathered the engine to prevent a fire. We climbed to 5,000 feet on the one engine and headed toward a hill that had been designated as a safe place to jettison armament.

Behind us, near the border of North Vietnam and Laos, we had left an inferno of blazing North Vietnamese Army (NVA) transport trucks. This large NVA convoy heading toward South Vietnam had been spotted crossing a sparsely vegetated clearing by a C-130 Lamplighter flare-ship. Several of the trucks were considerably larger than most NVA trucks seen along the Ho Chi Minh Trail. The length of the convoy and the larger size of some of the trucks had undoubtedly contributed to their detection. We had survived a fierce gun battle with three antiaircraft guns, but one surviving NVA .50-caliber antiaircraft gun had left us with only one engine and other possible battle damage.

Nimrod 36 came up under us to inspect for battle damage. Besides the damaged and now feathered number two engine, they noted a fire in our wheel-well, probably a burning tire. They also suspected that some fuel might be leaking onto the fire. We tried one of two fire extinguishers for the wheel-well area that could be remotely operated from the cockpit. Then Nimrod 36 came up under us again and informed us that it did not work. We made a second try with no results, and that was the last of our fire extinguishing capability. Our hearts sank at the disappointing news. By this time we were over the uninhabited area designated as a safe armament drop zone and dumped our flares, anti-personnel bombs, and the remaining rockets. Nimrod 36 came under us again and reported that there was still a fire in the wheel-well, and leaking fuel was feeding the blaze.

McCleskey, whose previous flying experience was with jet fighter/trainer-type aircraft, had one more trick up his sleeve to put the fire out. I think I had seen this before in a WWII movie, but I never thought I would have to live through it. He put the twin-engine aircraft, now with only one engine, into a very steep dive (nearly straight down) to try to blow the fire out. Putting a burning A-26 with only one engine into a steep 4000-foot dive is not for the faint-hearted, and I was greatly relieved when we pulled out of the dive at an altimeter reading of 1200 feet, just 700 feet from the ground. But Nimrod 36 came up under us again and reported the discouraging news that the wheel-well fire was still blazing.

By this time I would have preferred to bail out. However, because the A-26 had no ejection systems, and there had been numerous fatalities and serious injuries trying to bail out of the A-26 and the old B-26, McCleskey thought it best to attempt a crash landing on the pierced steel planking runway at NKP. Making a crash landing with one engine, unusable landing gear, and a fire on the underside of the aircraft near a fuel tank did not seem like an attractive alternative. But we were down to only two alternatives, and neither of them was good. We were within a few minutes now of NKP, and we started going down the checklist for a crash landing. Besides Nimrod 36, the C-130 flare-ship was also following us home and had alerted Air Rescue at Udorn Air Base in Thailand.

McCleskey told the tower at NKP that we were on fire and coming in for a crash landing. Two Jolly Green Giant helicopters were now on their way. Ground crews, fire trucks, and ambulances at NKP were already prepared and standing by. They searched the night sky for our burning and barely flyable aircraft to come into sight.

There was a great deal of adrenaline in my system as I went down the checklist, and I had to try hard to concentrate on my duties and responsibilities. I had been praying all along, but a favorite Bible verse popped into my head as we crossed the Mekong River into Thailand about ten miles from NKP. It was Matthew 10:29, probably the favorite of many aviators: "Are not two sparrows sold for a penny. Yet not one of them will fall to the ground apart from the will of your father." Verses 30 and 31 continue the thought: "And even the very hairs of your head are numbered. So do not be afraid. You are worth more than many sparrows."

We began making our approach to NKP at only 700 feet off the ground, but Nimrod 36 came under us again to make a final inspection. I remember vividly the words: "Your wheel-well is still on fire. My God, your whole wing's on fire. Get out. Get out." I quickly blew the canopy so we could bail out. With one wing of the aircraft on fire, McCleskey reported difficulty keeping it stable, making bail-out more difficult. To bail out of an A-26 after blowing the canopy, you must dive for the wing on your side and pull the cord on your chute when you clear the aircraft's tail. I unfastened my lap and shoulder belts and grabbed hold of my parachute ring. Since I had always been afraid that I might not have the presence of mind to find the parachute cord ring on the way down, I had my hand on it and pulled out several inches as I crouched low and lunged for the right wing. The 130-mph wind-stream, however, knocked me back into the cockpit, and I had to untangle myself from the seat harnesses again. As the fire increased, the aircraft was becoming more unstable and difficult to handle. At that point I believed I had almost no chance of survival. I made another lunge for the wing, this time with McCleskey giving a push with his right boot. As I made the second lunge for the wing, I prayed a prayer that I had just read in both the New Testament and Psalms. "Lord, into your hands I commit my spirit." This was the prayer Jesus uttered with his last breath, as recorded in Luke 23:46. Psalm 31:5 reads: "Into your hands I commit my spirit; redeem me, O Lord, the God of truth."

A second later, in the black of the night, I had cleared the tail, and my chute opened. A moment later at NKP, the Wing Commander, Col. "Heinie"Aderholt, looked up to see the brightest flash of light he had ever seen, almost as bright as the sun.

But the silly thought was running through my head that parachuting is really fun. I looked down and could see somehow in the dark night the top of a small tree. Then I hit—and hard! Disregarding all previous training on getting out of the chute by the quick releases, I unbuckled the chute harness, stepped out of it and let the chute blow away. My right foot was injured and hurting, so I remained seated on the ground, while I pulled out one of two radios I was carrying and started asking for the rescue helicopters. I thought I was talking to the other A-26, but it turned out to be the C-130 that had followed us. The voice on the radio assured me that two Jolly Greens were on the way. I sat there and nervously loaded my revolver. I never carried it loaded for fear of shooting myself in the hip or leg while trying to bail out. Although only ten miles from NKP and in Thailand, I was in an area that had recently reported as many as 2,000 North Vietnamese insurgents, and there had been some casualties. It worried me that I did not hear McCleskey on the radio. I wondered if he had made it or how far away he might be.

Within thirty minutes that seemed like a lifetime, I saw two Jolly Green rescue helicopters approaching from the Northwest. I got on the radio and guided them toward me by giving sort of a gyro-GCA (Ground Controlled Approach), telling them to turn left 30°, then corrected back to the right 10°, and so on. When the first was approaching me, I flashed a bright signal light, but the crew did not see it. Fortunately, the pilot of the second chopper spotted me and set down about twenty yards away.

Out came a young pararescue medic, Sergeant Duane Hackney. Since I could not walk on my right foot, he carried me into the helicopter. They had nothing for the pain in my foot, so they offered me a couple of small, complimentary bottles of bourbon whiskey of the kind that used to be given away on commercial airline flights. I quickly downed them both. Two weeks before, McCleskey and I had flown combat support for a rescue mission at Mu Gia Pass. On that mission, the pilot of a small FAC (Forward Air Control) spotter/observer plane from our Air Commando Wing at NKP and all of a rescue helicopter crew from Udorn, except Hackney, had been killed. This was Hackney's first mission since that night. He later received the Air Force Cross for the Mu Gia Pass mission and was to become one of the two most highly decorated Air Force enlisted men in the Vietnam War. I got to know him better about a year later when we were both assigned to the 41st Air Rescue Squadron in California. On this particular night, he later told me, he was very anxious, not having completely recovered from the previous experience.

The Jolly Green flew for a few more minutes—looking for McCleskey, I thought—but in a short while we landed at NKP, and I was transferred to a waiting ambulance. To my surprise, McCleskey was already in the ambulance. He asked if I had heard anything about Nimrod 36 being missing. The tragic part of this story, which we did not know for sure until the next day, is that our aircraft had exploded in midair about three seconds after we bailed out, and the debris from the explosion had hit Nimrod 36 in the cockpit and killed our two friends instantly. This was an especially grievous loss to both of us.

McCleskey had broken both ankles on his parachute landing and was badly scratched up and bloody from scraping along the fuselage as he bailed out. The arch of my right foot was broken with substantial muscle damage, and I had a good many small cuts, scratches, and bruises. I believe a part of the debris from the exploding aircraft may have hit my right foot since a metal grommet of my boot looked as if it had been hit with a sharp ax. Of course, we were only about 700 feet from the ground when we bailed out, so the chutes may not have completely deployed. McCleskey and I were sent to Clark AFB Hospital in the Philippines within a few days. After two months, McCleskey was back with the 606th at NKP and distinguished himself another night, winning the Silver Star. I would not recover as quickly, and after ninety days at

Clark, I was shipped back to the States to a series of three more hospitals. After a few more months, I was assigned to the 41st Air Rescue Squadron in California to fly HC-130s. It took still another three months of physical therapy before I regained flying status. During all those months, I had time to read and contemplate for what providence God had pulled me from a burning warplane.

McCleskey and I received the Distinguished Flying Cross and the Purple Heart for the action on February 22, 1967, as did Campbell and Scholl, the crew of the Nimrod 36, posthumously. While with the 41st Air Rescue at Hamilton AFB, California, I sent a letter back to the commander at NKP noting McCleskey's particular heroism in staying with the plane long enough to give me a shove with his boot to make sure that I could get out. I also noted the courageous action of Campbell and Scholl in coming under a burning aircraft at a low altitude. Had it not been for their warning, we would not have survived. I had hoped that McCleskey, Campbell, and Scholl might get some additional recognition, but I never received a reply or any news to that effect.

I will add one final note to this account. During the war there was much criticism and protest in the press, on college campuses, and by politicians both sincere and opportunistic, over American involvement in Vietnam. Much misinformation and misunderstanding of that war is still prevalent today. But I believed then, and still believe today, that defending Southeast Asia from Communist aggression and the brutal treatment of its people that followed was a worthy cause. Not all the political strategies, not all the military strategies and tactics, and not all the restrictions imposed on our armed forces were wise, but the cause was just.

USAF CH-3C Jolly Green Giant

USAF A-26K Counterinvader

CHAPTER 6

Rolling Thunder

American involvement in Vietnam remained largely advisory until late 1964. By June of that year, President Lyndon Johnson realized that North Vietnam was infiltrating regular army units into South Vietnam with five times the fire power of the South Vietnamese Army units.[45] Following attacks by North Vietnamese patrol boats on the destroyers *Maddox* and *Turner Joy* in the Tonkin Gulf in August 1964, Johnson allowed U.S. Navy aircraft to retaliate against North Vietnamese patrol boat installations.

On October 30, a Viet Cong attack on Bien Hoa Air Base destroyed six U.S. B-57 bombers and killed five American servicemen. Perhaps because the attack occurred on the eve of the presidential election and just after the Chinese tested their first atomic bomb, Johnson decided against any retaliation. Aside from domestic political considerations, Johnson wanted to demonstrate restraint to our European allies and the Soviet Union and show his willingness to settle differences by negotiation. Johnson's decision was against the strong advice of the Joint Chiefs of Staff (JCS), the Ambassador to Saigon, retired general Maxwell Taylor, and Admiral U.S. Grant Sharp, Commander-in-Chief, Pacific Command (CINPAC). The JCS proposed a non-nuclear, twenty-four- to thirty-six-hour, intense B-52 and fighter-bomber attack on North Vietnam and major transportation targets in Laos. The North Vietnamese targets included all major fuel storage facilities and military airfields around Hanoi and the port city of Haiphong. In addition, the port of Haiphong was to be mined. This was to be followed immediately by strikes against industrial facilities and other airfields, military installations, and important transportation centers. Such an attack would have had a crippling effect on North Vietnam's ability to wage a war against South Vietnam. Vetoing this JCS plan over their strong protest, Johnson established a pattern of ignoring experienced military advice.

It is interesting to contemplate what would have been the results if the JCS plans had been approved and executed accordingly. At the time, North Vietnamese air defenses were extremely weak. They had no jets, only a few limited airfields, fewer than twenty radars, and a mere handful of obsolete antiaircraft guns. In contrast, by mid-1967 the Soviets had supplied the North Vietnamese with a more formidable air defense system than U.S. bombers encountered over Germany in 1944.

On February 7, 1965, a barrage of mortar rounds unexpectedly crashed into the American airbase at Pleiku in the Central Highlands of South Vietnam, destroying or badly damaging twenty U.S. aircraft, killing eight Americans, and wounding 109 others. On February 10, Viet Cong sappers blew up an American hotel in Qui Nhon, killing twenty-three Americans as they slept. Now convinced that South Vietnam's survival was seriously threatened, Johnson allowed Admiral Sharp to retaliate by executing a contingency plan called "Flaming Dart." U.S. Navy jets bombed a North Vietnamese Army barracks and port just north of the DMZ, and the South Vietnamese Air Force was allowed to bomb a barracks about fifteen miles north of the DMZ. Thereafter, Johnson decided upon a slowly escalating "sustained" bombing of North Vietnam under an operation named by Washington as "Rolling Thunder."

The Rolling Thunder operation was initiated on March 2, 1965, and lasted for three and a half years, but it could hardly be called "sustained." Johnson insisted on many bombing halts in hopes that the North Vietnamese would negotiate peace, but the North Vietnamese consistently took advantage of the breaks in bombing to intensify the shipment of men, arms, and supplies into South Vietnam and to beef up their air defenses. Furthermore, the escalation was quite slow and gave the North Vietnamese a generous opportunity to build their ground forces and air defenses before they were seriously threatened. Bombing was also very restricted geographically. At first bombing was only allowed in the very southern part of North Vietnam, whereas the vast majority of really important targets were around Hanoi and Haiphong in the northeast. The types of targets were also restricted. Amazingly, U.S. aircraft were not allowed to fire on a surface-to-air-missile (SAM) site unless it had first fired on them.[46]

This theory of warfare—variously called "graded escalation," "gradual escalation," "the doctrine of gradualism," or sometimes just "the slow squeeze"—was the brainchild of Harvard academics, and Secretary of Defense Robert McNamara was its foremost ranking advocate. Lyndon Johnson became its most faithful and powerful executive disciple.

However bright the strategy of graded escalation might have seemed to Harvard whiz kids and game theorists, it went against the accumulated military wisdom of centuries.

The JCS, Admiral Sharp, the Central Intelligence Agency, the Defense Intelligence Agency, the State Department Intelligence Agency, and Secretary of State Dean Rusk all strongly opposed it.[47] Rather, the JCS and the intelligence agencies consistently advocated quick and decisive action against North Vietnam, including bombing critical military, air, naval, transportation, industrial, and fuel storage targets in all parts of North Vietnam, especially those near Hanoi and Haiphong. Conventional military wisdom is to hit an enemy as hard and fast as you can to maximize his costs and minimize your own risks and costs. A Marine Gunnery Sergeant once gave the advice, "Hit 'em as hard as you can, when they ain't looking." Giving the enemy plenty of time has few experienced survivors. Despite these objections, Johnson and McNamara, with the apparent consent of General Maxwell Taylor, who was acting as the U.S. Ambassador to Vietnam, decreed the graded escalation concept for Rolling Thunder. Taylor, however, was evidently misled on the degree of restraint.[48]

Operation Rolling Thunder kicked off on March 2, 1965, by sending several squadrons of USAF and Navy aircraft to bomb two minor targets just north of the DMZ. Then Johnson delayed two weeks before allowing another strike. General Taylor, a retired former Chairman of the JCS, doubted the enemy was impressed and sent a blistering rebuke to McNamara for risking aircrews and expensive aircraft in such a paltry and timid action.[49]

From the beginning of Rolling Thunder to late 1967, all the planning for air strikes was done at a Tuesday luncheon in Washington. Those attending were Johnson, McNamara, Secretary of State Rusk, Presidential Assistant Walt Rostow, and the Presidential Press Secretary, initially Bill Moyers. Assistant Secretary of Defense John McNaughton, a former Harvard faculty member and mathematical game theorist, was not an official member of this luncheon committee but wielded enormous influence on McNamara, who considered him his most trusted advisor. No military or naval officer was included in the planning, not even the Chairman of the JCS, until late 1967. The targets, the dates, the hour, the number and type of aircraft, the bomb loads, and many of the tactics were specified in Washington and passed through each intermediate headquarters to the USAF squadrons and Navy carriers affected. Thus, Johnson super-centralized even tactical decisions and micromanaged the air war.[50]

On one occasion Johnson bragged, "I won't let those Air Force Generals bomb the smallest outhouse without checking with me." On another occasion he said, "I spent ten hours a day worrying about all this, picking the targets one by one, making sure we didn't go over the limits."[51]

Johnson and McNamara were surprised and disappointed that their gradual escalation of the air war failed to bring Ho Chi Minh to the negotiating table—though no senior military commander or advisor was at all surprised. Yet the obvious failure of their gradual escalation policy during the first months of Rolling Thunder in 1965 and the relentless objections of senior military advisors and the intelligence community did not convince Johnson and McNamara of the folly of what Admiral Sharp called "powder-puff" air warfare doctrine.[52] Rather, on April 20, 1965, McNamara announced that the U.S emphasis would now turn to the ground war in South Vietnam. Bombing enemy targets in the south would take precedence over those in the north. In his 1978 book, *Strategy for Defeat*, Admiral Sharp stated, "This fateful decision contributed to our ultimate loss of South Vietnam as much as any other single action we took during our involvement."[53]

Sharp has also stated that the U. S. could have won the war in early 1965, when North Vietnamese air defenses were minimal, if we had used our enormous air power advantage aggressively rather than pursuing the misguided strategy of gradual escalation.[54]

On February 7, 1967, I again wrote my parents about the frustrations USAF and Navy aircrews were feeling about the debilitating target restrictions placed on air warfare by the Johnson Administration. "I am tired of dallying around in this war. If we want an end to the war, we're going to have to make the North Vietnamese suffer the consequences of war. We're not really doing that now. . . There's not much else I can say about it."

We were flying in an increasingly hellish antiaircraft environment but were restricted from delivering really devastating blows against North Vietnam's major air defenses and critical logistical and administrative concentrations. We were successful in reducing and slowing the manpower, weapons, and supplies flowing down the Ho Chi Minh Trail, but simply reducing and slowing this flow was not enough to prevent a steady build-up of North Vietnamese Army (NVA) strength in South Vietnam. The air warfare restrictions over North Vietnam resulted in higher allied casualties and more aluminum coffins going back to the States.

Air Force General William Momyer, 7th Air Force Commander, summarized the frustration of USAF aircrews flying over North Vietnam and Laos perfectly: "To wait until he (the enemy) has disseminated his supplies among thousands of trucks, sampans, rafts, and bicycles and then to send out multimillion dollar aircraft after these individual vehicles—this is how to maximize our costs, not his."[55]

Within weeks of my February 7 letter to my parents I would experience firsthand the impact of the NVA build-up in Laos and South Vietnam. Wounded on February 22 and evacuated to the USAF hospital at Clark AFB in the Philippines, I found myself among thousands of wounded Army, Marine, and South Korean Army (ROK) personnel who were casualties resulting from Soviet-made AK-47's, grenades, mines, artillery, and mortars that could have easily been stopped when concentrated in Haiphong or Hanoi.

The buildup of North Vietnam's air defenses dramatically illustrates the terrible folly of the Johnson-McNamara graduated escalation doctrine of air warfare. At the beginning of 1965, North Vietnam had no SAMs, few radars, and only a handful of obsolete anti-aircraft guns. The first SAM was detected by USAF photo reconnaissance planes on April 5, 1965. But Assistant Secretary of Defense John McNaughton advised McNamara that they should not be a threat, because the Soviets were only humoring the North Vietnamese and would discourage use of what few SAMs they allowed them. In a memo, McNaughton said, "We won't bomb the sites, and that will be a signal to North Vietnam not to use them." Reacting to the concern of USAF Lt. Gen. Thomas Moore, McNaughton told him, "You don't think the North Vietnamese are going to use them! Putting them in is just a political ploy by the Russians to appease Hanoi."[56]

However, several months later, on July 24, 1965, a Soviet missile crew shot down an F-4C. By the end of 1966 there were 150 SAM sites, and another 100 became operational in 1967 alone. In the three and a half years of operation Rolling Thunder, SAMs fired more than 5,000 missiles, bringing down 101 U.S. aircraft.[57]

Navy pilots spotted 111 SAM missiles loaded on railcars near Hanoi, but McNamara's rules of engagement prohibited bombing close to Hanoi, and the Navy's request to destroy them was denied. As one Navy pilot remarked, they would later have "to fight all 111 of them one at a time." The North Vietnamese and Soviets also took substantial advantage of the U.S. policy of prohibiting or restricting bombing in many areas around Hanoi and Haiphong. SAMs located in prohibited areas were able to engage U.S. aircraft as much as seventeen miles outside the area prohibited to U.S. bombing, thus firing on U.S. aircraft with impunity.[58]

In addition, most of the logistical systems supporting the North Vietnamese Army were within thirty miles of Hanoi and could not be attacked. By the end of 1966, over seventy MiGs challenged the USAF and Navy in the air over North Vietnam. Yet their airfields were prohibited strike areas, and USAF and Navy planes were not allowed to attack a MiG until it had taken off. North Vietnam had sixteen MiG-17 and Mig-21 aces!

Failure to throttle the import of conventional antiaircraft guns at their source resulted in far more U.S. aircraft casualties. While the North Vietnamese possessed only a few obsolete antiaircraft guns at the beginning of 1965, by the end of 1968 they had deployed 5,795 antiaircraft guns, many of them radar-controlled. About 68 percent of U.S. aircraft losses in Vietnam were due to conventional antiaircraft fire.[59] U.S. planes were often able to avoid SAMs by diving to a lower altitude but were then caught in a deadly barrage of flak and antiaircraft machine gun fire. As the number of SAMs and conventional antiaircraft weapons increased in North Vietnam and Laos, U.S. aircraft losses rose accordingly.[60]

Moreover, failure to pursue an air war necessitated a build-up of ground forces. In April 1965, when McNamara announced that the U.S. would concentrate on stopping the NVA and Viet Cong guerillas (VC) on the ground in South Vietnam rather than substantially accelerating air warfare against North Vietnam, there were not much more than 25,000 U.S. military personnel in Vietnam. By early 1967, we had more than 400,000 there. By the end of 1967, over 16,000 U.S. personnel had been killed in action.[61]

U.S. Army and USMC combat units countered the massive flow of enemy soldiers and weapons into South Vietnam by an aggressive strategy of attrition, which became the primary American ground war strategy. Given McNamara's substantial restrictions on air warfare in North Vietnam, Johnson's constant bombing halts, and engagement rules allowing enemy sanctuaries in Cambodia, Laos, and North Vietnam, our ground war strategy of aggressive attrition was really the only alternative. It was one which made good use of superior American fire power. By the end of the war Communist forces had suffered between 700,000 and 1,200,000 battle deaths, equal to between three and five percent of the total population of North Vietnam.[62] Yet Communist leaders were willing to sustain such casualties and press on.

While our strategy of attrition was very costly to our enemy, such a strategy always comes with a price tag. By the end of the war, U.S. forces had suffered 47,000 battle deaths. This was not a small price to the American people. The Communist strategic hope, which turned out to be correct, was that growing anti-war sentiment in the U.S. would eventually result in American withdrawal. Their hope was buttressed with well-organized leftist agitation on U.S. college campuses and in key urban areas.[63] In the end, this did, in fact, result in eventual U.S. abandonment of South Vietnam to a heavily armed and equipped North Vietnamese Army.

Another failure of the gradual escalation doctrine of air warfare involved U.S. attempts to destroy North Vietnam's fuel storage facilities. North Vietnam has no petroleum resources. One hundred percent of its petroleum, oils, and lubricants (POL) had to be imported from the Soviet Union or China. In late June 1966, President Johnson finally relented and allowed U.S. aircraft strikes on POL facilities in North Vietnam, including those near Hanoi and Haiphong. More than 80 percent were destroyed, but by that time the North Vietnamese had disbursed much of their POL storage. The sixteen-month delay in striking North Vietnam's major POL storage facilities had allowed the North Vietnamese to develop underground storage facilities and disburse POL stores in drums along the streets of populated areas, which were off limits to U.S. attack. Petroleum tankers, which were prohibited targets, often unloaded POL drums directly on to small barges and boats that transported them to hundreds of concealed locations along inland waterways. The June 1966 damage to Hanoi's petroleum inventory was severe but too late for maximum effectiveness.[64]

Air Force historian Wayne Thompson has pointed out a peculiar aspect of Johnson's air warfare policies in his book, *To Hanoi and Back*: "In Rolling Thunder, the Johnson Administration devised an air campaign that did a lot of bombing in a way calculated *not* to threaten the enemy regime's survival. . . President Johnson repeatedly assured the Communist rulers of North Vietnam that his forces would not hurt them, and he clearly meant it. Government buildings in Hanoi were never targeted."[65]

Judging by their actions, especially the bombing halts that hampered the effectiveness of our air power and endangered allied ground forces, Johnson, McNamara, and Assistant Secretary of Defense McNaughton apparently believed the widespread academic myth that Ho Chi Minh was a reluctant follower of Moscow and would be amenable to negotiating a just peace. That Ho was a heroic liberator of his people who had only reluctantly aligned his career with Soviet power was a common theme of anti-war propaganda during the war and is still popular with academic historians today. Ho often said things like, "It was patriotism, not communism, that inspired me."

But the curious calculation that Ho was a paternalistic nationalist open to sincere and reasonable peace negotiations on any terms other than eventual Communist takeover of South Vietnam ignored his record of deception and murder. In 1959, as part of his insurgency plan in South Vietnam, his terrorist cadre assassinated 250 government officials, village leaders, and uncooperative schoolteachers. Such terrorist murders increased to 1,400 in 1960, while Communist propaganda cultivated the image of a humble and kindly "Uncle Ho."[66] Johnson and McNamara were apparently unfamiliar with the Marxist doctrines that a lie that advances Communism is the truth and that whatever advances Communism is just. Reviewing the history of negotiations with North Korean leaders during the Korean War should have given any U.S. leaders cause to be wary Communist duplicity. That Ho consistently took maximum military advantage of Johnson's bombing halts and hopes for negotiation speaks for itself.

The North Vietnamese only negotiated in earnest when Nixon's Operation Linebacker II nearly bombed them into oblivion in December 1972. Sadly, the U.S. Congress threw that victory away and abandoned South Vietnam to a renewed North Vietnamese invasion in December 1974 and early 1975.

Navy A-4E Skyhawk

USAF F-105D Thunderchief

USAF F-4D Phantom

Navy A-6 Intruder

Lyndon Johnson

Robert McNamara

Admiral Grant Sharp

Gen. Maxwell Taylor

Gen. Earle Wheeler

CHAPTER 7

The Great Logistics Race
and the Battle of Ia Drang

On April 20, 1965, U.S. Secretary of Defense Robert McNamara held a conference in Honolulu to inform General Wheeler, the Chairman of the Joint Chiefs of Staff, and his top commanders in the Pacific of the Johnson-McNamara strategy to prevent the fall of South Vietnam to the Communist regime in Hanoi. Attending this meeting were Admiral Sharp, Commander-in-Chief of all U.S. forces in the Pacific (CINPAC); General Westmoreland, Commander of the Military Advisory Command in Vietnam (MACV); and retired General Maxwell Taylor, the U.S. Ambassador in Saigon. McNamara brought with him his most influential advisor, Assistant Secretary of Defense John McNaughton, and National Security Advisor Walt Rostow. This was a mere seven weeks following the commencement of Operation Rolling Thunder, Johnson's plan to bring Hanoi to the negotiating table by a gradually escalating campaign of bombing targets in North Vietnam.

The Joint Chiefs of Staff and U.S. intelligence agencies, however, had recommended a rapid and devastating escalation of air warfare against North Vietnam and warned Johnson that the Communist regime in North Vietnam would view a slow escalation of bombing as a demonstration of weak U. S. resolve. They also warned that a gradual escalation of air warfare against North Vietnam would dissipate the decisive advantage of American airpower and allow the North Vietnamese time to build up their army and air defenses—which could result in a considerable cost to U.S. and allied forces in the future.[67]

Despite the objections of his chief military and naval commanders, McNamara announced that the Johnson strategy for halting North Vietnamese aggression in South Vietnam would rely principally on allied ground forces. The chief role of U.S. airpower would be ground support of allied forces in South Vietnam rather than strategic bombing of the source of war materials in North Vietnam.[68]

This decision had several immediate influences on the conduct of the war. First, it implicitly removed any danger of invasion of the enemy's home territory by allied forces. The war had moved from a Viet Cong guerilla insurgency inspired and supported by the North Vietnamese to an outright invasion of South Vietnam by the North Vietnamese Army (NVA). South

Vietnam was being invaded, but North Vietnam was safe from invasion. Second, North Vietnamese troops would be allowed sanctuaries in Cambodia and Laos, on the western border of South Vietnam—at one point only thirty miles from Saigon. Third, the Johnson-McNamara restrictions on air warfare prohibited bombing around Hanoi, the port of Haiphong, and much of the railway system leading from China to Hanoi. These areas contained more than 80 percent of North Vietnam's most lucrative concentrations of enemy port facilities, airfields, railroads, fuel storage, weapons, supplies, and troops.[69] Trying to interdict the enemy's supplies and soldiers on their way to South Vietnam along the jungle roads of the Ho Chi Minh Trail would be far less effective and more costly than bombing them at their source. Johnson's strategy was essentially defensive and left most of the initiative to Hanoi.

The Johnson-McNamara strategy also caused an immediate logistical crisis. North Vietnam's most acclaimed military hero and strategist, General Vo Nguyen Giap, famous for his defeat of the French at Dien Bien Phu in 1954, was in the process of infiltrating three fully equipped NVA divisions into Cambodia and from there planned to cut South Vietnam in half. By such a feat, he hoped to demoralize the South Vietnamese Army (ARVN) and cause the collapse of the politically vulnerable regime in Saigon.

Giap's supply lines to Hanoi and Haiphong were relatively short and full. Few of the 25,000 American military personnel in Vietnam were combat troops. Most were support troops and training cadres for the still poorly armed and trained ARVN, whose firepower in 1965 was only about one fifth that of the Soviet- and Chinese-supplied NVA.[70] Moreover, the allied pipeline to the United States was long and dependent on tediously slow merchant marine traffic. Furthermore, Saigon was South Vietnam's only deep water port. Its facilities were antiquated, and its access to the sea by the Saigon River was vulnerable to Viet Cong interdiction. In addition, South Vietnam had only three airfields capable of handling larger transport aircraft. Meanwhile, the NVA, under Giap's close supervision, was working feverishly to have the men, weapons, and supplies in place to cut Vietnam in half on a line through Pleiku, An Khe, and Qui Nhon by early 1966. Saving South Vietnam would be a logistics race.

Many of the first and as yet unsung heroes of this race were the Army Corp of Engineers; Army, Air Force, Navy, and Marine construction battalions; the Merchant Marine; U.S. construction companies; and the transport squadrons of the USAF Military Airlift Command. In addition, General Westmoreland was permitted to use USAF, Marine, and Navy tactical fighters and bombers to support the ARVN in the field, and U.S. helicopters were used to transport ARVN troops to reinforce areas under NVA and VC attack. This support made a critical difference that the ARVN had not enjoyed before, and they were able to hold the NVA and VC at bay while a new port (called Newport) was built near Saigon; Nha Trang was made into a major port and airfield; and new airfields were built at Da Nang, Phan Rang, and Tuy Hoa. Even docking piers were shipped from Charleston, South Carolina. Roads and tactical airfields were built, support bases sprang up, and millions of tons of American supplies and weapons came pouring into to halt the North Vietnamese advance. By November there were over 150,000 U.S. personnel in South Vietnam.[71]

General Westmoreland felt he needed 300,000 men to save South Vietnam from military and political collapse, but he knew he would not have them before General Giap could attempt his death blow to South Vietnam. Westmoreland decided he must take decisive offensive action and deal Giap a crushing blow before the NVA could repeat a military and psychological victory—like that at Dien Bien Phu—against the ARVN and Saigon government.

In late September, Westmoreland saw his chance to stun Giap's gathering NVA divisions. Westmoreland noted with satisfaction the arrival of the First Cavalry Division (Airmobile), better known as the First Air Cavalry, under the command of a tough-minded Texan, General Harry W. O. Kinnard, since its inception. The First Air Cavalry was a combination infantry-artillery-helicopter division that went to war to the thumping sound of rotary helicopter blades. With 450 helicopters, it was a war machine of astonishing mobility and devastating firepower.

Westmoreland immediately dispatched the First Air Cavalry to a base hacked out of the jungle near An Khe, astride Highway 19 and blocking Giap's path from Pleiku to Qui Nhon. The soldiers of the division immediately began their aggressive mission of "unlimited offense" to "find and destroy North Vietnamese forces." The NVA, however, decided the First Air Cavalry was too far from its concentration near the Cambodian border to interfere with its planned ambush of an ARVN column and capture of an American Special Forces camp near Plei Me, about twenty-five miles southwest of Pleiku. This turned out to be a disastrous underestimation of the First Air Cavalry's mobility by the NVA.

The initial confrontations between NVA troops and First Air Cavalry units on November 1 led to a series of ferocious battles between three NVA regiments and units of two First Air Cavalry brigades along the Ia Drang (River Drang), near the Chu Pong massif on the Cambodian border. These clashes lasted until November 26, when the badly mauled NVA regiments retreated into their Cambodian sanctuary with only a remnant of their original strength. Ia Drang was a decisive American combat victory, and thereby General Westmoreland also won the strategically critical logistics race. But 305

Americans were killed in action. Over 1,500 NVA dead were counted. Total enemy dead probably exceeded 2,000.[72]

The Battle of Ia Drang is the subject of the critically acclaimed book, *We Were Soldiers Once...and Young* by Lt. Gen. Harold G. Moore and Joseph L. Galloway. Part of the movie, *We Were Soldiers,* starring Mel Gibson as Moore when he was a Lt. Col. and commander of the 1st Battalion, 7th Regiment, is based on the events at Ia Drang.

First Air Cavalry UH-1 liftship puts troops on the ground.

First Air Cavalry troops disembarking from UH-1 at Ia Drang

Army UH-1 Gunship

Heavily armed UH-1 liftship delivers troops to
mountain outpost

Gen. William Westmoreland

CHAPTER 8

Military Victories and Political Surrender

During the year 1966, the U.S. effort in Vietnam continued with its attrition war against enemy troops on the ground in South Vietnam. Army and Marine operation after operation—with code names like Utah, Texas, and Masher—were launched to run up the North Vietnamese Army (NVA) and Viet Cong (VC) body count. But the Army and Marines could never strike at major enemy forces until they emerged from their Cambodian and Laotian sanctuaries. Thus allied forces were never allowed the initiative, even on the ground. That was always left to the NVA.

Nevertheless, North Vietnam lost over 50,000 men killed in action during 1966, but it did not seem to matter to Ho Chi Minh or General Giap in the least.[73] During the same time there were just over 6,000 American battle deaths, but that was the cause of considerable public and political anti-war agitation in the U.S.[74] Any increase in bombing targets in North Vietnam met with an intense escalation of anti-war news in the U.S. media, agitation on college campuses, and hand-wringing in Congress.

The air war against North Vietnam actually declined during 1966. McNamara's priority for air warfare was, first, to support American and allied ground actions in South Vietnam and, second, to interdict Communist supplies coming through Laos. Strategic bombing of targets in North Vietnam ranked a distant third, and McNamara frequently urged its discontinuation altogether. Johnson, McNamara, and most of his civilian staff were obsessed with the fear of Chinese or Soviet intervention.

In early October 1966, McNamara made a brief visit to South Vietnam and, against the united advice of U.S. commanders there, recommended to President Johnson that the U.S. should avoid any bombing escalation and seek a negotiated peace with Hanoi. As an alternative he recommended a physical barrier across the DMZ and Laos. On October 14, in a memorandum to McNamara, which they explicitly urged to be passed on to the President, the JCS reacted strongly:

> The Joint Chiefs of Staff do not concur in your recommendation that there should be no increase in the level of bombing effort and no modification in areas and targets subject to attack. They believe our air campaign against North Vietnam to be an integral and indispensable part of our overall war effort. To be

effective, the air campaign would be conducted with only those minimum constraints necessary to avoid indiscriminate killing of population. The Joint Chiefs of Staff do not concur with your proposal that as a carrot to induce negotiations, we should suspend or reduce our bombing campaign against North Vietnam. . . Additionally, the Joint Chiefs of Staff believe that the likelihood of the war being settled by negotiation is small, and that, far from inducing negotiations, another bombing pause will be regarded by the North Vietnamese leaders, and our allies, as renewed evidence of lack of U.S. determination to press the war to a successful conclusion.[75]

Nevertheless, President Johnson halted the bombing during Christmas and New Year's truces and again during the Tet holidays on February 8-12. To his disappointment, no progress was made toward a negotiated settlement, but the North Vietnamese took full advantage of the lull in bombing and fighting to re-supply and strengthen their positions.

It was then that Johnson, because of relentless urging by the JCS and the Pacific Command, began to allow more strategic targets to be bombed in North Vietnam. Although the increase in bombing was rather modest, by the spring of 1967, there were fewer war materials getting through to the NVA in South Vietnam than were being destroyed by Allied forces in South Vietnam. The result was a continual net depletion of enemy combat capabilities.[76]

By mid-July, our modest and still restricted bombing raids on North Vietnam had at least temporarily destroyed 76 percent of ammunition depots, 87 percent of POL storage, 36 percent of railroad yards, 12 percent of maritime ports, 100 percent of iron and steel plants, 20 percent of naval bases, 23 percent of airfields, 78 percent of power plants, and 26 percent of military barracks. But no authorization had yet been given to bomb the majority (59 percent) of desirable strategic targets—which were generally the most vital targets.[77]

Yet McNamara visited Saigon in July 1967, hoping to find some reason to de-escalate or discontinue the bombing altogether. Again, he met with unanimous, strong opposition from military and naval commanders. By contrast, they proposed mining or bombing Haiphong harbor, mining inland waterways to China, and destroying all electrical generation capacity, maritime ports, airfields, transportation centers, military complexes, and war-supporting industry. In addition, they recommended extending the bombing to all of North Vietnam except some heavily populated areas of Hanoi.[78]

The JCS had also warned McNamara and Johnson again and again of the lessons we had learned in Korea: any negotiations with Communists must be accompanied by relentless tightening of military pressure on them—they understood force and force alone. Yet time after time Johnson removed the military pressure on Hanoi and offered them important one-sided concessions in hopes of a breakthrough toward negotiation.

As the strong disagreement between the JCS and McNamara over military strategy and especially the use of airpower began to spill over into Congressional dining rooms and the news media, the relatively conservative membership of the Senate Armed Forces Subcommittee on Military Preparedness, chaired by Senator John Stennis (D) of Mississippi, called for hearings. Every member of the JCS, the overall commander in the Pacific, Admiral Sharp, and many other qualified witnesses were called. The last witness was Secretary of Defense Robert McNamara himself. On August 9, Senator Stennis put the reasons for inquiry into Defense Department war policy succinctly: ". . .[T]he question was growing in Congress as to whether it is wise to send more men if we are just going to leave them at the mercy of the guerilla war without trying to cut off the enemy's supplies more effectively."[79]

The President had declined to escalate the bombing of North Vietnam in July; however, faced with having his policies subjected to the harsh scrutiny of the Stennis Subcommittee, he authorized bombing sixteen additional targets just hours before Admiral Sharp was scheduled to give his testimony. But Sharp's testimony was persuasive to the conservative membership of the subcommittee and backed by a common-sense interpretation of irrefutable data. Secretary McNamara gave testimony defending his policies on the last day, August 25. McNamara's articulate but evasive testimony, especially on his airpower policies, was unsuccessful in refuting the powerful statistical data and reasoning of the JCS and Admiral Sharp.

In the end, the subcommittee felt the military view sound and McNamara's view highly questionable. The subcommittee report was emphatic:

> In our hearings we found a sharp difference of opinion between the civilian authority and the top level military witnesses, who appeared before the subcommittee, over how and when our air power should be employed against North Vietnam. In that difference we believe we also found the roots of the persistent deterioration of public confidence in our air power because the plain facts, as they unfolded in the testimony, demonstrated clearly that civilian authority consistently overruled the unanimous recommendation of the military commander and the Joint Chiefs of Staff for a systematic, timely and hard-hitting integrated air campaign against the vital North Vietnam targets. Instead, for policy reasons, we have employed military aviation

in a carefully controlled, restricted and graduated build-up of bombing pressure which discounted the professional judgments of our best military experts and substituted civilian judgment in the details of target selection and the timing of strikes. We shackled the true potential of air power and permitted the build-up of what has become the world's most formidable anti-aircraft defenses.[80]

On September 1, Johnson called a press conference to distance himself from McNamara's policies and to deny any differences among his civilian and military advisors. On September 10, Johnson began to overrule McNamara's targeting decisions and allowed the USAF and Navy to bomb more important North Vietnamese installations. McNamara resigned by the end of the year. Johnson, however, continued his consistently unsuccessful policy of frequent bombing halts to persuade the North Vietnamese to negotiate. But, even with the bombing halts, the expanded bombing of targets in North Vietnam was devastating the North Vietnamese economy and Hanoi's ability to continue the war. An American victory was in sight had we only kept up the bombing pressure. However, political developments in the U.S., especially after the enemy offensive during the Tet holidays in early 1968, caused Johnson to order a drastic reduction in bombing for the rest of the year. Once again the politicians threw away victory for a bogus peace.

CHAPTER 9

Hanoi's Bloody Plans for Tet

Until April 1967, Ho Chi Minh and the Communist leaders of North Vietnam believed they could win the war by wearing down the political will of the Americans and South Vietnamese to fight a protracted war. However, new military and economic circumstances forced them to reconsider their previous strategy. Communist forces had not won a single significant victory in 1966, while suffering over 50,000 battle deaths. Allied forces suffered a combined total of less than 20,000 battle deaths, of which about 6,000 were Americans. The Communists had, in fact, lost more men in 1966 than the South Vietnamese had lost during the entire war to that date.[81] That very month General Westmoreland met with President Johnson in Washington to inform him of the "crossover" with respect to NVA manpower. The U.S. strategy of aggressive attrition, with its many "search and destroy missions," was killing more North Vietnamese soldiers each month than the number of North Vietnamese men coming of military age who could be trained and sent to the front.[82]

Westmoreland, however, also informed Johnson that the war would last another five years unless he could bring total U.S. strength to just over 700,000, approximately 200,000 more than previously planned. He believed the additional troops could shorten the war by three years. This, of course, assumed continuation of the Johnson-McNamara policy of only limited strategic bombing of North Vietnamese military, transportation, and port facilities.[83]

In early 1967, Johnson finally responded to the insistent demands of the JCS and Admiral Sharp, Commander-in-Chief Pacific Area Command (CINPAC), and approved some additional strategic bombing targets in North Vietnam. Although overall U.S. strategic bombing remained at a relatively modest level, by mid-1967 this new bombing effectively squeezed the North Vietnamese supply chain enough to result in a logistical "crossover." The allies were destroying more North Vietnamese war materials every month than the North Vietnamese could replace.

In addition, things were not going well for the Viet Cong (VC), either militarily or politically. Viet Cong casualties had been so high that their remaining forces were largely composed of North Vietnamese.[84] President Thieu and Prime Minister Ky had also brought enough stability to the government in Saigon to remove any doubt that the VC would be an improvement. The ham-fisted despotism and terrorist tactics of the VC had also made them extremely unpopular with the South Vietnamese people. Hanoi had not recognized it yet, but they had few friends left in South Vietnam.

By mid-1967 the NVA's escalating casualties and tightening logistical circumstances convinced the leaders of North Vietnam that they could not sustain a protracted war against the U.S. Time, they thought, was no longer on their side. They decided to abandon their protracted war strategy and go for a swift and decisive victory that would quickly collapse the government in Saigon and result in a humiliating U.S. withdrawal. General Giap envisioned another Dien Bien Phu, where his astonishing victory against a French expeditionary force in 1954 resulted in such public disillusionment in France that sustaining a war to defend its economic interests in Indochina became politically impossible.

General Vo Nguyen Giap was a former history teacher who became a self-taught soldier after the age of thirty. A shrewd student of both history and warfare and a dedicated nationalist and Communist zealot, he soon became Ho Chi Minh's most trusted military advisor. That trust was later validated by Giap's brilliant victory at Dien Bien Phu and the subsequent French withdrawal from Indo-China.

In 1953 and 1954, Giap had faced a technically superior French Army concentrated around Hanoi and other major population centers. His strategy was to create many military diversions in the outer periphery of French military concentrations, forcing the French to divide their forces to maintain control of the countryside. By these means he hoped to lure a major French force far enough from support to cut it off and annihilate it. With the French already involved in a costly civil war in Algeria, he correctly calculated that the French people were so war-weary that a major military catastrophe in Indochina would collapse the resolve of French political leaders to maintain a presence there.

In November 1953, seeking to cut off Vietminh supply routes from Laos, the French dropped over 5,100 paratroopers on an old airfield and military base surrounded by mountainous terrain near the border of Laos and northwestern Vietnam. By March 1954, the French expeditionary force—which could only be supplied and reinforced by air—had grown to nearly 12,000 men. Giap viewed the isolated French garrison at Dien Bien Phu as a fortuitous opportunity to implement his military and political strategy and subsequently invested the surrounding mountains with nearly 100,000 men. This was a remarkable military feat in itself, but most astonishing to the French was that this enormous Vietminh force was well equipped with Soviet and Chinese heavy artillery and nearly 200 antiaircraft guns. On March 13, the Vietminh began their assault on Dien Bien Phu with a tremendous artillery barrage. In the next fifty-seven days of hell the French brought in another 4,000 men, but by May 6, despite heroic efforts, logistical support and reinforcement became almost impossible. On May 7, with little ammunition left, the remaining 11,700 French troops, including 4,500 wounded, were overrun and captured. The resulting military catastrophe broke the French political will as expected. Fewer than 5,000 French POWs were ever returned.[85]

In early 1968, Giap planned to collapse the Saigon government and break American will by inflicting a similar military victory and political embarrassment in South Vietnam. Giap knew that South Vietnam would be most vulnerable to attack during the generally relaxed week of Tet holidays celebrating the Chinese lunar New Year, which began that year on January 30. During the holidays many people—including South Vietnamese soldiers on leave—would be traveling and relaxing.

General Giap formed five assumptions in calculating his chances for another "Dien Bien Phu."[86]

1. U.S. politics would prevent American military strength from being increased significantly above the 485,000 already there.
2. President Johnson would not loosen his restraints on American airpower or allow American ground forces to enter NVA sanctuaries in Cambodia and Laos or enter into North Vietnam.
3. Anti-war sentiment in the U.S., especially in an election year, would force U.S. political leaders to throw in the towel quickly following a Communist victory.
4. The South Vietnamese Army would quickly disintegrate in the face of a powerful NVA onslaught.
5. Seeing that a Communist victory was imminent, the South Vietnamese people would rise up as one to overthrow the remnant of the Saigon government.

Giap started laying the foundations for this victory during the previous fall. In October 1967, he had begun a series of bloody diversionary attacks around South Vietnam. A U.S. Marine base at Con Thien near the DMZ was attacked with such force that it took B-52 bombers to drive off the determined NVA units. Then NVA shock troops attacked Loc Ninh, a district capital near the Cambodian sanctuary. Then they hit nearby Song Be. In November, the NVA struck Dak To in Kontum Province. The battle there raged for twenty-two days, and Westmoreland had to deploy elements of the 4th Infantry and First Air Cavalry divisions, an airborne brigade, and six South Vietnamese Army (ARVN) battalions to break the NVA assault. In December, there were battalion-size VC attacks in the Delta.

U.S. and ARVN troops were suffering many casualties in these battles, but the NVA losses were staggering. General Giap took these losses stoically.

He once said, "The life or death of a hundred, a thousand, or tens of thousands of human beings, even if they are our own compatriots, represents really very little. . ."[87]

Giap was only concerned with the results. In this case, he felt the results he wanted had been achieved. American and ARVN forces were being pulled to places remote from major population and government centers. In fact, despite heavy losses, Giap prolonged and intensified his peripheral campaign in order to create the bloodiest headlines possible for the American media.

On January 21, 1968, two NVA divisions besieged the 6,000 Marines based at Khe Sanh near the DMZ and the Laotian border. The NVA began by pounding the Marines with artillery hidden in the nearby ring of hills. NVA infantry then began digging trenches closer and closer to the American perimeter. Khe Sanh became one of the fiercest battles of the war with NVA tactics strikingly reminiscent of Dien Bien Phu. At one nearby outpost the Marines drove off NVA attackers in hand-to-hand fighting. American television news programs reported on Khe Sanh nightly. President Johnson became obsessed with daily developments there and had his aides construct a minutely accurate photomural of the base and surrounding area, which covered several tables and showed trenches, gun placements, and other details. The battle lasted seventy-seven days. B-52s and tactical fighter-bombers constantly blasted NVA positions.

But Khe Sanh was only a diversionary feint. Giap never intended to overrun it. His scheme was more breath-taking: While the NVA engaged in diversionary battles for the most part outside South Vietnam's major population and political centers, Giap planned to attack and capture thirty-six of the forty-four provincial capitals and five of six autonomous cities in South Vietnam by surprise attacks during the relaxed Tet holidays. Then through a coordinated effort of the NVA and VC, he hoped to instigate a general uprising to overthrow most provincial governments and cause the government in Saigon to collapse.[88]

Vo Nguyen Giap

Le Duan and Castro

CHAPTER 10

The 1968 Tet Offensive

As 1968 began, President Johnson continued to make negotiations with North Vietnam his top priority for ending the war. Moreover, he was so anxious to negotiate that he made frequent offers to stop U.S. bombing over North Vietnam on no precondition other than that North Vietnam come to the negotiating table and talk. No demand was made on them to halt any military or logistical action as a concession to the U.S. and South Vietnam. This was despite their treacherous record of taking military and logistical advantage of past truces and bombing halts without making a single concession. They simply demanded more and waited for the Johnson Administration to give it to them. The new Secretary of Defense, Clark Clifford, was in complete agreement with such a negotiating strategy.

At that time, I was assigned to the 41st Air Rescue Squadron in California, flying HC-130s. I was dumbfounded when our squadron commander gave me a Department of Defense (DOD) memo requesting suggestions on how the armed forces could be used more effectively in the "War on Poverty." The DOD under Clifford would not be friendly to strategic bombing or tough-minded negotiations. Admiral U.S. Grant Sharp summarized my own frustration: "We could have flattened every war-making facility in North Vietnam. But the handwringers had center stage; the anti-war elements were in full cry. The most powerful country in the world did not have the willpower needed to meet the situation."[89]

In 1968, the first day of the Chinese Lunar New Year and thus the beginning of the week-long Tet holiday fell on January 30. During previous years, both sides had honored the Tet holiday by a cease fire, either officially or unofficially. But with several intense battles between the North Vietnamese Army (NVA) and allied forces raging around the country—especially the Dien Bien Phu-like siege of Khe Sanh—most military commanders and intelligence officers knew something big was in the making. Given the enormous importance of Tet in both Vietnams, they assumed that the big push would come after the seven-day holiday and that it would probably be the final assault on Khe Sanh. Had they studied their history and General Giap better, however, they would have found that the successful overthrow of the Chinese occupiers of Hanoi in 1789—an immensely important event in Vietnamese history—had occurred during the Tet holiday.[90]

The overthrow of the Chinese in 1789 was important in another respect: It had not been a palace coup or battle between rival warlords, but a general uprising of the people. Thus the concept of a general uprising against oppression was ingrained in Vietnamese political thinking.

It was just such a general uprising that General Giap hoped to instigate in South Vietnam to bring down the Saigon government and force a humiliating American withdrawal. Phase I of Giap's plan, creating diversionary conflicts outside the major population and government centers, was working extremely well. The NVA was paying an incredibly high price in blood, but U.S. and South Vietnamese (ARVN) troops were being deployed away from Giap's real target—the people. Giap made sure that peripheral battles like Dak To and Khe Sanh were as long and bloody as possible for maximum U.S. media impact.

Phase II would require stealth and surprise. If there is anything the North Vietnamese are famous for in history, it is their extraordinary ability to move large numbers of men and supplies to a battle field without detection. More than 70,000 Viet Cong (VC) were to infiltrate thirty-six of the forty-four provincial capitals, six major cities, and numerous secondary administrative and population centers. In addition, they would strike every allied airfield in the country. Yet they would have to avoid any area of allied strength where deadly American firepower might be brought against them.

Meanwhile, thousands of tons of war materials were being brought into Cambodian ports. These would be transported to the NVA's Cambodian sanctuaries and then to secret stockpiles in South Vietnam from which thousands of new AK-47 assault rifles, B-40 rockets, and tons of food, fuel, and ammunition could be distributed. Even propaganda leaflets were being stockpiled.

Only a few high ranking NVA officers knew the date on which VC units would be sent surging into unsuspecting and vulnerable cities. The principal targets would be symbols of South Vietnamese government power: government offices, administrative buildings, radio stations, newspapers, police stations, and political headquarters. Once in place, VC political agitators and organizers would announce that the government in Saigon had fallen and that a new "coalition government," whose main goal was peace, was in charge. Amnesty would be offered to ARVN soldiers and units who came over to the "coalition government" side.

The third and final phase of Giap's plan would be an NVA sweep to clean up pockets of South Vietnamese resistance, destroy any intervening American and allied forces, help promote the general uprising, and make sure that Hanoi remained in control of the new "coalition government."

Giap's Grand Strategy assumed that the South Vietnamese Army would melt away by desertions and defections and that the people would embrace the general uprising and the victorious new coalition for peace.

In mid-January, VC troops and political organizers began filtering into South Vietnamese provincial capitals, district capitals, and large cities by tens and hundreds. As usual, they did so with minimal detection. But Lt. Gen. Fred Weyand, commander of the Saigon sector, was becoming uneasy. There were many signs of unrest. Consequently, he convinced General Westmoreland to move fifteen combat battalions from the Cambodian border to the Saigon area, giving Weyand twenty-seven U.S. combat battalions to protect Saigon.

With much fanfare, Hanoi and the VC announced a seven-day truce beginning on the 29th and implied that there might be an extension. By 6 p.m. Saigon time on January 29, half of the ARVN was on leave, but 70,000 VC assault troops were in place, ready to strike the most important administrative and population centers in the country. Six hours later the Tet offensive began. The suddenness and magnitude of the offensive stunned the allies and especially the American media.

However, Giap's plan had several flaws. Because the timing of the action had been kept secret, resulting communications problems led to a lack of coordination. Rather than a simultaneous assault, VC action and NVA coordination occurred hours or even days after the start—in one case, twelve days late. These delays forfeited the surprise effect in about two-thirds of the provinces. In addition, the VC were everywhere, but nowhere in strength, and Giap had forfeited the traditional military advantage of mass.

More importantly, Giap was disastrously wrong in his assumptions that the ARVN would crumble and that the South Vietnamese people would rally to the Viet Cong. Although only at half strength because of the Tet holiday, the ARVN rallied and fought with surprising spirit and toughness. As a result of furious ARVN and American counter-attacks, by February 12 nearly 32,000 VC had been killed in action.[91] Moreover, the South Vietnamese did not view the Communist invaders as liberators. They knew well the invaders' bloody and despotic style of "liberation." Rather than a general uprising against the Saigon government, there was a general uprising to support the Saigon government and throw the VC and NVA out. The VC assault during Tet was an utter failure in all but ten provinces. Tet proved that, despite political differences in South Vietnam, the overwhelming majority of the South Vietnamese people were strongly anti-Communist. Tet also turned out to be one of the South Vietnamese Army's finest hours.

The most successful VC and NVA assault was on Hue, where street fighting continued for twenty-five days. The Communists used their 25-day reign of terror in Hue to execute 3,000 civilians presumed to have anti-

Communist political views. The tough street fighting in Hue resulted in 500 American and ARVN battle deaths. As usual the VC and NVA paid an even dearer price—4,500 dead.[92] But on American TV coverage of Hue, Vietnam did not look like a war we were winning.

The VC's greatest psychological victory, however, was scored by a suicide platoon of just twenty VC from Sapper Battalion C-10. At 2:45 a.m. on the second day of Tet, they drove a taxi and a small truck to the U.S. Embassy compound and opened fire on the two Marine guards as they approached the gate. The Marines, however, closed the gate and shot down several of the VC, including their leader, before they themselves were killed. The VC blew a large hole in the fence, but found that other Marine guards had locked all the buildings. At dawn American military police reinforcements rushed the gate, and airborne assault troops were landed on the roof. By 7 a.m. all twenty VC sappers were dead. Five Americans, including the two Marine guards, had been killed.[93] The news media, however, erroneously reported that the VC had captured the U.S. embassy. Walter Cronkite exclaimed to his TV audience, "I thought we were winning the war." The erroneous reports were corrected, but Cronkite's remarks helped convey a completely false impression that Tet was a great Communist victory.

More than 1,000 VC were also able to entrench themselves in scattered pockets of Cholon, the Chinese sector of Saigon, for several days. Seven of Westmoreland's maneuver battalions wiped out all who could not manage to escape in civilian dress. Westmoreland's timely reassignment of troops from the Cambodian border to Saigon probably negated any realistic chance for a Communist victory in Saigon.

Due in large part to the U.S. media's excited misreporting and distortions, the Tet offensive was viewed by many in Congress as a Communist victory. In reality, it was a complete failure, probably the most costly Communist defeat of the war. Of the 85,000 NVA and VC troops involved, over 45,000 were killed in action. Just over 1,000 Americans and 2,100 allied soldiers were killed.[94]

USAF AC-47D Spooky
(Puff the Magic Dragon

CHAPTER 11

Throwing Away a Great Victory

By the end of February 1968, the four weeks of Tet battles were over. Not one of South Vietnam's forty-four provincial capitals remained in enemy hands or was under enemy attack. But 45,000 of the 85,000 Vietcong (VC) and North Vietnamese Army (NVA) troops who participated in the attacks were dead, while allied losses were relatively light: slightly more than 1,000 Americans and 2,100 South Vietnamese Army (ARVN) troops had been killed. Communist forces had suffered the most costly and stinging defeat of the war, and the VC were demoralized and reduced to nominal combat effectiveness. Moreover, the ARVN had proved itself a capable and highly motivated fighting force, and the South Vietnamese people had proved themselves to be stubbornly and overwhelmingly anti-Communist.[95]

American television coverage, however, made the unsuccessful VC attack on the U.S. Embassy and the ferocious and bloody street fighting in Hue appear like astonishing Communist victories. Tragically, the Communists had managed to execute almost 3,000 civilians suspected of anti-Communist political sentiments during their three-week control of part of Hue. This number unfortunately included the wives and children of prominent anti-Communists.[96] Indeed, American and South Vietnamese forces had been caught somewhat off guard, but despite their surprise, they still launched smashing counter-attacks that devastated the VC and NVA forces. In the end, North Vietnamese General Vo Nguyen Giap's grand strategy to collapse South Vietnam was an utter failure, and his forces were in disarray. In addition, the North Vietnamese economy was being slowly strangled by increased U.S. Air Force and Navy bombing. It was now the long North Vietnamese struggle to bring South Vietnam under its control that was about to collapse.[97]

Yet in the U.S., the news coverage continued to imply that America's effort to defend South Vietnam's freedom was a costly failure that promised more frustration, failure, and endless battle casualties in the future. Ironically, this was at the very same time that Ho Chi Minh and his politburo were seriously considering throwing in the towel until such time as future events or political developments restored their chances of success.

According to Admiral U.S. Grant Sharp, Commander-in-Chief of all Pacific forces at that time, had President Johnson listened to the Joint Chiefs of Staff and his military and naval commanders in the Pacific and implemented their plans to mine the harbor at Haiphong and lift the bombing restrictions on military, transportation, and logistics targets in North Vietnam, the war would have ended in an American and allied victory within a few months. That is my opinion as well. Military historian, S. L. A. Marshall, summarized the opinions of many American officers that the Johnson Administration's failure to exploit the remarkable success of the allied counter-attack following the 1968 Tet Offensive was "a potential major victory turned into disastrous retreat through mistaken estimates, loss of nerve, bad advice, failure in leadership, and a tidal wave of defeatism."[98]

There were two American intelligence shortcomings, however, that contributed to our failure to exploit our tremendously successful counter-attack. First, although the Tet Offensive turned out to be a major Communist defeat and a major allied victory, the surprise of the attacks alarmed the U.S. media, the public, and Congress. This alarm was a major factor in turning public opinion and key political leaders against the war and making rational and informed decisions on future war strategy politically difficult. There was evidence of large shifts in VC positions but no one took it seriously. All focus was on Khe Sanh. Several documents captured one to two months before Tet outlined General Giap's plan but were dismissed as propaganda. The war had been going extremely well on the ground and the NVA and VC were beginning to experience a shortage of manpower and war materials—this was in fact the reason for their desperate attempt to win a quick victory.[99] U.S. successes in 1966 and 1967 had led to unrealistic optimism, and Allied officers just could not believe the enemy could pull off such a vast operation.

Second, but understandably, military intelligence in the field did not recognize the full and enormous extent of enemy casualties for several weeks. As a result, General Wheeler and General Westmoreland gave rather cautious first appraisals of conditions following Tet. This unfortunately preconditioned President Johnson and the already dovish civilians in the Defense Department toward negotiation rather than aggressive exploitation of North Vietnam's military calamity. Nevertheless, both Wheeler and Westmoreland viewed the failed Communist Tet Offensive as a golden opportunity to go for North Vietnam's jugular and complete victory. However, their plan required another 206,000 men to push the NVA out of its Cambodian and Laotian sanctuaries within a year. This would have brought total U.S. strength to about 731,000, which Johnson viewed as politically impossible, and his dovish civilian Defense Department advisors viewed as extremely alarming.

Unfortunately, many faulty decisions were made before it was realized just how badly the VC and NVA had been beaten up during their disastrous Tet enterprise. The Wheeler-Westmoreland plan could have been accomplished with no increase in troops, and the victory would have been swift had the U.S.

Air Force and Navy been released to mine Haiphong harbor and destroy strategic military, shipping, and rail targets in North Vietnam.

In addition, the flow of news from late January through the end of February 1968 was especially likely to undermine public optimism about the war and the credibility of the Johnson Administration. Just four days before Tet, General Westmoreland's optimistic assessment of 1967 became available to the press. Westmoreland accurately described the situation: North Vietnam and the VC were suffering military defeat after defeat; the VC had declined substantially as a military threat, and North Vietnam's ability to replenish the NVA's heavy losses in manpower and war materials in the field was faltering; the North Vietnamese economy was being strangled, and North Vietnamese leaders were finding themselves in an increasingly desperate situation. Hanoi would have agreed with Westmoreland's optimistic assessment. But Westmoreland did not know that Hanoi was desperate enough to stake the outcome of the war on a single but comprehensive offensive plan designed to collapse the South Vietnamese government and humiliate the U.S. into withdrawing under the pressure of American public opinion. Captured documents indicate this comprehensive plan included disseminating "peace-movement" propaganda and agitating political and social unrest in the United States. Hanoi was going all out for a decisive, grand victory.[100]

Four days after Westmoreland's optimistic statements circulated in the press, the nightly TV news was filled with scenes of battle and gore . This went on for more than a month. Many news announcements were politically untimely and further undermined public confidence in our war efforts. On February 13, the Pentagon announced that 10,500 troops were leaving to reinforce American units engaged in the Tet Offensive. On February 17, the highest weekly casualties of the war to that date were announced—543 Americans killed and 2,547 wounded.[101] On February 23, there was a new draft call for 48,000 men, the second highest of the war. On the same day, the NVA bombarded Khe Sanh with 1,100 high explosive artillery shells, and there was a VC mortar attack on Saigon. On February 27, *CBS Evening News* anchorman, Walter Cronkite, pontificated that the war was a hopeless stalemate and that the U.S. should negotiate a withdrawal from Vietnam. It did not seem to the public that victory was anywhere near.

Johnson and much of the Democratic Party were in a state of near panic as these events unfolded in an election year. On March 10, the Wheeler-Westmoreland request for 206,000 more troops was leaked to the press and printed in the *New York Times*. Two days later, Senator Eugene McCarthy (D, MN.) came very near defeating the President in the New Hampshire Democratic Primary with 42 percent of the vote to Johnson's 46 percent. On

March 16, New York Senator Robert Kennedy, sensing Johnson's vulnerability on the war, entered the Democratic race for President.

In mid-March, Johnson gathered a Senior Informal Advisory Group to get members' recommendations on the war. The group was heavily weighted with former cabinet members and other high ranking State Department and civilian Defense Department officials in Democratic administrations but included several retired generals, among them General Maxwell Taylor. The majority of the group favored de-escalation of the war. According to Taylor, who was one of the strong dissenting votes, the group was overly influenced by the civilian "doves" in the Pentagon and the anti-war bias of the East Coast media. Taylor also believed that many members of the group were already of a mindset that no military solution was possible. Meanwhile, Johnson was being pressured by dovish Senate Democrats and a few liberal Republicans to negotiate American withdrawal from Vietnam. During his entire tenure as President, Johnson consistently leaned toward his many dovish advisors from government and civilian think-tanks and away from military advice, no matter how experienced or close to the ground on military matters.

Finally on March 31, Johnson publicly called for a negotiated peace in Vietnam, and ordered a halt to all bombing north of 20° latitude in North Vietnam—which contained more than 85 percent of the important military and logistical targets.[102] He invited the North Vietnamese to join the peace talks without any preconditions or similar gestures, and announced he would not be a candidate for President in 1968.

A military calamity for the Communist rulers of North Vietnam was thus turned into a substantial political victory for them in the United States, and a golden opportunity for American and allied victory was again thrown away.

CHAPTER 12

Fruitless Negotiations

On March 31, 1968, President Lyndon announced that he would not seek reelection to a second full term in the White House. At the same time he unilaterally halted all USAF and Navy bombing north of 20° latitude in North Vietnam and invited the North Vietnamese to join in peace talks without insisting on any preconditions on their part. The bombing halt and unconditional peace talks were against the strong advice of the Joint Chiefs of Staff (JCS) and his chief military and naval commanders in the Pacific. As usual Johnson listened to his civilian Defense Department staff and his political advisors rather than experienced military commanders close to the action.

Unfortunately, the bombing halt and call for unconditional peace talks came just as the Communist regime in Hanoi, reeling from its heavy losses during their unsuccessful Tet campaign, were ready to throw in the towel. Had Johnson approved the JCS plan to mine Haiphong harbor and bomb all strategic targets in North Vietnam outside of heavily populated areas, the North Vietnamese would have had no choice but to withdraw their troops from South Vietnam and negotiate a peace on American terms. Instead, Johnson gave them the chance to gain on the negotiating table what they were clearly losing on the battlefield.

Moreover, the left began more intense organization of anti-war propaganda and protests in the United States. On April 26, nearly 200,000 people in New York City demonstrated against the war.[103] This was only the first of many such orchestrated events. Anti-war protestors instigated demonstrations in Chicago during the August 1968 Democratic Convention that resulted in riots. The organizers included some of the most famous names of the radical left—Jerry Rubin, Abbie Hoffman, David Dellinger, Tom Hayden, Rennie Davis, and Bobby Seale. These six were found guilty of crossing state lines to incite a riot and contempt of court, but the convictions were later overturned on appeal.[104]

On May 10, the North Vietnamese agreed to enter into negotiations in Paris. By May 20, they had already infiltrated another 80,000 men into South Vietnam to replace their losses. They were accompanied by thousands of tons of new Soviet and Chinese arms, ammunition, and supplies.[105] Meanwhile, and for the rest of Johnson's term, the progress of peace negotiations in Paris was fruitless, just as had been two years of negotiations with North Korean Communists from 1951 to 1953.

The North Vietnamese Army (NVA) replacements were only barely trained, but months of disingenuous negotiations with no concessions gave them time to train. The poor training of these recruits continued to add to NVA losses. In the first half of 1968 alone, which included the bloody weeks of Tet, Communist battle deaths accumulated to over 100,000.[106] Yet rather than taking the opportunity to finish off Hanoi's capacity to make war, the U.S. continued its fruitless negotiations in Paris without the Communists making a single concession.

Earlier in the spring the Republicans in Congress had gathered a team of distinguished military experts to assess the situation in Southeast Asia. This group was composed of former Secretaries of Defense Neil McElroy and Thomas Gates; former Assistant Secretaries of Defense Wilfred McNeil and Perkins McGuire; and a panel of retired four-star flag and general officers, including Navy admirals Arleigh Burke, Harry Felt, and Arthur Radford; Army generals George Decker and Alfred Gruenther; and Air Force generals Bernard Schriever and Nathan Twining. Congressional members included Senator James Pearson of Kansas, Congressman Craig Hosmer of California, and Senator John Tower of Texas, as Chairman.

Their report, released on April 18, was entitled "The Failure of Gradualism in Vietnam." The report cited the failure of the doctrines of "measured escalation" and "flexible response," largely the ideas of former Secretary of Defense Robert McNamara, as dangerously unrealistic and disastrous. It further stressed the necessity of quick and decisive action once the nation resorts to arms. The report also emphasized the folly of assuring an enemy that it would only pay a moderate or limited price for aggression.

Lyndon Johnson and his Democratic Administration paid little heed to this report and continued to hope for a "breakthrough" in negotiations, while American air and naval power were muzzled and American and allied soldiers were dying on the battlefield. Approximately 14,600 American servicemen and 28,000 South Vietnamese soldiers were killed in action in 1968 while the Johnson Administration all but kissed the posteriors of North Vietnamese diplomats in Paris.[107]

Admiral U.S. Grant Sharp, Commander of all U.S. forces in the Pacific, later expressed the frustration that most American officers felt as the NVA prepared for another offensive thrust on Saigon: ". . .[T]he fruitless negotiations droned on in Paris, with no real progress in sight. We were sitting back and allowing these bandits to do just as they pleased in South Vietnam without retaliating on their own country at a time when we had aircraft carriers and airfields full of planes that could have gone up and blasted Hanoi and Haiphong wide open, if we had just been given the 'go' sign. It was the most asinine way to fight a war that could possibly be imagined."[108]

On October 31, just days before the November 5 presidential election, Johnson announced a complete bombing halt of all targets in North Vietnam, thoroughly emasculating allied chances for victory. The next Tuesday, Republican Richard Nixon was elected President of the United States.

Nixon, however, did not immediately heed the advice of Senator Tower's Republican Task Force or the JCS. He came into office politically handicapped by widespread public misunderstanding of the war and strong public and political pressures to de-escalate military activity and withdraw. Nixon at first attempted to disengage by a program of "Vietnamization," as suggested by his Secretary of Defense, Melvin Laird. This had become increasingly feasible following Tet as the South Vietnamese government had gained considerable credibility with the South Vietnamese people, while Communist credibility—owing both to their failure and their totalitarian form of "liberation"—had been destroyed. The South Vietnamese Armed Forces (SVNAF) were able to recruit and build from 798,000 in late 1968 to 1,050,000 in late 1971.[109] However, Nixon soon found that Vietnamization could not work while Soviet and Chinese arms and logistical support for North Vietnam continued to pour unhindered into Haiphong and Hanoi and Allied forces were being attacked from NVA and VC sanctuaries in Cambodia and Laos. In 1972 Nixon finally took some decisive actions that had the North Vietnamese pleading for mercy, but by then he was involved in the Watergate scandal that ended his presidency. Congress quickly threw another victory away and left the South Vietnamese to face the whole Communist world by itself.

Had the U.S. used its Air Force and Navy airpower decisively, the war could have been won easily and without much cost in early 1965, before the Soviets and Chinese helped North Vietnam build the greatest air defense system in history. We could have won in mid-1967, when the Communists were unable to fully replace lost manpower and destroyed supplies. We missed a perfect opportunity after the battles of Tet in early 1968, when the Viet Cong and NVA had been so mauled and devastated that the leaders of Hanoi were on the verge of conceding defeat except for encouraging political developments in the U.S. In fact, we could have won at any time our national leaders had the will to use our naval and airpower to its fullest advantage—without resorting to nuclear weapons.

One of the lessons learned from Vietnam is that Communists do not negotiate in good faith. They take advantage of negotiations and truces to build up strength. Deceit and patience are their primary negotiating weapons. They will win at the negotiating table if they can, but they will not give up winning. Any loss in battle or at the negotiating table is regarded as a temporary loss to be recovered as soon as they can gain the upper hand.

The "Cold War" against Communism is largely in the past, but its negotiating lessons should not be lost. While the deeper theology of fundamental Islam and Communism are far apart, their operational doctrines on war, negotiation, truces, and justifying deception are remarkably close. Robert Spencer, author of six books on Islam, has aptly described Islam's overarching moral principle: "If it is good for Islam, it is right."[110] European historian and political commentator Serge Trifkovic makes a stinging comparison in regards to operational doctrines: "Islam and Communism differ from Nazism only in their inability to create a viable economy."[111] In other words, both Communism and fundamental Islam embrace the idea that whatever advances them is true and just. I am not talking about the naïve understanding of Islam as a "religion of peace and tolerance" taught by Islamic apologists and gullible secular scholars and believed by many naïve, multiculturalism-indoctrinated Western leaders. I am talking about the Islam of the Koran and the Teachings of Muhammad. Unfortunately, the "radical" Islam we hear about is simply mainstream fundamentalist Islam armed with Islamic literacy, money, and guns. Much of Western experience with Muslim leadership in the past has been with secularized "moderate" Islam, but the growing influence of the fundamentalist Islam of the Koran and Muhammad will present a much greater challenge to Western diplomacy.

The lessons of Korea were not learned by President Johnson and his advisors, and I fear that the lessons of Vietnam are being ignored by many—especially in his party—today. People who refuse to learn from history and those who are committed to false ideologies keep repeating the same mistakes, each time with more painful and potentially calamitous results. The Greeks had a saying: "Those whom the gods would destroy, they first make mad." Romans 1: 22 ESV has: "Claiming to be wise, they became fools."

CHAPTER 13

Nixon Takes Command
Vietnamization and the Cambodian Incursion

By the time Richard Nixon took the oath of office as President of the United States in January 1969, peace negotiations with North Vietnam had droned on for eight months without progress. In May 1968, President Johnson had discontinued bombing all but the southern panhandle of North Vietnam, an area which contained less than 15 percent of the enemy's significant targets, in order to lure Hanoi's leaders to the peace table in Paris. He had discontinued all bombing of North Vietnam just before the November election. Meanwhile the North Vietnamese made not a single concession but continued to call for American surrender and withdrawal from South Vietnam.[112]

Nixon's inaugural address in January 1969 was a curious contrast to what might have been expected from his support of Barry Goldwater in 1964 and his generally friendly relations with hawkish Congressional conservatives in 1968. His words were reminiscent of Lyndon Johnson's utopian belief in negotiation: "After a period of confrontation, we are entering a period of negotiation... Those who would be our adversaries, we invite to a peaceful competition—not in conquering territory or extending dominion but in enriching the life of men." On March 25, he told the National Association of Broadcasters, "So I can tell you that it is our conviction and our belief that it is through private talks with the North Vietnamese and others involved that real progress towards peace will be made.[113]

Nixon's dovish words may have been meant to calm the American people, but the Communist world took note. On April 14, the North Koreans tested him by shooting down a U.S. Navy reconnaissance plane over international waters in the Sea of Japan. All twenty-one men on board were lost. Nixon's only reaction was a formal protest and a promise to provide fighter escorts to future reconnaissance missions. On May 14, in a nationally televised address to the nation he stated, "We have ruled out attempting to impose a purely military solution on the battlefield... I reaffirm now our willingness to withdraw our forces on a specified timetable. We ask only that North Vietnam withdraw its forces from South Vietnam, Cambodia, and Laos into North Vietnam, also in accordance with a timetable."[114]

Nixon had not yet learned that basic Marxist doctrine recognizes only three reasons to negotiate: to consolidate a victory, to stave off defeat, and to open a new front. Readers should be forewarned that Marxist doctrine in this regard is very similar to that of the Koran and the teachings of Muhammad. In both Marxist and Islamic doctrine, truces are used to build up enough strength to overcome enemies.

Vietnamization

On July 25, Nixon announced the "Nixon Doctrine": that in the future the U.S. would continue to support its allies, but they would have to supply most of the manpower. In regard to South Vietnam the President noted, "We have adopted a plan which we have worked out in cooperation with the South Vietnamese for the complete withdrawal of all U.S. combat ground forces and their replacements by South Vietnamese forces on an orderly scheduled timetable."[115]

First warning the North Vietnamese that there could be no greater mistake than to assume that an increase in enemy action would be to their advantage, he summarized his conclusions:

> My fellow Americans, I am sure you recognize from what I have said that we really only have two choices open to us if want to end the war.
>
> I can order an immediate, precipitate withdrawal of all Americans from Vietnam without regard to the effects of that action.
>
> Or we can persist in our search for a just peace, *through a negotiated settlement, if possible* (my italics), or through continued implementation of our plan for Vietnamization if necessary—a plan in which we will withdraw all of our forces from Vietnam on a schedule in accordance with our program, as the South Vietnamese become strong enough to defend their own freedom.
>
> I have chosen the second course.[116]

This policy stood in stark contrast to Eisenhower's dealings with the North Koreans shortly after his election. Eisenhower quickly recognized that nothing was being resolved at the negotiating table. He sent notice to China through India that, unless he got a prompt cease-fire, the U.S. would go on the offensive. The fighting quickly ended.

Nixon's initial policies in Vietnam did not follow Eisenhower's model; however, by this time Nixon recognized that negotiations with Hanoi's Communist leaders were largely futile. He placed his real hope on Vietnamization, which would have worked had not the North Vietnamese been allowed sanctuaries in Cambodia and Laos and unlimited logistical and weapons support from the Soviet Union and China coming through Haiphong and Hanoi. After some hard lessons, Nixon would finally apply the strategy that the Joint Chiefs of Staff (JCS) and his commanders in the Pacific had been recommending since 1965. That strategy combined intensive strategic bombing of all North Vietnamese military, logistical, and transportation targets supporting their ability to make war, after which the South Vietnamese would take over responsibility for their own defense on the ground.

In fairness to Nixon, upon taking office, he believed his options were very limited, and he believed his election mandate was to end the war with honor, but he did not believe any aggressive military action against North Vietnam was politically feasible. In addition, despite the South Vietnamese victories during and following Tet, there was a general, but erroneous, consensus that the South Vietnamese Army and government could not stand alone. Furthermore, the constant drumbeat of an anti-war press convinced him that the American people and especially the Democratic majority in Congress would not stand for any escalation of the war. On March 18, however, he authorized the secret B-52 bombing of North Vietnamese positions up to five miles inside the Cambodian border. Within a week, Women Strike for Peace picketers were demonstrating in Washington. This was the forerunner of the many orchestrated anti-war demonstrations aimed at intimidating the Nixon Administration. These factors caused Nixon to act very cautiously until he had surer footing. During Nixon's first months in office it seemed that he was continuing the same unsuccessful policies as Johnson.

But also during his first days in office, Nixon ordered a comprehensive top-to-bottom study of every factor needed to understand the situation in Vietnam and more broadly Southeast Asia. A Vietnam Special Studies Group was formed to include inputs from the Joint Chiefs of Staff (JCS), the Department of Defense, the State Department, and the Central Intelligence Agency. He also consulted Sir Robert Thompson, the respected British authority on guerilla and insurgency warfare, who had successfully put down a Communist insurgency in Malaya. All this was filtered through former Harvard Professor Henry Kissinger, his National Security Advisor.

Gradually a picture emerged which was very different from the gloomy consensus in Washington. All the inputs confirmed that the Viet Cong (VC) had suffered devastating casualties during the Tet Offensive and that the North Vietnamese Army (NVA) was now unable to threaten areas protected by allied forces. The South Vietnamese Army (ARVN) had proved itself highly capable of meeting any NVA opposition, and the VC had been reduced to a mere nuisance. Furthermore, the South Vietnamese people had proved themselves strongly anti-Communist.

In fact, the NVA had been so reduced in strength that it was unable to launch a single offensive during 1969. Furthermore, the charismatic leader of North Vietnam, Ho Chi Minh, died on September 3. It seemed to retired General Maxwell Taylor that these new seeds of victory were ready for Nixon's harvesting, if he could somehow "hold the country together for the time required for reaping."

Armed with this information, Nixon would have done well to unleash the full brunt of USAF and Navy airpower against North Vietnam. That would have brought quick victory—as it should have in 1972 had not Congress thrown it away. There is nothing that the American people support more heartily than quick and decisive military victory. Unfortunately, Nixon did not yet feel comfortable with going for Hanoi's jugular. The unfruitful peace talks in Paris continued, with the North Vietnamese using them as a propaganda microphone.

Thus Nixon began the "Vietnamization" of the war. American troops would be slowly replaced by South Vietnamese troops. This was made easier by the thorough defeat of the VC during the 1968 Tet holiday. This ferocious series of battles had also proved the South Vietnamese Army to be an effective and highly motivated fighting force. The death of Ho Chi Minh in September 1969 allowed additional time for making Vietnamization a success militarily and politically. By the end of 1969, SVNAF strength increased from 820,000 to 897,000, and U.S. strength decreased from a peak of 543,000 to 475,000. Another 9,600 Americans were killed in action.[117] In addition, over 90 percent of South Vietnam was relatively secure. In fact, Vietnamization was so successful that Hanoi made thwarting further success its primary goal.[118]

The Cambodian Incursion

Unlike Lyndon Johnson, Richard Nixon listened attentively to his military and naval commanders. He soon realized that something had to be done about the NVA sanctuaries in Laos and especially in Cambodia. In order for Vietnamization to be a complete success, North Vietnam's Cambodian's sanctuaries had to be destroyed. The NVA had fourteen major bases inside neutral Cambodia. Some of them were only thirty miles from the South Vietnamese capital of Saigon. Eliminating these threatening enemy strongholds was also necessary to effect a safe and orderly withdrawal of American troops. Withdrawal is the most hazardous of all military operations. It is particularly dangerous as your forces become smaller and less able to defeat enemy attacks. This lesson should not be forgotten in Iraq.

Fortunately, the North Vietnamese overplayed their hand in Cambodia. Prince Norodom Sihanouk had previously navigated a neutral course in the war but had become an unwilling accomplice to North Vietnam as it occupied Cambodian territory and began to push the Cambodians around, impress them into labor, and confiscate their property, actions that only exacerbated Cambodians' deep, historical enmity toward the Vietnamese. In addition, Sihanouk's fifth wife, Monique, had become the ringleader of black market corruption in Cambodia, making her extremely unpopular with the Cambodian people. When Sihanouk returned from negotiating with the North Vietnamese after Ho Chi Minh's funeral in September 1969, he had become so unpopular that he feared a coup. He departed the country for a prolonged vacation in January 1970, leaving his prime minister, General Lon Nol, in charge. In the prince's absence unrest grew into violent anti-Communist demonstrations in Phnom Penh. In response, Lon Nol demanded that the North Vietnamese and Viet Cong leave Cambodia. On March 18, the Cambodian General Assembly voted to oust Sihanouk. Reacting to Lon Nol's demand and the coup in Phnom Penh, however, the NVA simply pushed the tiny and largely ceremonial

Cambodian Army aside. On April 13, Lon Nol asked Washington for help. He was quickly obliged. The next day South Vietnamese troops scattered NVA troops in Cambodia during a three-day raid on the more northern sanctuaries.

The highest concentration of NVA troops—21,000—along with prodigious amounts of stored supplies, arms, and ammunition, were located in the central sanctuary area called the "Fishhook," dangerously close to Saigon. This area also contained the headquarters of the VC's National Liberation Front.[119] On April 30, General Creighton Abrams commenced a coordinated attack by 10,000 U.S. troops from several Air Cavalry regiments and armored tank battalions and 5,000 South Vietnamese armored and airborne troops. These were supported by intensive B-52 bombing and other coordinated air support. Due to political considerations in Washington, they were delayed twenty-four hours and thus did not enjoy the complete impact of surprise. Most of the NVA troops in the Fishhook were able to escape the multi-pronged allied envelopment, but they left behind about 2,000 dead. Moreover, they also left behind a huge "city" of supplies, arms, and ammunition.

Logistically, the NVA suffered a substantial disaster. Allied troops captured enough crew-served weapons and ammunition for thirty-three Communist infantry battalions and enough individual weapons and ammunition for fifty-five Communist infantry battalions. In addition, tens of thousands of rockets, mortars, and recoilless rifle rounds were captured or destroyed, along with tons of food and other supplies. The 11th Armored Cavalry Regiment destroyed more than 800 reinforced bunkers and cleared nearly 1,700 acres of jungle cover.[120]

The Cambodian incursion was very unpopular on U.S. college campuses and with liberal Democrats in Congress, but it enhanced Vietnamization, lessened future allied losses, and allowed American withdrawal to stay on schedule. Enemy action was relatively light for the rest of 1970. By the end of 1970, U.S. strength in South Vietnam had been reduced to 335,000, while South Vietnamese strength increased to 968,000. Cumulative American battle deaths had reached just over 44,000.[121]

The year 1970, however, was marked by a continued escalation in anti-draft and anti-war demonstrations. On May 4, four students were killed by Ohio National Guardsmen during an anti-war protest. On December 22, Congress prohibited the use of U.S. forces or advisors in Cambodia and Laos.

Richard Nixon

Admiral Thomas Moorer

CHAPTER 14

Lam Son 719—Bloody War in Laos

In late April 1970, American and South Vietnamese Army (ARVN) troops launched a major ground operation into Cambodia to clear the North Vietnamese Army (NVA) out of fourteen bases being used to strike into South Vietnam. This operation was complete by June, having destroyed more than 800 enemy bunkers and many massive stockpiles of weapons, ammunition, and supplies. Known enemy casualties accumulated to more than 10,000.[122] This reduced future allied casualties, gave the South Vietnamese more time to prepare for taking over the allied war effort, and allowed U.S. withdrawal to continue on schedule. However, it also caused an escalation of anti-war demonstrations in the U.S. In December, Congress reacted by hamstringing the flexibility of American combat forces, prohibiting them from entering Cambodia or Laos.

Deprived of their Cambodian sanctuaries, the North Vietnamese immediately began to reinforce and fortify their bases along the Ho Chi Minh Trail in Laos. In December, allied intelligence reported unusually heavy stockpiling of weapons and supplies at NVA bases near Tchepone, threatening the two northernmost provinces of South Vietnam and the city of Hue. With American forces steadily departing according to Nixon's Vietnamization plans, these two provinces were soon to be defended by ARVN forces alone. Meanwhile, NVA troop strength along the border was building daily.

As a former ARVN general, President Thieu knew that he could not just sit back and wait for the enemy to take the initiative. But attacking the well-defended enemy bases across difficult terrain would be dangerous and possibly costly. He weighed the decision and took the bolder course of attack, which in war is more often the greater wisdom. He named his operation Lam Son 719, after the village in North Vietnam where the Vietnamese national hero, Le Loi, had defeated an invading Chinese army in 1419.

Weather often dictated operations during the Vietnam War. Taking the weather and previous experience into account, allied planners set early February 1971 as a time when enemy stockpiles would be at their fullest and most vulnerable to destruction. Thieu's plan was not to occupy Laotian territory but to disrupt the enemy buildup so thoroughly that the NVA would be prevented from attacking again before ARVN strength was fully capable of hurling it back. The Saigon government placed Lt. General Hoang Xuan Lam in command of Operation Lam Son with orders to stay in a corridor no wider than fifteen miles either side of Highway 9 to Tchepone and to go no deeper into Laos.

American forces were assigned to seize approaches to Highway 9 inside South Vietnam up to the border with Laos, but they would not be allowed to follow the ARVN into Laos. For the first time in the war, no American advisors would accompany the ARVN into battle. U.S. helicopters and tactical aircraft would, however, support the ARVN over Laotian airspace, and U.S. artillery would assist from within its range just across the border.

The Cambodian incursion had put Hanoi on guard that its Laotian sanctuaries might soon be given the same rough treatment. Hence the NVA was ready with 20,000 men including 13,000 first-line combat troops. They had rehearsed their defense and their counter-attack plans. Their roads had been improved and their artillery and antiaircraft capabilities heavily reinforced.

The operation began on January 30 with a concentrated artillery barrage laid down by the U.S. 101st Airborne Division on NVA Base 611, just across the Laotian frontier. A regiment of the 1st ARVN Division moved up Highway 1 toward the DMZ in a feint. Meanwhile, U.S. Army Engineers hustled to make Khe Sanh a major forward supply base again to support Operation Lam Son. The engineers hoped to make the airfield there operational in four days but had to abandon the project and build a new one. That and rain delayed the first aircraft landing there to February 15, which was too late to support the air assault and armored advance by two ARVN divisions on February 8.

The ARVN advance was deceptively easy until February 12, when NVA troops were reinforced by the 308th Division. As NVA resistance stiffened, small arms fights erupted everywhere, and even tank battles raged. At some locations ARVN and NVA infantry engaged in bitter hand-to-hand combat.

In previous engagements, American advisors on the ground had coordinated U.S. air strikes. But too few ARVN replacements had the training and experience to be as effective. Antiaircraft fire was far denser than anticipated. In addition, NVA units purposely moved close enough to ARVN perimeters to make allied air support difficult.

But although the fighting grew more savage and desperate, the South Vietnamese moved relentlessly toward Tchepone. They captured it on March 6 and stayed ten days, destroying enemy supplies and facilities. Despite the delays, poorly coordinated air support, high casualties, and fierce NVA resistance, the raid was a success. The NVA had suffered tremendous logistical losses and heavy casualties, and the Ho Chi Minh Trail had been temporarily severed.[123] But General Lam still had to extricate his tired and bloodied troops from Laos. He would have to bring them through a fiery gauntlet of NVA fury.

In a furious effort, North Vietnam's great war hero, General Giap, threw everything he had into annihilating the ARVN expeditionary force as it withdrew to South Vietnam. He hurled 36,000 troops, including two armored regiments equipped with Soviet T-34 tanks, into the task of destroying and humiliating the already battered ARVN divisions. NVA infantry attacked them in suicidal human waves, oblivious to the staggering losses that mounted to as many as 15,000 battle deaths. Despite this furious assault, most ARVN units performed and fought magnificently.[124]

U.S. air support played an equally magnificent role in helping to extricate the beleaguered South Vietnamese expeditionary force. American helicopter pilots flew over 160,000 sorties to extract ARVN troops, losing 107 choppers to intense enemy fire. USAF tactical aircraft made more than 10,000 strikes, and B-52 bombers dropped 46,000 tons of bombs.

Although the outcome was frequently in doubt, General Lam got most of his men out. But losses were heavy: Lam's 15,000-man force suffered a 50 percent casualty rate, of which more than 2,000 were killed in action or presumed dead.[125] On March 24 the last ARVN troops were back in South Vietnam, and U.S. forces evacuated Khe Sanh. Operation Lam Son, one of the bloodiest campaigns of the war, was history.

The most important result of Operation Lam Son was to delay the possibility of another North Vietnamese invasion for nearly a year. Hanoi would not fully recover from Lam Son until early 1972. This gave the South Vietnamese ample time for Vietnamization of the war and helped assure the safe withdrawal of American troops on schedule. By July, the northern provinces of South Vietnam were defended by the ARVN alone.[126]

However, denying sanctuary to NVA troops in Cambodia and Laos in 1970 and 1971 should have been essential military objectives in 1966 and 1967. Letting an enemy operate and strike from safe sanctuaries is an insane military and foreign policy. It is an appeasement so extreme as to guarantee eventual surrender or defeat. Many recognized this truth. In April 1961, South Vietnamese President Ngo Dinh Diem had told U.S. Army General Thomas A. Lane that South Vietnam could not be defended by waiting within its boundaries for the enemy to attack. It could only be defended by moving out to strike the forces and installations of the attacking enemy. General Lane agreed that such truths are as old as warfare. And in June 1961, Walt Rostow, a special national security advisor to President Kennedy, told a group of Army officers at Fort Bragg, N.C., "The truth is that guerilla warfare, mounted from external bases—with rights of sanctuary—is a terrible burden to carry for any government. . ."[127]

Unfortunately, at the same time in Geneva, President Kennedy agreed with Soviet Premier Nikita Khrushchev to neutralize Laos. Perhaps he was intimidated by Khrushchev's threatening bombast or too anxious to establish some progress for peace and too naïve about the nature of Communist promises. Whatever the reasons, the U.S. and its allies honored the neutrality while the Communists flagrantly ignored it and made the Ho Chi Minh Trail along the eastern border of Laos a major North Vietnamese logistics route to invade South Vietnam. Thailand would have launched a military effort to cut Laos in half and block the North Vietnamese invasion of South Vietnam, but the U.S. would not support it.[128]

By the end of 1971, U. S. strength in South Vietnam had been reduced to 157,000. Cumulative American battle deaths stood at 45,600. The strength of the South Vietnamese armed forces stood at 1,046,000, but they had suffered 156,000 battle deaths during their long war against Communist aggression.[129]

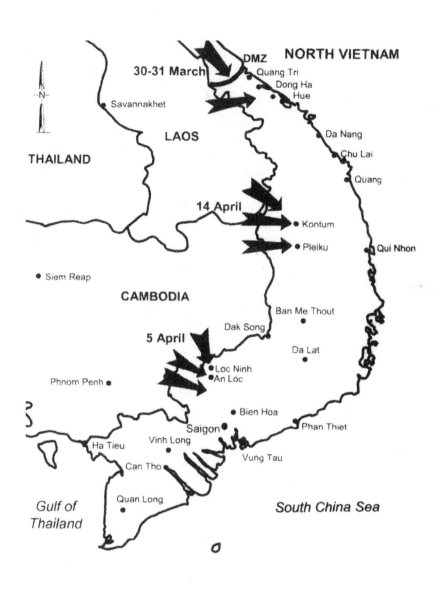

1972 NVA Easter Offensive

CHAPTER 15

North Vietnamese Blitzkrieg

By the end of 1971 the North Vietnamese Army (NVA) had recovered from the manpower and logistics losses it suffered in February and March during the South Vietnamese Army's Lam Son 719 raid into Laos. The Soviets and Chinese had amply replenished the NVA's stock of weapons, vehicles, and ammunition. These flowed largely unmolested through the port of Haiphong and along the railroad connection between China and Hanoi. The NVA had also scoured the countryside, drafting almost every male from ages fourteen to forty-five. Consequently, some areas of North Vietnam were nearly bereft of males of military age.[130]

With American troops rapidly departing, Hanoi was determined to make another grand attempt to rout the South Vietnamese Army (ARVN) and topple the South Vietnamese government in Saigon. The decision-makers calculated that the best timing would be after most American combat troops had withdrawn and before the South Vietnamese were strong enough to repel an NVA invasion unaided. This calculation pointed to the early spring of 1972, which coincided with the monsoon season in Vietnam. Typified by rain and overcast skies, often with ceilings less than 500 feet, the monsoon season promised optimal weather for defending against American airpower. Hanoi's new invasion plan would become known as the "1972 Easter Offensive."

Because the capabilities of the Viet Cong had been all but destroyed during the 1968 Tet offensive and by the success of the South Vietnamese pacification program in securing 90 percent of South Vietnam from significant guerilla attacks, the North Vietnamese were essentially forced to place their hopes for success on a massive conventional-warfare attack.[131] Remembering how their military defeat during the 1968 Tet offensive had been turned into a propaganda victory by the U.S. news media, the Communists would also step up their propaganda war on the American home front during the 1972 presidential election campaign.

The North Vietnamese were willing to throw twelve of their fifteen combat divisions—totaling more than 150,000 men—into the attack. While these divisions were filling up and training new recruits, the Soviets were busy pouring a new generation of modern weapons into North Vietnam, which would provide the NVA with a frightening technological advantage over the ARVN. Included were scores of heavy artillery pieces, upgraded antiaircraft weapons, and over 500 of the most modern battle tanks. A new, 130mm long-range cannon would give the NVA a stand-off capability considerably exceeding that of the ARVN. These new weapons would give the NVA the advantages of surprise and shock in their initial encounters with the ARVN.[132]

Allied intelligence predicted that a major attack would come early in 1972 and pinpointed the areas of South Vietnam that the NVA would most likely attack. However, the Communists again proved their expertise in concealing movements of equipment and men. By slipping hundreds of tanks down through the Ho Chi Minh Trail, NVA General Giap set the stage for an unexpected armored blitzkrieg across South Vietnam's borders. The allies were prepared for an attack, but a German Panzer-style blitzkrieg coupled with a shocking superiority in firepower would throw them off balance.

General Giap's plan was to knock the ARVN so badly off balance that the NVA could drive it from the northern half of South Vietnam before it could recover. Then he would seriously threaten Saigon. As ARVN reserves in the southern part of the country were sucked into meat-grinder battles in the northern and central highland provinces, he would infiltrate NVA regiments into lightly defended population centers in the southern half of the country. Giap believed that somewhere along this course the Saigon government would collapse and the Americans would lose any further resolve to defeat Hanoi's purposes. At the very least, driving the ARVN out of a large part of northern South Vietnam would humiliate Saigon and the Nixon administration, achieving an important and perhaps decisive propaganda victory in the U.S.

This plan was similar to his 1965 campaign to sever South Vietnam. In 1965, he had hoped to advance from the southern tip of Laos to Pleiku and then, astride Highway 19, through An Khe to Qui Nhon on the east coast. This he hoped would cause the Saigon government to collapse. His advance, however, was stopped in the Ia Drang Valley near the Cambodian border by the U.S. First Air Cavalry Division, backed by the herculean logistical efforts of the U.S. Army, Air Force, and Navy, as well as the U.S. Merchant Marine fleet.

Meanwhile, without renewed bombing of North Vietnam, the enemy's own territory remained a sanctuary from which to attack South Vietnam. Although Giap calculated that Nixon would not resume bombing North Vietnam so close to a U.S. election, it was a major risk to NVA success. In addition, if the North Vietnamese Blitzkrieg stalled before the NVA could capture at least the major population centers of the northern and central highland provinces of South Vietnam—Quang Tri, Hue, Kontum City, and Pleiku—the North Vietnamese troops could be chewed to pieces by murderous American airpower. Against this North Vietnam could offer only mobile antiaircraft fire and minimal resistance from its relatively small air force. If used to its full capacity, American airpower had the potential for devastating tactical and strategic dominance.

On March 23, frustrated by the futility of peace talks with the North Vietnamese and National Liberation Front in Paris, the U.S. delegation announced an indefinite suspension of negotiations until the Communist delegates entered into serious discussions on concrete issues determined beforehand. One week later, on March 30, 1972, General Giap sent his armored columns crashing across the DMZ in violation of a 1968 "understanding" President Johnson had made with North Vietnamese peace negotiators in exchange for a cessation in the bombing of North Vietnam. On the basis of this "understanding," allied intelligence had presumed that Giap's attack would come from the mountains on the western border. Thus the best ARVN divisions were facing west toward Laos.

In the first days, the NVA advanced with remarkable success. Initially the South Vietnamese had few weapons capable of knocking out hundreds of rapidly advancing Soviet tanks. Under intense pressure from artillery and armored firepower and outnumbered three to one, the new ARVN 3rd Division fell back in disorder. On April 15, after a four-year lull, the USAF resumed bombing targets near Hanoi and Haiphong, provoking a wave of new anti-war demonstrations across the U.S. On May 1, the provincial capital of Quang Tri fell despite a valiant counter-attack by an ARVN tank regiment. Rainy weather had curtailed the use of allied airpower. The enemy advance was only stopped at the gates of Hue by the battle-hardened 1st ARVN Division.

The NVA thrust soon opened on two other major fronts: from Laos an enemy column of armor-supported infantry overran the outer defenses of Kontum City in the Central Highlands and threatened the town itself; on the Cambodian border just fifty-six miles north of Saigon, an NVA assault thrust through Loc Ninh and besieged An Loc. Giap's immediate objective for this front, however, was to divert ARVN reinforcements in the southern half of the country away from defending the northern and Central Highland provinces and Saigon. President Thieu declared a national emergency.

A fourth smaller front developed on the coast. Insurgent National Liberation Front regiments took control of a large part of sparsely populated Binh Dinh Province. Only a tough-willed South Korean Division stopped them from taking Highway 19 and linking to enemy forces in Kontum. The South Koreans had such a fierce combat reputation in Vietnam that the Communists generally avoided them.

The NVA advance was finally stalled by determined ARVN defenders belatedly equipped with anti-tank rockets and by B-52s and tactical fighter-bombers equipped with all-weather navigation and bombing systems. But a major victory was still within Giap's grasp if he could only resupply and restore his forward momentum. Consequently, he advanced his final reserves in an effort to overwhelm South Vietnamese resistance.

Meanwhile, President Nixon determined to halt the North Vietnamese Blitzkrieg. With fewer than 15,000 American combat troops and one Korean Division left in South Vietnam, there was little alternative but the decisive use of American airpower—advice senior military and naval officers had been giving both Nixon and Johnson since 1965.

The taping system built into his desk recorded Nixon's determination: "The bastards have never been bombed like they're going to be bombed this time."[133]

This was the beginning of Operation Line Backer I.

CHAPTER 16

Operation Linebacker I

The North Vietnamese 1972 Easter Offensive was the result of many months of buildup and infiltration by North Vietnamese forces. Prior to launching their heavily armored attack across the DMZ on March 30, they had assembled a force of 200,000 men. This included twelve North Vietnamese Army (NVA) combat divisions with over 150,000 men, 500 tanks, new long-range artillery, and another 50,000 support troops. It was a force with frightening new Soviet-made firepower but many inexperienced draftees.[134]

Determined to halt the three-pronged North Vietnamese blitzkrieg threatening first Quang Tri and then Hue, Kontum, and An Loc, President Nixon initially implemented U. S. Navy Operation Freedom Train which unleashed air attacks on many targets in North Vietnam from the aircraft carriers *Hancock, Coral Sea, Kitty Hawk,* and *Constellation.* Restrictions on North Vietnamese targets were gradually lifted.

On April 10, a dozen USAF B-52s stationed at Guam, accompanied by USAF and Navy tactical aircraft, obliterated the North Vietnamese fuel storage areas at Vinh, an intermediate logistics facility between Hanoi and NVA troops attacking Quang Tri and Kontum. Three days later eighteen B-52s destroyed North Vietnamese airfields at Thanh Hoa and Bai Thuong. On April 16, eighteen B-52s and 100 tactical aircraft hit the fuel storage areas at North Vietnam's chief port, Haiphong. The smoke could be seen for 110 miles. Shortly thereafter, USAF and Navy fighter-bombers battered a tank farm and warehouses just outside Hanoi. This strategic bombing, however, did not have any immediate effect on the North Vietnamese advance.

With the fall of Quang Tri on May 1 and the NVA threat to Hue and Kontum City, Nixon implemented the Navy's 1965 plan, called "Pocket Money," to mine Haiphong harbor and other strategic waterways in North Vietnam. At exactly 0900 local time on May 8, six Navy A-7 Corsair IIs and three A-6 Intruders, protected by the guided missile cruisers, *Chicago* and *Long Beach,* and F-4 Phantom fighter escorts, dropped thirty-six one-thousand-pound mines in Haiphong Harbor. Timers delayed their activation until late on May 11 so that ships would have three days to leave the harbor without damage.

At the same time, President Nixon informed the Soviets and Chinese of U.S. actions, assuring them that the U.S. was still interested in peaceful co-existence and participating in strategic arms talks (SALT I). He immediately dispatched Henry Kissinger to meet with them.

Immediately following these naval and diplomatic actions, in a brief broadcast to the American people, Nixon explained, "The way to stop the killing is to take the weapons of war out of the hands of the international outlaws of North Vietnam."[135]

USAF and Navy operations over North Vietnam were known as Operation Linebacker from that date—called here Linebacker I. In the next three days, U.S Navy planes dropped another 11,000 smaller mines in secondary North Vietnamese waters. The Navy mining operations blocked approximately 85 percent of North Vietnamese imports. Both North Vietnam's economy and its capacity to make war on South Vietnam began to crumble.[136]

In the following days, use of the new, guided "smart" bombs opened up a new era of increasingly accurate and effective air strikes. On May 13, USAF F-4Ds dropped the Than Hoa bridge into a pile of twisted debris with the first use of guided bombs. In the previous seven years, 873 sorties, in which eleven aircraft were lost, had failed to bring down this key transportation target.[137] A railroad and highway bridge over the Song Ma River, that allied pilots had nicknamed "the Dragon's Jaw," also came down. Antiaircraft batteries defending the Dragon Jaw's had claimed twenty-nine allied planes from 1965 to 1968.[138]

Strategic bombing during Linebacker I was aimed at isolating North Vietnam from its sources of supply. In addition to halting marine commerce, there were four other main objectives: destroying the railroad bridges and rolling stock serving Hanoi from the Chinese border; destroying all railroad marshalling yards, connections, and equipment around Hanoi; destroying primary supply storage and transshipment points; and severely damaging North Vietnamese air defense systems.

The build-up of U.S. air attack forces had been underway for only a month. At the beginning of 1972, the USAF had only 76 aircraft stationed in South Vietnam and another 114 fighter-bombers in Thailand. In April, 176 F-4s and 12 F-105s were reassigned from Korea to Thailand. Between April 3 and May 23, the Air Force's Strategic Air Command relocated 124 B-52s from the U.S. to Guam, bringing the total number of B-52s available for Linebacker I to 209 aircraft. The Navy ordered the aircraft carriers *Saratoga*, *Midway*, and *America* to augment the *Coral Sea, Hancock, Kitty Hawk,* and *Constellation* off the coast of North Vietnam. Nixon's Operation Linebacker I was going to be a far cry from the gradually escalating powder-puff air strikes of Johnson's Rolling Thunder.

As Air Force and Navy squadrons relentlessly pounded previously prohibited North Vietnamese targets, the North Vietnamese Politburo watched in dismay as Hanoi felt the full fury of American airpower. Its ports were closed, its overland routes to China blocked, and its internal waterways and highway systems seriously disrupted. Power plants and factories were destroyed by smart bombs, one after another. Supplies of every sort dwindled to dangerously low levels.

On the battlefield, North Vietnamese soldiers were dying by the tens of thousands as they encountered stiffened ARVN resistance while having to conserve their dwindling stocks of ammunition and supplies. Only 30 percent of the requested logistical support survived allied bombing.[139] Now armed with hand-held antitank rockets, ARVN infantry began exacting a punishing toll on NVA armor. In addition, helicopters armed with antitank missiles were rushed to the battle areas. Meanwhile, allied tactical aircraft pounded NVA armored columns and positions twenty-four hours a day. Consequently, NVA tank crews soon began abandoning tanks as certain death traps. Moreover, huge USAF C-5 jet transports began flying in replacement tanks for the ARVN, and allied smart bombs took out the NVA's fearsome 130mm long-range cannons one by one. ARVN counterattacks began to rout many enemy units, especially those with many new, inexperienced draftees. In these ferocious battles, American advisors fought with their South Vietnamese units.

The siege of An Loc—one of the three objectives of North Vietnam's Easter Offensive—ended on June 18 as NVA units withdrew into their recently reestablished Cambodian sanctuaries, leaving behind more than 10,000 dead.[140] This removed the most direct threat to Saigon. Finally on September 15, Quang Tri, the nearest provincial capital to the DMZ, was recaptured. The Easter blitzkrieg ended with over 100,000 North Vietnamese battle deaths. A substantial number of these undoubtedly resulted from B-52 strikes and other tactical USAF and Marine air support.[141] The ARVN suffered approximately 25,000 battle deaths—nearly 13 percent of the 195,000 South Vietnamese battle deaths from the beginning of the war until the end of 1972 and half what the Americans suffered during the entire war—a grim testimony to the furious intensity of the Easter Offensive.[142]

While the Easter Offensive was raging on the ground in South Vietnam and North Vietnam's economy and ability to sustain an offensive war were being devastated day after day by U.S. bombing, a frenzy of air warfare thundered in the skies over North Vietnam. The 200 MiG interceptors of the North Vietnamese Air Force (NVAF) doggedly contested USAF and Navy destruction of North Vietnamese infrastructure, transportation networks, and air defense systems. The Navy's superior aerial combat tactics and highly trained pilots, however, resulted in a 6:1 kill ratio over NVAF pilots during May and June. Thereafter the NVAF avoided contact with Task Force 77 carrier aircraft. The Air Force realized no better than a 1:1 ratio in those same months. By August, however, new tactics, more experience, and a new real-time early warning system resulted in a much improved 4:1 kill ratio over the NVAF.[143]

Two-thirds of the sixty-three MiGs shot down during Linebacker I were USAF kills. Of the fifty-one USAF combat losses, twenty-seven were shot down by MiGs. Only four of the fifty-three Navy and Marine combat losses were due to MiGs. The U.S. lost a total of 134 aircraft on Linebacker I missions, 104 to combat and 30 to operational accidents. No B-52s were lost during Linebacker I, although they dropped an astonishing 150,000 tons of bombs on North Vietnam and well over 100,000 tons on NVA positions in the south. Antiaircraft fire downed fifty-five American planes, while SAMs (surface-to-air missiles) downed eighteen. The South Vietnamese lost ten aircraft.[144]

Operation Linebacker I had a greater impact on North Vietnam's ability and will to make war than had Operation Rolling Thunder in three and one-half years. By early October the leaders of Hanoi were convinced that their Easter blitzkrieg had failed and that negotiations were preferable to the economic collapse of their country. In addition, Henry Kissinger's diplomatic inroads with the Soviets and Chinese had weakened their resolve to respond to North Vietnam's military and economic emergency. Consequently, Hanoi's leaders dropped their demands for President Thieu's replacement by a coalition government that included the National Liberation Front. Sensing that a major diplomatic impasse had been overcome and negotiations now promised genuine steps toward peace, Nixon ordered a halt to all bombing north of the 20th parallel on October 23.

Nixon's actions during Linebacker I proved him to be a decisive leader willing to make forceful use of American airpower as well as diplomacy. Unlike Johnson, he paid considerable attention to his experienced commanders and gave them much greater latitude in targeting and tactics. It soon became apparent, however, that the North Vietnamese were only using negotiations to gain time for military and economic recovery. In less than two months Nixon would have to launch Linebacker II.

Navy A-7 Corsair

USAF B-52D Stratofortress

Navy F-8 Crusader

USAF F-4C Phantom

CHAPTER 17

Operation Linebacker II—Decisive Victory

Operation "Linebacker I" had severely damaged North Vietnam's economy and ability to support their invasion of South Vietnam. This persuaded Hanoi's leaders that peace negotiations were preferable to further devastation of their country. On October 23, 1972, optimistic about the progress of peace talks, President Nixon suspended all bombing above the 20th parallel, leaving Hanoi, Haiphong, the railway connections to China, and most other major North Vietnamese targets temporarily safe from U.S. bombing. Three days later Henry Kissinger held a televised news conference in Washington and made the presumptuously optimistic declaration, "We believe peace is at hand."[145] However, remembering past Communist deception and treachery, South Vietnam's President Thieu was justifiably apprehensive about the sincerity of North Vietnam's willingness to negotiate. He also feared being abandoned by the United States.

By late November it became apparent that the North Vietnamese were stalling the negotiation process in the hope that their position would be stronger when the new Democrat-controlled Ninety-third Congress was seated on January 3. Nixon and Kissinger agreed with the North Vietnamese assessment of the new Congress and thus preferred to get an agreement as soon as possible. Hence they were not inclined to tolerate the usual delaying tactics experienced during the last four fruitless years of negotiations. More important, aerial reconnaissance showed that the North Vietnamese were making a frantic effort to repair the Linebacker I bombing damage and thereby increase war materials shipments from China by railroad and truck. They were obviously planning another invasion of South Vietnam once American airpower was at a safer distance and a more dovish U.S. Congress was in place. Meanwhile, no American combat troops remained on the ground in South Vietnam. Consequently, on December 14, Nixon gave Hanoi a 72-hour ultimatum to return to the negotiating table and work out a viable peace agreement without delay. He would get no response except the usual propaganda charade.

Nixon realized that the only way to persuade the North Vietnamese to sign a peace agreement on terms acceptable to South Vietnam and the United States was a renewed and even more massive escalation of force. Previously, B-52 bombers had been used sparingly over North Vietnam. This time Nixon was determined to make full use of American airpower—short of using nuclear weapons. He would use the huge all-weather B-52 bombers accompanied by

USAF and Navy fighter-bombers equipped with laser-guided precision bombs. As future admiral and U.S Senator Jeremiah Denton (R-AL), a POW in the "Hanoi Hilton" in December of 1972, later put it, "Linebacker II . . . wasn't the straw that broke the camel's back; it was the sledgehammer that hit the camel in the head where he should've been hit back in 1964. . ."[146]

Linebacker II would differ from Linebacker I in several respects: It would hit Hanoi and Haiphong hard and with few restrictions except to avoid civilian and allied POW casualties. It would concentrate on railroad transportation, power plants, fuel storage, arms storage, communications centers, and North Vietnam's formidable air defense system, including surface-to-air missile sites (SAMs) and MiG airfields. Because of its all-weather radar bombing capability and the enormously destructive power of its 25–30-ton bomb-load, the primary weapon would be the B-52. The B-52s would be assisted by USAF and Navy fighter-bombers and support aircraft. At least five Navy aircraft carriers—the *Enterprise, Saratoga, Oriskany, America,* and *Ranger*—would take part. Each carried between seventy and ninety combat aircraft. One of the first Navy tasks in Linebacker II was to reseed Haiphong harbor and other North Vietnamese waterways with mines.

The Strategic Air Command in Nebraska committed almost half of its B-52 force, a total of 207 aircraft, to Operation Linebacker II. Included were fifty-four B-52Ds stationed at U-Tapao Air Base in Thailand, and fifty-five B-52Ds and ninety-eight B-52Gs stationed at Anderson AFB on Guam. All of the B-52Ds had been modified with updated and more powerful electronic counter-measures (ECM) equipment, but only about half the B-52Gs had been modified.

Because of Nixon's short notice to the Air Force's Strategic Air Command (SAC), the first three of eleven B-52 missions were planned at SAC headquarters in Omaha, Nebraska. No B-52 had ever gone into the intensely defended areas within ten miles of Hanoi and Haiphong. B-52s are particularly vulnerable during their bombing run because they must fly straight and level toward the target for accurate bomb release. They are even more vulnerable when they turn away from the target; during the turn away from Hanoi, for instance, head winds slowed their speed, and the aircraft's profile was larger to antiaircraft and SAM radars. In addition, their ECM antennas—especially those of the unmodified B-52Gs—were much less effective when turning away from a target. The B-52s would carry enormous destructive power to their targets, but flying a huge plane into the most concentrated antiaircraft environment in the world for the first time entailed grave risks. At the same time they were vulnerable to North Vietnam's 145 modern MiG fighter-interceptors.

The B-52s and F-111s would fly only at night, but North Vietnam would be pounded around the clock by other USAF and Navy fighter-bombers.

On a typical Linebacker II bombing raid, the B-52s—nicknamed "BUFFs" (Big Ugly Fat Fellow)—would be accompanied by many other combat and support aircraft. The electronic-warfare (EW) aircraft—F-105G and F-4G "Wild Weasels"—would arrive first to suppress enemy air defenses. The crucial but extremely hazardous job of the Wild Weasels was to "bait" the enemy and attract their fire so that their radars, antiaircraft batteries, and SAM sites could be located, jammed, and destroyed. The F-111 was used effectively for night-bombing and air-defense suppression. Chaff dispersal to block and confuse enemy radar was typically performed by USAF EB-66s and Navy EA-6s. Escort protection was provided primarily by Air Force F-4s and Navy F-4s, A-6s, and A-7s. In addition, KC-135s were needed to refuel B-52s on their grueling 12-hour mission out of Guam. Backing everyone up were rescue HC-130s and rescue HH-53 "Jolly Green" helicopters.

Most B-52s carried a crew of six: pilot, copilot, navigator, radar navigator (and bombardier), electric-warfare officer (EWO), and a tail-gunner. The fighter-bombers, reconnaissance aircraft, and most of the fighter-interceptors carried a crew of two: a pilot and a weapons-systems officer (WSO) or EWO.

On the first night, December 18, a total of 129 B-52 bombers in three waves would be launched from Guam and U-Tapao. A small armada of 102 USAF and Navy fighter-bombers, EW/ECM aircraft, and fighter-interceptors would accompany them.

The crews on the first missions were told that they would be taking the Buffs "downtown." They knew that meant Hanoi and inestimable danger. B-52D pilot, Major Craig Mizner, recalled his first reaction: "And I went back and gathered my crew together and I told them to prepare to go 'downtown' and start making your final arrangements to do that. Of course, we couldn't tell them that we were going into Hanoi, but I think that we all just called and said how things are going and how's the children and kind of small talk to make it possibly a last contact with them."[147]

Lt. Col. John Yuill, another B-52D aircraft commander, remembered the first briefing: "And I remember sitting in there looking around and thinking, you know, this is probably it for some of us. . . You knew there was a pretty good probability that at least some of the people in that room weren't coming back that night."[148]

Yuill was shot down on his third mission. He and his whole crew were captured.

Ed Rasimus, an F-105 pilot, remembered the first Linebacker II mission: "And you can just imagine what it was like on December 18 . . . when all of a sudden all hell goes up around you... It was like the symphony of fireworks."[149]

John Petelin, a pilot with the 43rd Strategic Wing in Guam who flew on three of the eleven Linebacker II missions, remembered having come close to death when a SAM came roaring up at his B-52D: "It's real easy to describe it as a telephone pole with a 15-foot stream of flame behind it... You don't actually see the missile until it's very, very, very close and then you can see the outline, if there's any moon at all. And the biggest thing you see is the tail of the thing. And of course, the next biggest thing you see is when it detonates ... a nice big elliptical ring of fire that's shooting steel ball bearings out at you... Actually it's real pretty if it doesn't kill you."[150]

The Rough Road to Victory

When the Paris peace talks between Henry Kissinger and North Vietnamese emissary, Le Duc Tho, broke down on December 13, 1972, President Nixon was determined to bring the full weight of American airpower to force Hanoi's leaders back to the negotiating table. He would no longer tolerate the usual Communist negotiating artifices or permit any sanctuary from U.S. bombing except POW camps and densely populated civilian areas. Because of the loud objections to the expanded bombing of North Vietnam voiced by the media, anti-war groups, and many in Congress during Linebacker I, Hanoi's leaders had badly miscalculated the mood of the American public toward the war. Most Americans wanted action to end the war and bring peace with honor. They despised the spineless political morality and radicalism they perceived in the anti-war movement and their allies in Congress. Nixon won a resounding victory over anti-war Democrat George McGovern in the November 1972 elections with 61 percent of the popular vote and 520 of 537 electoral votes. (McGovern carried only Massachusetts and the District of Columbia.) Thus in December, Nixon held a stronger political hand than the North Vietnamese had anticipated.

On the afternoon of December 18, 1972, the flight line at Anderson AFB on Guam was jammed with ninety-nine B-52Gs and fifty-three B-52Ds. In addition, there were over 15,000 USAF personnel there to support Operation Linebacker II. Their mission was to bomb the most important and heavily defended targets in North Vietnam, a long overdue decisive use of American airpower in the Vietnam War.

That afternoon it took nearly two hours for eighty-seven B-52s to taxi and takeoff on their way to Hanoi. The grueling 12-hour round trip would be fraught with unknowns and inestimable dangers that would require in-flight refueling by KC-135 tankers and extraordinary focus by every crewmember. They would be joined by another forty-two B-52s from U-Tapao Air Base in Thailand. U-Tapao was a much smaller airfield than the immense base on Guam, but the round trip to Hanoi was less than five hours. The combined mass of 129 aircraft constituted the largest bomber force assembled since World War II. Their immense collective bomb load of over 3,500 tons of high explosives probably exceeded that of any bombing mission in history. They would be accompanied by 102 USAF and Navy fighter-bombers, fighter-escorts, and ECM aircraft.

The F-105G and F-111G Wild Weasels would arrive at the target areas first to suppress enemy air defenses. The main targets for the B-52s were three North Vietnamese MiG bases, three railroad marshalling and repair yards, and the main Radio Hanoi station. Strategic Air Command considered the MiGs to be a greater threat to the B-52s than the twenty-six SAM complexes. Nine F-111s were assigned special targets. The F-111 was especially feared by the North Vietnamese because its terrain-avoidance radar allowed it to fly below the effective altitude for SAMs to target and fire at them. Other USAF and Navy fighter-bombers, many equipped with laser-guided smart-bombs, would follow the B-52s—unfortunately, overcast weather with 1,000- to 3,000-foot ceilings would hamper their effectiveness. USAF and Navy fighter-interceptors would defend against any MiG threats.

Col. George E. "Bud" Day (ret)—a Medal of Honor Winner and the most decorated officer since MacArthur—who had been a prisoner in the Hanoi Hilton for 2,027 days, recalled the reaction of his fellow POWs: "Nine o'clock at night . . . all of a sudden. just out of nowhere, the bombs started falling. No sirens, no lights going out, none of the normal stuff that would happen that you would expect in an air raid. And it was all pretty clear they'd been surprised...And, you know, when that first raft of bombs fell everybody just started screaming. . . they knew we were free."[151]

According to other POWs, their North Vietnamese guards were shaking in fear. They considered the B-52 something between an earthquake and the Apocalypse.

That night the North Vietnamese fired more than 200 SAMs, often in volleys of four to six. At one point there were more than forty SAMs in the air at the same time. Meanwhile, the sky lit up with antiaircraft fire. Two B-52Gs, a B-52-D, and a Navy A-7C were lost to SAMs, and an F-111 was lost to unknown causes.

While the North Vietnamese Politburo was still reeling from the shock and extensive damage of the first bombing raid, on the night of December 19 a second raid of 93 B-52s and 104 supporting aircraft smashed them again. This time the targets were power plants and railroad and vehicle-repair facilities. The bombers attacked using the same routing, headings, altitudes, and turn-points as on the previous night. Although the North Vietnamese launched 185 SAMs against them, and several B-52s received battle damage, no U.S. aircraft was lost on the second raid.

The third Linebacker II mission on December 20 targeted more railroad facilities, power plants, and a major warehouse complex. But the Strategic Air Command (SAC) plan to attack on the same routing, headings, and altitudes, using the same formations and turn-points, had run out of luck. SAC had planned the first three missions this way because Nixon had given them so little notice. They especially wanted to avoid the danger of midair collisions. But it was also meant to facilitate preparing the aircrews for their first combat missions and to give the B-52s the best MiG defense—a defense, however, that never fully materialized.

This time ninety-nine B-52s and an equal number of supporting aircraft flew into what was the best ambush the North Vietnamese could manage. As an official USAF history put it, "All hell broke loose." They greeted the three waves of bombers with 300 SAMs. Six B-52s and a Navy A-6A were lost. Many others suffered battle damage. But, in Air Force tradition, they never wavered from their targets and delivered their devastating bomb-loads. Four of the B-52s lost were G-models without updated ECM equipment. Three were hit approaching their targets, and three were hit during their turn when they were most visible on enemy radar and least able to use their ECM equipment against enemy missiles. Because of in-flight mechanical problems, only ninety of the ninety-nine B-52s ever made it to North Vietnam, making the effective loss rate nearly seven percent. Such a loss rate could not be sustained, so there was much controversy over tactics and ECM equipment and even whether the missions should continue.

Photo-reconnaissance and other intelligence, however, indicated that North Vietnam's economy and war-making capabilities had been severely damaged by the B-52 raids. In addition, the North Vietnamese were rapidly expending their supply of antiaircraft missiles, and their resupply channels were acutely diminished. President Nixon gave the go-ahead to continue the missions, and SAC commander, Gen. John C. Meyer, was determined to make them successful. He was particularly intent on destroying SAM complexes and missile storage. Tactics on routings, headings, altitudes, formations, and turn-points would start changing. All the B-52Gs were grounded until their ECM equipment could be changed to match the battle environment. Only B-52Ds from U-Tapao would be used until the deficiency was corrected. On the insistence of Brig. Gen. Glenn R. Sullivan, commander of the 17th Air Division at U-Tapao, specialized ECM for SAM communications would be added to the B-52Ds.

On December 21, thirty B-52Ds from U-Tapao, accompanied by forty-five USAF fighter-bombers and support aircraft, attacked airfields and storage areas near Hanoi. Two B-52Ds were lost attacking heavily defended Bac Mai Airfield just south of Hanoi. Unfortunately, an errant string of bombs hit one wing of Bac Mai hospital, only 200 yards from a large petroleum storage facility. The hospital had been evacuated, but twenty-eight hospital personnel were killed. Naturally, Hanoi made maximum use of this bombing error in its propaganda. The incident was soon a major talking point in the American media and by anti-war activists. Neither the press nor the anti-war movement ever mentioned that 25,000 South Vietnamese civilians had been killed during North Vietnam's Easter 1972 blitzkrieg into South Vietnam's northern provinces.

At this point, General Sullivan insisted that local commanders have more input into tactics. On December 22, thirty B-52Ds, accompanied by fifty-seven fighter-bombers and other aircraft, struck petroleum storage and railroad targets near Hanoi. One F-111 fighter-bomber was lost attacking a railroad complex.

On December 23, SAC approved SAM sites as B-52 targets and added several MiG fields to the list. Previously, F-111G and F-105G Wild Weasels had destroyed SAM sites only after having baited them into firing first. Not only was direct B-52 bombing of SAM sites more dangerous for the B-52s, but it was also politically sensitive. Many SAM complexes had Soviet advisors, and it was likely that many were actually manned by Soviet crews. In addition, it is likely that many of the latest North Vietnamese MiGs were flown by Soviet and Chinese pilots. SAMs and MiGs were the vanguard of the Soviet Union's proxy war against the United States. That night thirty B-52Ds and twenty-eight other aircraft attacked airfields and SAM sites northeast of Hanoi. The F-111s attacked first and successfully suppressed SAM firings and MiG takeoffs. No aircraft was lost to combat—although a USAF E-66B was lost due to engine failure.

Finally, on Christmas Eve, thirty B-52D bombers supported by fifty-four other aircraft destroyed the railroad yards at Kep and Thai Nguyen, northeast of Hanoi, with no losses of U.S. aircraft. Moreover, Airman First Class Albert Moore, a B-52G gunner on Ruby 03, shot down an attacking MiG.

The B-52 and F-111 attacks only occurred at night, but on each night they flew, an average of sixty-nine USAF, Navy, and Marine fighter-bombers attacked during the day. Because the North Vietnamese were saving their ammunition for the B-52s, losses of fighter-bombers had been relatively light.

There was a 36-hour stand-down beginning on Christmas Day. The time would be used to plan more extensive attacks using both the B-52Ds and the now ECM updated B-52Gs.

Decisive Victory

The North Vietnamese interpreted the 36-hour Christmas stand-down by the B-52s as weakness and spent the time in urgent restocking of their SAM complexes with missiles to be ready for the next strike. On the night of December 26, an enormous air armada of 120 B-52s and 75 other aircraft attacked twenty railroad and storage targets evenly spread between Hanoi and Haiphong. Seventy-eight B-52s attacked Hanoi simultaneously from four different directions; at the same time, forty-two B-52s attacked Haiphong from three directions. Their altitudes were varied, and their vulnerability to enemy targeting was reduced by eliminating wide post-target turns.

The North Vietnamese air defenses were overwhelmed by so many B-52s hitting Hanoi and Haiphong from all directions in such a short period of time. In addition, they were thoroughly confused by the huge blankets of chaff laid down by fighter-bomber and ECM aircraft. They were able to fire only sixty-eight SAMs, but unluckily two B-52Ds were hit. One went down in North Vietnam, and a second, badly damaged, made it back to U-Tapao but crashed just short of the runway, killing four of the six crewmembers.

By the night of December 27 there were fewer worthwhile targets left in North Vietnam, and only sixty B-52s were launched against SAMs and railroad storage areas. They were accompanied by seventy-eight other fighter-bombers and combat aircraft. Unfortunately, two B-52s were downed by SAMs, two USAF F-4Es were downed by MiGs, and a "Super Jolly Green" HH-53 helicopter was downed by small-arms fire while attempting a rescue.

The next night sixty B-52s and fifty-eight support aircraft hit five SAM support and railroad targets at a major transportation and storage depot connecting to China. During that action a Navy RA-5C was downed by a MiG 21.

The eleventh and final mission of Operation Linebacker II was flown on December 29, by which time there were few important targets left in North Vietnam. Two SAM storage sites and adjacent railroad complexes were destroyed by the sixty B-52s accompanied by sixty-nine supporting aircraft. Only twenty-three SAMS were fired, and no MiGs contested American air superiority. No American aircraft was lost. North Vietnamese air defenses were exhausted and in distress. They were almost out of SAMs; their MiGs were effectively grounded; and their radar and communication links were seriously disrupted. North Vietnam was now at the mercy of American airpower.

Nixon promised the leaders of Hanoi that he would cease bombing north of the 20th parallel if they would resume negotiations on January 3 and accept the terms proposed by the United States in October. They quickly agreed to this and to a cease fire on January 15. On January 27, a peace pact was signed in

138

Paris by the U.S., South Vietnam, the National Liberation Front, and North Vietnam. By the end of March, North Vietnam released its 591 American POWs, and the United States withdrew its remaining 24,000 troops from South Vietnam.

Eleven days of B-52 bombing had not only crushed North Vietnamese communications and air defenses, it had destroyed 80 percent of their electrical power. It further reduced imports to only 30,000 tons per month, a decline of 81 percent from the already low level in November.[152] Their ports were blocked, and their railroad system was in shambles. In addition, 372 railroad cars and three million gallons of petroleum had been destroyed. The North Vietnamese economy was reeling, and its leaders were without the logistical support necessary to continue their war against South Vietnam.[153]

There is no record of their military casualties, but the North Vietnamese claimed 1,624 civilians had been killed by the bombing. However, many of these deaths were probably caused by the 1,242 SAMs they had fired, many of which fell into civilian areas. Such collateral casualties are always regrettable, but they were made more likely by the North Vietnamese practice of using population density as a protection against U.S. air strikes. Many SAMs were placed near thickly populated areas in order to deter air strikes or to make them more difficult.[154] The North Vietnamese did the same thing in dispersing petroleum storage, placing barrels of fuel along crowded city streets. Nevertheless, a great protest was raised over these civilian casualties in the U.S. media and in Congress. However, the media never mentioned the 25,000 South Vietnamese civilians killed during North Vietnam's 1972 Easter offensive or the tens of thousands of South Vietnamese civil servants, school teachers, village elders, land owners, and anti-Communists murdered by the Viet Cong over the course of a decade in promoting their savage brand of "democracy."[155,156] Linebacker II also took its toll on the Air Force and Navy: The Air Force had lost fifteen B-52s and six other aircraft on the eleven Linebacker II missions. The Navy had lost another six aircraft. A great cry in Congress was raised over this, especially over the loss of the B-52s. No one likes taking losses, but twenty-seven aircraft were a relatively small price to pay considering that North Vietnam was rendered militarily helpless and was forced to negotiate peace terms, a cease fire, and the return of our POWs. Of the ninety-two B-52 crewmembers involved in these losses, eight had been killed in action or died of wounds, twenty-five were missing in action, thirty became POWs, and 26 were recovered by Air Rescue.[157]

By comparison, the Air Force lost 922 combat aircraft over North Vietnam during the three and a half years of President Johnson's Operation Rolling Thunder from 1965 to 1968. Of these, 382 were F-105 Thunderchiefs—nicknamed "Thuds" by their crews.[158]

This was nearly half of the 833 F-105s ever produced. Johnson wasted the equivalent of a sizeable Air Force practicing McNamara's "graded response" or "gradualism" doctrine of warfare. Under this doctrine, targeting was very restricted, and these restrictions were removed only gradually as the enemy took the initiative to escalate warfare. In addition, air strikes were purposely limited in destructive power, only gradually escalating as the enemy continued to escalate their warfare. This allowed plenty of time for the enemy to build up its forces. One accomplishment of Linebacker I and II was to completely repudiate the gradualism doctrine of Johnson and McNamara. Both operations proved the enormous advantage of airpower properly and aggressively employed.

However, Linebacker I and Linebacker II came seven years too late. The Joint Chiefs of Staff (JCS) had recommended such plans in 1965 and had been consistently recommending their implementation for seven years. They only needed to dust them off, update them, and fill in the details when Nixon finally got serious about using the full force of USAF and Navy airpower to quickly bring Hanoi to terms. How many thousands of American and allied lives would have been saved if Johnson had implemented the JCS's recommendations in early 1965? In addition, American and allied objectives to build South Vietnam's armed forces into an adequate deterrent to Communist invasion could have been achieved with far fewer Americans than the 543,000 who were there at their peak in 1970.

We could also have won the war in late 1967 when North Vietnam could not sustain manpower and logistical support levels in the field because of more aggressive U.S. bombing. We could certainly have won in 1968 following the devastating and costly defeat of the North Vietnamese and Viet Cong in their Tet offensive. The only thing that was needed in 1965, 1967, and 1968 was to implement the JCS plans that became Linebacker I and Linebacker II in 1972.

Rear Admiral James B. Stockdale, a former POW, speaking to the Armed Forces Staff College in April 1975, told the officers there:

> If I learned nothing else in North Vietnam it is that Clausewitz is as right today as he was during the Napoleonic Wars. . . [T]rue progress toward victory is, and I think always will be, simply a direct function of the degree to which the enemy "will" is being subdued. Arms are effective only to the degree that they transmit a message of the ultimate futility of further resisting them. The essence of deterrence is to demonstrate a commitment that your adversary will find unprofitable, if not downright frightening, to challenge. If our escalation, our creeping up the panhandle with graduated

bombing raids, our bombing pauses, conveyed any message
to the enemy, it was a lack of commitment.[159]

Linebacker II demonstrated a commitment to subdue North Vietnam's
will to resist America's vast power. That commitment essentially defeated
North Vietnam and won the war.

This is the view of Sir Robert Thompson, famed British expert on
counterinsurgency, who had frequently been consulted by three U.S. presidents
on strategy and tactics during the Vietnam War: "In my view, on December 30,
1972, after eleven days of those B-52 attacks on the Hanoi area, you had won
the war. It was all over! They had fired 1,242 SAMs; they had none left, and
what would come overland from China would be a mere trickle. They and their
whole rear base at that point were at your mercy. They would have taken any
terms. And that is why, of course, you actually got a peace agreement in
January, which you had not been able to get in October."[160]

I believe most senior military and naval officers who served in the
Vietnam era would agree with Sir Robert Thompson's assessment. Linebacker
II is the classic example of the successful use of overwhelming military and
naval force to end enemy resistance and to quickly achieve a political end.
Fortunately, it became the future model of American airpower rather than the
costly failure of Operation Rolling Thunder.

We had won in the war in December 1972, but Congress, with the aid of
the mainline media, had already sown the seeds of defeatism that would throw
this great victory away and place South Vietnam and Cambodia in the hands of
murderous totalitarian regimes.

Navy A-6 Intruder

USAF F-105F Wild Weasel

USAF F-111 Aardvark used for SEAD

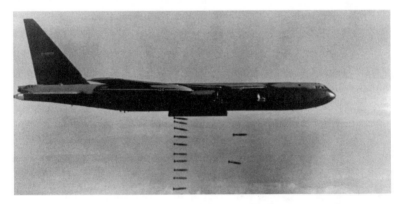

USAF B-52D Stratofortress

Henry Kissinger

CHAPTER 18

Political Betrayal

The United States had essentially won the Vietnam War in December 1972. President Nixon finally used previously restricted American airpower to mine North Vietnam's ports and reduce their railroad transportation and electrical power systems to shambles. Military airfields and the vast majority of their major petroleum and munitions storage facilities were devastated. The North Vietnamese economy was reeling, and the country's once formidable air defense system was out of ammunition and in a state of confusion. Supplies from its Soviet sponsors were cut off, and only a trickle of truck traffic was coming from China. North Vietnam was at the mercy of American airpower.

We were in a position to demand unconditional surrender, but we settled for a ceasefire, the return of our prisoners of war, and North Vietnamese pledges to end their invasion of South Vietnam. The ceasefire took place on January 15, 1973, only three days after negotiations in Paris had resumed. A peace pact was signed by North Vietnam, the National Liberation Front (the Viet Cong), South Vietnam, and the United States on January 27. It was not a perfect agreement in the eyes of President Nixon and South Vietnam's President Thieu, but it would have worked if the U.S. Congress had been willing to enforce its terms. But in the end, Congress was not willing and so betrayed a great victory, the sacrifice of over 57,000 American lives, the trust of the South Vietnamese people, and the honor of the United States.[161]

As soon as the last American troops were gone, the North Vietnamese began to violate the ceasefire and to infiltrate tens of thousands of additional troops into South Vietnam. Article 7 of the peace agreement effectively committed the United States to sustain the South Vietnamese Army, Navy, and Air Force with the same level of equipment, weapons, ammunition, and supplies that existed in January 1973. But Congress reduced its support from $2.27 billion in fiscal year 1973 to $1.03 billion in 1974 and less than $700 million in 1975.[162] Meanwhile the Soviets and Chinese increased their support for the North Vietnamese by 50 percent over 1972 levels and 10 percent over peak 1971 levels to prepare for a final invasion of South Vietnam.[163] Hanoi's leaders correctly read U.S. Congressional signals that a future Communist invasion of South Vietnam would be unopposed by the United States.

In August of 1964, the U.S. House had approved the Gulf of Tonkin Resolution, giving President Johnson sweeping powers to defend South Vietnam and the other member nations of the Southeast Asia Treaty

Organization against Communist aggression. The vote was 416 to 0 in favor. The Senate passed it by a vote of 88 to 2. Although Congress had been provoked by two incidents of North Vietnamese torpedo boats attacking U.S. destroyers in the Tonkin Gulf, there was a larger purpose in the resolution: short of a declaration of war, it was necessary for President Johnson to get immediate and substantial Congressional backing to prevent the imminent North Vietnamese takeover of South Vietnam and a subsequent threat to Cambodia and Laos. Johnson and his advisors feared a full declaration of war might provoke the Soviets and Chinese into coming to the aid of North Vietnam more directly and forcefully.[164]

Until late in 1965, there were few doves in either house of Congress. Many who later became leaders of the Congressional anti-war faction were strongly supportive of U.S. efforts to defend freedom in Southeast Asia:

> "I think we must defend freedom in that area, or else see the balance of a large segment of the world tipped against freedom."—Senator Jacob Javits (R-NY), August 6, 1964.[165]

> ". . .I would hope that we would be prepared to wage such a conflict rather than surrender the area to Communism."—Senator George McGovern (D-SD), January 15, 1965.[166]

> "Do we want to defend freedom? We do, because this is our commitment, our heritage, our destiny."—Senator Edward Kennedy (D-MA), November 1965.[167]

Hanoi's leaders were ruthless tyrants, but they at least had the wisdom to appreciate and study history. They remembered that a key reason for their success against the French in 1953 and 1954 was that they had paid as much attention to undermining the French people's will to win the war in Indochina as they had to the strategies and tactics of the battlefield. Hence, as they began to escalate their attacks on American installations in South Vietnam, they also stepped up their propaganda efforts on the American home front. With the help of their Soviet and other international Communist allies, they began to sow the seeds of protest in the U.S. through Communist front organizations, sympathetic media, and radical or left-leaning community organizers able to influence the anti-war and anti-draft movements.

On April 17, 1965, Students for a Democratic Society (SDS), a radical leftist student and political activist organization, sponsored a public anti-war demonstration in Washington. On October 15 and 16, there were anti-war protests in forty major cities, organized by the National Coordinating

Committee to End the War in Vietnam, an umbrella coalition of New Left organizations headed by radical leftist organizer Jerry Rubin.

In February 1966, the Senate Foreign Relations Committee, chaired by Democratic Senator J. W. Fulbright of Arkansas, held televised hearings on the war. By March 1, there was an attempt to overturn the Gulf of Tonkin Resolution in the Senate. On April 15, 1967, over 100,000 anti-war protestors gathered for a huge rally in New York City. Another 20,000 protested the war in San Francisco.[168] Two days later, sixteen U.S. Senators signed a letter drafted by Senator Frank Church (D-ID) warning Hanoi that although they were critical of the Johnson administration's war policies, they opposed unilateral American withdrawal. However, most of them eventually took stronger anti-war positions tantamount to unilateral withdrawal. On the other side of the issue—Senator John Stennis (D-MS) of the hawkish Senate Armed Forces Committee, chaired hearings that criticized Secretary of Defense McNamara for his costly and ineffective policy of timid gradualism in air warfare. Senator Stennis particularly berated McNamara for risking the lives of USAF and Navy pilots on missions that restricted them from doing much damage to the enemy.

On October 21, 1967, over 50,000 protestors marched on the Pentagon. With casualties mounting, no end to the war in sight, and a strategy that seemed to be designed for defeat rather than victory, American opinion began to shift against the war. By December 1967, the U.S. had 483,000 troops in South Vietnam and had suffered over 16,000 battle deaths.[169]

On January 3, 1968, Senator Eugene McCarthy (D-MN) announced his candidacy for president as a "peace" candidate.

The 1968 Tet offensive, which began on January 30 and lasted through February, resulted in a significant Communist defeat, but it was portrayed in the American press as an embarrassing Allied defeat. Television coverage following the attack on the U.S. Embassy and fighting in Saigon and Hue helped create attitudes of alarm, skepticism, and defeatism among the public and Congress. It did not help that there were 543 American battle deaths during the week ending February 17—the highest one-week total of the war. Shortly thereafter, it was revealed that General Westmoreland had requested 206,000 more troops to assure victory—based on Johnson's continued opposition to cleaning out Communist military sanctuaries in Cambodia and Laos and using the full brunt of American airpower against North Vietnam.[170] Yet the Communists lost probably more than 55,000 killed in action during Tet, and these losses accumulated to more than 100,000 in the first half of 1968 alone.[171] Hanoi's leaders were psychologically devastated and were seriously considering throwing in the towel and postponing their objective to conquer South Vietnam for three to five years.[172] Had the U.S. decided to do some substantial strategic bombing of North Vietnamese targets near Hanoi and

Haiphong at the time, we could have forced their withdrawal from South Vietnam. When the North Vietnamese Politburo realized that anti-war protests and an increasingly anti-war American media had turned their devastating military defeat into a political victory, it bolstered their resolve to persevere and to pay even more attention to propaganda and agitation on the U.S. home front.

Despite the South Vietnamese Army's victorious Tet counterattack, President Johnson continued to be influenced by the media and pressure from anti-war Democrats more than by the facts on the ground. On March 12, Eugene McCarthy received 42 percent of the vote in the Democratic presidential primary in New Hampshire, coming close to defeating Johnson who got 48 percent. On March 16, Senator Robert Kennedy announced his candidacy for the Democratic presidential nomination and took an anti-war campaign strategy. Two weeks later, the President's Senate advisory group recommended de-escalating the war. On March 31, it was Johnson who threw in the towel. He announced the de-escalation of the war and his withdrawal from the U.S. presidential race.

On April 26, more than 200,000 demonstrators gathered in New York City to protest the war. Meanwhile, Robert Kennedy was assassinated on June 6, following his victory in the California Democratic primary. The Democratic Convention in Chicago, held from August 26 to August 29, was marred by anti-war demonstrations, violence, and arrests.[173]

On October 31, President Johnson called a halt to all bombing of North Vietnam. Six days later, Richard Nixon was elected President of the United States, defeating Vice-President Hubert Humphrey in an electoral landslide. At the end of the year, there were 536,000 American troops in South Vietnam. Battle deaths had accumulated to 30,600.[174] Nixon was inaugurated on January 20, 1969, and only six days later, witnessed demonstrations by Women's Strike for Peace protestors in Washington. Meanwhile, the Communist Party in the United States (CPUSA) continued to expand its anti-war agitation and began to link it to racial, economic, and social issues.

CHAPTER 19

The American Front

After a thorough analysis of the military and political disasters suffered in their 1968 Tet campaign in South Vietnam and their American media-aided propaganda victories in the United States, the North Vietnamese Politburo ordered a comprehensive offensive for the fall of 1969. It would be a three-pronged assault: on the battlefield in South Vietnam; at the negotiating table in Paris; and in the streets, on the campuses, and in the halls of Congress on the American home front.

The Soviet Union and China poured more weapons, equipment, and supplies into Haiphong, and Hanoi's Communist leaders scoured every corner of North Vietnam for fresh manpower to build a new invasion force. It was never the policy of Ho Chi Minh and the Politburo to negotiate in good faith. Their strategy was to keep fighting while using negotiations as a means for deceiving and manipulating Allied diplomats into making one-sided concessions. During his term, President Johnson had unilaterally declared 16 bombing halts lasting from 24 hours to 36 days, in hope of concessions and negotiating "breakthroughs" that never materialized.[175] The North Vietnamese consistently used American bombing halts to build up and resupply their forces in safety, while Allied airpower stood down.

To coordinate their agitation and political assault on the American homeland with international Communist leadership, the North Vietnamese organized the Stockholm Conference on Vietnam, held May 16-18, 1969. Nguyen Minh Vy represented North Vietnam and Mme Nguyen Thi Binh represented the National Liberation Front (NLF)—the political arm of the Viet Cong (Communist guerillas and terrorists in South Vietnam). Dr. Carleton Goodlett, leader of the National Mobilization Committee to End the War in Vietnam (MOBE) and an official of the World Peace Council, was the chief American delegate. He was accompanied by Professor William C. Dawson and John Wilson of the Student National Coordinating Committee (SNCC).

Subsequently, more detailed planning was accomplished at the World Peace Assembly held in Communist East Berlin on June 21-24. The chief American delegates to the East Berlin conference included Dr. Goodlett and Irving Sarnoff, a member of the Communist Party in the United States (CPUSA). The assembly received formal greetings from the Soviet Union's top leaders: Leonid Brezhnev, General Secretary of the Communist Party of the

Soviet Union (the highest office of the USSR) and Alexei Kosygin, Chairman of the Council of Ministers of the USSR.[176]

In his address to the assembly, Sarnoff closed with a charge: "Our task is to broaden the base of understanding of our movement to include the many organized groups who are in motion around specific issues—wages, welfare, prices, taxes, racism, repression, housing—and to make them understand that there can be no improvements until the war in Vietnam is ended and the national priorities are reordered."[177]

Next the leaders of the principal American anti-war groups assembled in Cleveland, Ohio, for a conference over the July 4 holiday. Included were the CPUSA, the Trotskyite Socialist Workers Party (SWP), The Young Socialist Alliance (YSA), and the Student Mobilization Committee to End the War in Vietnam (SMC). Sarnoff and Wilson were active organizers of the event. As a result of their planning and discussions, a new, overall coordinating organization was formed: the New Mobilization Committee to End the War in Vietnam, or "New Mobe." Subsequently, New Mobe leaders announced plans for an intensive campaign against the war. A two-part, fall offensive would include a nationwide moratorium on October 15 and a march on Washington on November 15. The November 15 march would be synchronized with agitation and demonstrations on the West Coast.

More detailed documentation of the strong Communist influences on New Mobe can be found in a Staff Study by the U.S. House Committee on Internal Security, second session, of the 91st Congress, entitled: Subversive Involvement in the Origin, Leadership and Activities of the New Mobilization Committee to End the War in Vietnam and its Predecessor Organizations, published in 1970.[178]

In mid-September, plans for the moratorium and Washington march were publicized at a New Mobe press conference in New York City. Shortly thereafter, Senator Fred Harris of Oklahoma, Chairman of the National Democratic Party, called twenty-four liberal Democrats to a secret caucus meeting in Washington. Among those attending the September 26 caucus were Senators Edward Kennedy, Edmund Muskie, George McGovern, Walter Mondale, Birch Bayh, and Representative John Conyers, Jr. These influential Democratic leaders agreed to support the nationwide moratorium and develop a set of resolutions calling for the withdrawal of all American troops from Vietnam. As they departed the secret caucus, Senator Harris declared, "It is time to take off the gloves on Vietnam."[179]

On October 6, Tran Buu Kiem, Chairman of the South Vietnam Liberation Students' Union, a front organization of the NLF, sent a message to American students and youth wishing them great success in their heroic struggle.

An estimated one million people across the nation participated in the October 15 moratorium. In Boston, Senator Edward Kennedy urged that the United States make "an irrevocable decision" to withdraw ground combat forces from Vietnam by the end of 1972. In Maine, Senator Edmund Muskie called for an orderly withdrawal from Vietnam and for Saigon to "widen its base"—evidently to include the Communists. However, Barry Goldwater and other Republican leaders made strong speeches in support of President Nixon's policies. Nixon himself took the opportunity to point out that his Vietnamization policy would allow honorable American withdrawal as the South Vietnamese were able to replace American forces on the battlefield.[180]

Support for the November 15 anti-war activities began to dwindle as Republicans and conservative Southern Democrats in Congress made it a daily practice to read reports of North Vietnamese atrocities into the Congressional Record. Senator Carl Curtis of Nebraska had this *Reader's Digest* quote by John Hubbell read into the Congressional Record: "Two VC battalions struck in the earliest hours. . . [W]hen every building was ablaze, the Communists took their flamethrowers to the mouth of each trench. . . The bodies of 252 people, mostly mothers and children, lay blistered, charred, burned to the bone. . . The massacre at Dak Son was a warning . . . to cooperate."[181]

Curtis also embarrassed Indiana Democrat Vance Hartke by reading one of Hartke's statements into the Congressional Record for the benefit of Indiana's conservative voters: "Both reality and reason impel us to declare our support for the formation of a coalition government that will include the significant participation of the National Liberation Front."[182]

On the evening of November 14, a rally sponsored by the "Revolutionary Contingent," a coalition of the Weathermen, the Revolutionary Youth Movement, the Mad Dog Caucus, and Youth Against War and Fascism, marched on the South Vietnamese Embassy in Washington., unfurled Viet Cong flags, and chanted: "Ho, Ho, Ho Chi Minh, the NLF is gonna win."[183]

By Saturday morning, 250,000 protestors had gathered in Washington to hear speeches by Democratic Senators George McGovern and Eugene McCarthy and Republican "moderate" Charles Goodell of New York. Self-professed Communist and Co-Chairman of New Mobe, David Dellinger, also addressed the crowd.[184] The unforgettable entertainment was provided by Pete Seeger, Arlo Guthrie, and Peter, Paul, and Mary. One group marched to the Justice Department shouting: "Ho, Ho, Ho Chi Minh." The West coast event drew 100,000 demonstrators.[185]

Unfortunately for the Nixon Administration, the My Lai atrocity, perhaps the greatest disgrace in recent American military history, that had occurred on March 16, 1968, under the watch of President Johnson, was revealed on November 16, 1969, the day following the march on Washington. Thirteen U.S.

Army officers and enlisted men were charged with war crimes resulting in the deaths of approximately 347 South Vietnamese civilians. Only one was later found guilty, Lt. William C. Calley. The My Lai incident is covered in more detail in an appendix article.[186]

An additional untimely event occurred on December 1: the first draft lottery since 1942 was held at Selective Service Headquarters in Washington.

Although constantly in the news, the anti-war demonstrations had comparatively little impact on the vast majority of the American public, who, regardless of their frustrations with the war, viewed anti-war demonstrators as distasteful and unpatriotic. Sadly, however, the anti-war movement had a major impact on Congress, especially the liberal wing of the Democratic Party, and became a major political constituency of that wing. Thus, though never really representing majority opinion in the U.S., the American anti-war movement bore a major responsibility for the eventual fall of South Vietnam and its bloody consequences.

The public opinion polls of the time failed to distinguish the varied political sentiments of those who "opposed" the war. It is a serious mistake to lump everyone who "opposed" the war or opposed various war policies and strategies into the category of fanatic anti-American leftists. Many were "anti-war hawks" opposed to sending American troops into combat under the perceived "no win" policies of the Johnson Administration. Some opposed the war because they believed Johnson, and later Nixon, were overstepping their Constitutional authority. Some libertarians viewed the draft as unconstitutional.

The real damage to the prospect of an honorable peace in Vietnam was done in Congress. It came in the form of misguided resolutions forbidding U.S. ground or air operations in Cambodia and Laos, thus allowing the North Vietnamese to strike at South Vietnam from enemy sanctuaries without fear of American interference or retaliation. Even more importantly, it came in the form of budget reductions and restrictions that eventually left the South Vietnamese unable to defend themselves against a North Vietnamese Army lavishly equipped and supplied by their Soviet and Chinese sponsors.

In early 1970, although the Nixon Administration's Vietnamization policy was progressing according to plan, Congressional attempts to limit military actions in Southeast Asia made Washington a major political battleground of the Vietnam War. In the first seven months of his Vietnamization program, Nixon had already withdrawn 68,000 U. S. troops, bringing U.S. strength down to 475,000, and the South Vietnamese Armed Forces and Territorial Reserves had increased from 820,000 to 897,000.[187] Yet the anti-war faction in Congress was growing larger and more partisan. Liberal Democrats and a few "moderate" Republicans were pushing hard to end U.S. involvement in Southeast Asia as quickly as possible—without much consideration for past commitments or future consequences. They were ready to desert our commitment to South Vietnam as soon as our prisoners of war could be returned. Many bills and amendments were offered to limit the administration's military flexibility and funding for the war. At first, most of these efforts failed.

Nixon was in a difficult position. He could not, with honor, desert the people of South Vietnam to the inevitable Communist takeover that precipitous American withdrawal would bring. He soon realized that peace with honor would require aggressive action against North Vietnam before South Vietnam could stand on its own. He was also acutely aware that aggressive actions against the enemy had the potential to aggravate anti-war sentiment in Congress, which could result in a vote to end our commitments to South Vietnam.

Also in January, the New Mobilization Committee to End the War in Vietnam launched an aggressive calendar of anti-war protests for the year. They began with campus discussions of alleged American "genocide" in Vietnam. But far more successful was their sponsorship of an anti-draft week beginning on March 16. This included demonstrations of civil disobedience at draft boards. On April 2, Massachusetts Governor Francis Sargent signed a bill passed by the Massachusetts Legislature challenging the legality of the Vietnam War. These actions, however, resulted in a significant public reaction. On April 4, a huge pro-war demonstration was held in Washington.

During this time, Nixon had concluded that pushing the North Vietnamese Army (NVA) out of their Cambodian and Laotian sanctuaries was absolutely necessary for the safe withdrawal of U.S. troops and the protection of South Vietnam until their Armed Forces were capable of turning back a North Vietnamese invasion. Eastern Cambodia was essentially occupied by the NVA, which had begun to push westward toward the Cambodian capital of Phnom Penh. The North Vietnamese sponsored forces of the Khmer Rouge (Red Cambodian Communist Party) were already besieging the capital and Cambodia's largest cities. On April 30, following a request for help by Cambodian Prime Minister Lon Nol, Nixon announced a Cambodian incursion by U.S. and South Vietnamese troops. Although this incursion was successful and necessary for South Vietnamese security and the subsequent safe withdrawal of American forces, anti-war Senators seized the opportunity to pass the Cooper-Church Amendment by a vote of 58 to 37, severely restricting spending on operations in Cambodia or assistance to the Cambodian Army. This was initially defeated in the House by 237 to 153 but was resurrected and passed by both Houses in late December 1970. This effectively barred funds for the introduction of U.S. ground troops or advisors into Cambodia and Laos. As a result, the defense of South Vietnam was undermined, and the people of Cambodia were exposed to the murderous assault of the Khmer Rouge.

Nixon's incursion into Cambodia also touched off hundreds of student strikes and other demonstrations. At the time, I was a graduate student in the MBA program at Stanford University. I remember well how student activists shut down Stanford classes for a day. As Treasurer of the MBA Student Association and an at-large member of the Student Senate, I had the opportunity to speak out against their actions and disruption of classes. It was a frustrating experience and to no avail. To the many Vietnam Veterans and conservatives in my class, it was disillusioning. Most of the students involved in the strike were totally ignorant of NVA and Khmer Rouge activities (and atrocities) in Cambodia and the grave threat they posed to the cause of freedom and the safe withdrawal of U.S. troops. Considering the ultimate cost of lives and freedom in Cambodia and South Vietnam, it was not a proud moment for Stanford, even though many of the students on campus that day were from other colleges and local high schools. The real political activists of New Mobe and their front organizations were relatively few in number. Their success was in organizing and misleading thousands of naïve college students and in charming the media, some opportunistic liberal politicians, and a few activist professors.

On May 4, 1970, four students were killed during an anti-war demonstration at Kent State University in Ohio by National Guardsmen. In August, student protesters set off a bomb at the Army Mathematics Center at the University of Wisconsin, killing a graduate student (the father of three small children) and injuring four others. This bombing revolted most Americans and further discredited anti-war demonstrators.

Anti-war demonstrations resumed their intensity in the spring of 1971. On April 18, John Kerry, a former Navy lieutenant and spokesman for "Vietnam Veterans Against the War," arrived in Washington and gathered 900 men to march on the capitol. There he demanded "immediate, unconditional, and unilateral withdrawal of all American forces in Vietnam." Later Kerry alleged that American troops were guilty of war crimes. Large demonstrations in Washington and San Francisco also urged Congress to end the war in Indochina. On May 3-5, a New Mobe front organization, the People's Coalition for Peace and Justice, conducted protest marches and rallies in Washington. These demonstrations reflected a disagreement over strategy between New Mobe's two most influential organizations: the Communist and Socialist parties. The CPUSA wanted to expand the anti-war movement by exploiting racial and economic issues, while the Socialist Workers' Party wanted to concentrate undivided attention on forcing the U.S. to withdraw from Southeast Asia. On June 13, *The New York Times* pitched in on the side of the anti-war movement by publishing stolen classified records of the Johnson Administration's deliberation on war policies, which they titled *The Pentagon Papers*. This was more embarrassing, however, to the liberal civilian bureaucrats who had overridden military advice and implemented McNamara's failed policies of gradualism than it was to top military advisors or President Nixon.

By late 1971, Nixon's Vietnamization policy was clearly working. U.S. troop strength had been reduced to 157,000, and Nixon announced on November 13 that U.S. ground forces were being used only for defensive operations. All offensive operations had been turned over to South Vietnam. Total American battle deaths, however, had risen to 45,000 by the end of the year.[188]

On January 16, 1972, liberal religious leaders from forty-six Protestant, Catholic, and Jewish denominations met in Kansas City, Missouri, and demanded that the U.S. withdraw from Indochina and refuse to aid the governments of South Vietnam and Cambodia. This was a stunning piece of propaganda, exploiting the religious left's muddle-headed ignorance of foreign policy issues, but it did not reflect the view of most American church-goers.

Meanwhile, Nixon was undermining the North Vietnamese by making diplomatic inroads with their Soviet and Chinese allies. In August of 1971, the U.S. ended opposition to admitting the People's Republic of China to the United Nations. February 1972 marked Nixon's highly publicized trip to China, while Henry Kissinger was in the Soviet Union discussing common Soviet-American interests. These diplomatic inroads had a payoff in late 1972. Soviet and Chinese interest in helping Hanoi declined as the prospects for American victory increased.

On December 29, 1972, the combined impact of the Linebacker I and II raids—which had unleashed the awesome destructive power of B-52s and laser-guided precision bombing on North Vietnam—brought the Communist leaders in Hanoi to their knees. We had won the war, but Congress continued to undermine the victory and the defense of Cambodia and South Vietnam.

Despite our military victory, a majority in Congress was ready to abandon our commitments to South Vietnam and Cambodia. In fact, on January 2, 1973, the House Democratic Caucus voted 154 to 75 in favor of cutting off all funds for military operations in Indochina as soon as our troops could safely withdraw and our prisoners of war were returned. Nixon and Kissinger both knew that unless our military victory resulted in a peace treaty soon, Congress would simply vote the U.S. out of the war. This pressure caused two unfortunate compromises. The peace treaty called for a ceasefire, the release of all prisoners of war within sixty days following withdrawal of all U.S. and other Allied troops from South Vietnam, and the withdrawal of all North

Vietnamese troops from Laos and Cambodia. However, it allowed North Vietnamese troops in South Vietnam to remain in place. This made South Vietnam extremely vulnerable to renewed Communist aggression if North Vietnam failed to withdraw from Cambodia and Laos. The treaty also set up an International Commission of four nations—Canada, Indonesia, Hungary, and Poland—to supervise the ceasefire; but the two Communist nations, Hungary and Poland, had an effective veto power over reporting violations. This made the International Commission essentially useless. Of course, North Vietnam also had a record of ignoring ceasefires and other agreements when violation was expedient to its cause.

In addition, both sides were allowed to keep their forces and supplies at current levels, but South Vietnam was dependent on the U.S. Congress to provide that level of assistance. Furthermore, with U.S. and other Allied troops out of Vietnam, the only real means of enforcing the treaty and deterring another major invasion of South Vietnam was U.S. airpower. Despite the treaty's weaknesses, continued material support for South Vietnam's Armed Forces and the threat of a formidable application of American airpower would have been sufficient to keep South Vietnam and Cambodia free.

The peace treaty was signed by the United States, South Vietnam, North Vietnam, and the NLF (Viet Cong) on January 27, 1973. A separate treaty on Laos was signed on February 21. The Khmer Rouge, however, continued to threaten Cambodia's government—theoretically without the help of North Vietnam. By March 29, all 591 American prisoners of war had been released. Two questions remained: Would North Vietnam honor the treaty and would the U.S. honor its commitments to South Vietnam?

CHAPTER 20

The Fall of Cambodia and South Vietnam
Abandoning the Cause of Freedom

On January 27, 1973, The United States, South Vietnam, North Vietnam, and the Communist National Liberation Front signed a peace agreement that should have ended the Vietnam War. By that time, there were only 24,000 American support troops and no American combat troops left in South Vietnam. Within a few months, the number was down to 50. On March 29, in accordance with the peace agreement, the North Vietnamese released the 591 known American prisoners of war. During a decade of war, the U.S. had suffered 46,000 battle deaths and another 11,000 non-battle deaths—a total cost of 57,000 American lives.[189]

The regular South Vietnamese Armed Forces had been built to a level of 551,000, and their Regional forces and reserves numbered another 550,000. Approximately 195,000 South Vietnamese soldiers, sailors, and airmen had been killed in action from 1959 through 1972. But in numbers, training, equipment, and morale, the South Vietnamese were at their peak. Approximately 80 percent of their territory and 87 percent of their people were considered safe from attack.[190]

The North Vietnamese Army (NVA) had been devastated. It lost 190,000 men in 1972 alone.[191] According to the North Vietnamese, nearly 1.2 million North Vietnamese and National Liberation Front (Viet Cong) soldiers were killed between 1959 and April 1975.[192] Perhaps one million of these had died by the end of 1972. NVA strength was at 550,000 men in January 1973. Of these forces, 148,000 remained in South Vietnam, 25,000 in Cambodia, and 70,000 in Laos. The rest remained in North Vietnam.[193]

Hanoi's leaders, however, never viewed the peace talks as anything but a device to get American troops out of Vietnam. North Vietnam ignored the ceasefire. As President Nixon said, "Hanoi's definition of a ceasefire was that we cease and they fire."[194] In fact, they attacked over 400 South Vietnamese hamlets in the first two weeks of the "ceasefire" but lost 5,000 men in furious counterattacks by South Vietnamese territorial forces. Poland and Hungary blocked any criticism of the North Vietnamese by the now demonstrably useless International Commission. Anti-war critics in the U.S. Congress claimed that both the South Vietnamese and North Vietnamese were violating the ceasefire, but the South Vietnamese were reacting defensively to North Vietnamese attacks.

The President and the Joint Chiefs of Staff also knew that to lose Cambodia was to lose South Vietnam. In May 1973, Nixon ordered USAF B-52 bombing of Khmer Rouge forces threatening the Cambodian capital of Phnom Penh. In reaction, anti-war senators and congressmen launched a frontal assault on Nixon's war policies. The North Vietnamese interpreted both U.S. failure to respond to NVA ceasefire violations and Congressional attempts to block aid to Cambodia as clear signals that the U.S. would not come to the aid of South Vietnam when the North Vietnamese were ready for another invasion. Hanoi immediately shipped another 35,000 troops and 30,000 tons of ammunition and supplies into South Vietnam to reinforce NVA positions. Roads and railroads were rebuilt, and even an oil pipeline was built parallel to the Ho Chi Minh Trail. The Soviets and Chinese enthusiastically resumed their relentless effort to rebuild the NVA in preparation for a final offensive to conquer South Vietnam.[195] The Ho Chi Minh Trail became a superhighway for war materials supporting a new invasion. Rather than withdrawing from Cambodia and Laos as the peace agreement required, the NVA sent another 18,000 trucks and 70,000 men to reinforce their positions. Yet the U.S. did not react to these violations of the peace agreement and obvious preparations for a new invasion of South Vietnam. President Nixon was forced to concentrate his efforts on stopping Congress from abandoning South Vietnam to its Communist enemies.[196]

Senator Edward Kennedy (D-MA), led the Congressional fight to prohibit U.S. bombing in Cambodia and Laos. He repeatedly demanded that the U.S. resolve the conflict in Indochina by diplomacy, once stating, "If we really want peace in Cambodia—and cease-fire arrangements for all Indochina—then we should be sending our diplomats to help negotiate these arrangements instead of sending our B-52s to bomb."[197]

Kennedy, like many of his liberal Democratic colleagues, seemed to think a satisfactory peace could be negotiated out of whole cloth. It never occurred to them that our primary negotiating tool was the use or restraint of bombing. Without any power to apply sticks as well as awarding carrots, negotiating is a process of surrender. Kennedy was effectively proposing a nominally negotiated surrender.

In June 1973, Congress passed a bill that prohibited funding for air strikes in Cambodia and Laos. Nixon successfully vetoed it on June 27, but realized Congress would soon have the upper hand. On June 30, he agreed to a bombing halt bill that would not be effective until August 15. The bill stripped Nixon of any ability to fund ground or air forces to defend Cambodia and essentially closed the door to any further American defense of Cambodia, Laos, or South Vietnam. With the U.S. safely out of the picture, North Vietnam put another 75,000 combat troops into South Vietnam.[198] Meanwhile, Congress cut the budget for supporting the South Vietnamese Armed Forces from $2.27 billion in fiscal year 1973 to $1.01 billion in 1974, and $700 million in 1975.[199] Major General John E. Murray, U.S. Defense Attaché in Saigon, warned that such reductions were equivalent to abandoning South Vietnam. In addition, Congress succeeded in restricting presidential war powers by passing the War Powers Act on November 7 over Nixon's veto. By these budget cuts and prohibitions against direct U.S. actions, Congress threw away the American victory of December of 1972 and doomed Cambodia and South Vietnam to fall.

Because the fighting never really stopped following the January 1973 peace agreement, reduced supplies to the South Vietnamese Army eventually resulted in critical material shortages. By May 1974, their original stockpile of 177,000 tons of ammunition had dwindled to 121,000 tons. About 35 percent of their tanks and 50 percent of their armored personnel carriers and aircraft were out of commission because of spare parts shortages. Due to a lack of spare parts and fuel, only 55 percent of its vehicles could be operated, thus robbing combat units of all-important mobility. Nearly 50 percent of medical supplies were out of stock.[200] North Vietnam interpreted Congress's lack of commitment and dwindling support to South Vietnam as a green light for invasion. At the same time, the Soviets and Chinese accelerated their support for North Vietnam to levels more than 10 percent above previous peak levels.[201] By the end of 1973, the levels of warfare and casualties were indistinguishable from that of previous years. Yet anti-war U.S. senators and congressmen persisted in an astonishing argument that our assistance to South Vietnam was fueling the war and that reducing assistance would bring the fighting to an end. Within two years, this remarkable reasoning would bring South Vietnam to an end.

By early 1973, the Watergate political scandals that began with the June 1972 arrest of five men for breaking into the National Democratic Headquarters at the Watergate Hotel in Washington had resulted in several of Nixon's top advisors being convicted of felonies. The building controversy and threat of impeachment forced Nixon to resign on August 9, 1974. His Vice-President, Gerald Ford, became President. Although Ford tried valiantly to restore Congressional support to South Vietnam and prevent the fall of South Vietnam and Cambodia, a majority in Congress persisted in denying our commitments in Indochina. In the November elections, the Democrats gained forty-three seats in the House and three seats in the Senate. This liberal victory gave the 94th Congress 291 Democrats and 144 Republicans in the House and 61 Democrats and 39 Republicans in the Senate, strengthening the already strong anti-war sentiment in Congress—and making Ford's attempt to prevent a Communist takeover of South Vietnam and Cambodia almost impossible.

It took the North Vietnamese Army until the end of 1974 to fully recover from its devastating defeat in 1972. On December 13, 1974, North Vietnam launched an 185,000-man expeditionary force against South Vietnam.[202] The offensive began with an assault on Phouc Long Province about fifty miles north of Saigon. Two NVA infantry divisions supported by tanks and heavy artillery were opposed by fewer than 2,000 South Vietnamese regional forces and reserves. The South Vietnamese resisted bravely, but under NVA artillery barrages of as many as 3,000 rounds per day, they were soon unable to return fire. The city of Phouc Long fell on January 6, 1975.[203]

This victory encouraged the North Vietnamese to bolder action. In a series of strategy meetings in Hanoi, North Vietnamese leader Le Duan argued that the failure of the United States to respond in any way demonstrated that we would not intervene with airpower to save Saigon. By this time, South Vietnam's air force had only enough fuel and spare parts to operate 30 percent of its aircraft. Over 200 aircraft had to be put in storage. It had lost 281 aircraft but received only eight replacements. Lacking spare parts and fuel, and running low on bombs and ammunition, the South Vietnamese Air Force was limited in its ability for aggressive action against the North Vietnamese invaders.[204]

The South Vietnamese Army had 4,000 vehicles idled because of the spare parts shortage. As South Vietnam faced an aggressive invader, its firepower had been reduced by 60 percent and its mobility by 50 percent because of reductions in American military assistance.[205]

On March 10, 1975, three NVA divisions assaulted the city of Ban Me Thout. South Vietnamese resistance was fierce, but overwhelming North Vietnamese numbers and firepower prevailed in less than 24 hours— threatening to split South Vietnam in half. On March 12, the House Democratic Caucus voted 189 to 49 against President Ford's $300 million emergency supplement for South Vietnam. The Senate Democratic Caucus voted against Ford's request 38 to 5.[206]

In Mid-March of 1975, South Vietnamese President Thieu gathered his generals at the former American airbase at Cam Ranh Bay on the east coast of South Vietnam. Anti-war sentiment in the U.S. Congress had resulted in a reduction of U.S. assistance to South Vietnam to $700 million per year, less than one-third of the minimal amount thought necessary to defend the country from another North Vietnamese invasion. Thus Congress had essentially defaulted on American obligations under the January 1973 peace agreement to maintain South Vietnamese defense capabilities at 1973 levels and to punish any further North Vietnamese attempts to invade South Vietnam. South Vietnam's situation was desperate. At current rates of usage, they would run out of ammunition in two months, and there remained only a thread of hope that President Ford could persuade Congress to prevent a Communist takeover of Cambodia and South Vietnam.[207] Reliable reports of recent Communist brutalities in Cambodia and South Vietnam were made available to them, but most refused to listen.

Now more than 250,000 North Vietnamese troops and 50,000 Viet Cong auxiliaries, heavily armed and equipped by their Soviet and Chinese allies, pressed upon the thinly spread South Vietnamese Army (ARVN). Due to supply shortages and the inability to replace equipment, ARVN firepower and mobility had been reduced to less than half of former levels. The South Vietnamese Air Force was so low on ammunition, fuel, and replacement parts that its remaining combat aircraft could only be used sparingly.[208] Thieu decided, quite rationally, that the ARVN no longer had the resources to defend all of South Vietnam. Two inadequately equipped ARVN divisions were now confronting four North Vietnamese Army (NVA) divisions attacking the Central Highlands. President Thieu's decision was to abandon the Central Highlands, including the cities of Kontum and Pleiku, and withdraw to defense perimeters along the eastern coastal enclaves, Saigon, and the Mekong River Delta. By regrouping, he hoped to retake Ban Me Thuot.

Rather than retreating over Highways 9 and 14, which were now subject to Communist interdiction, Thieu decided to use Highway 7B, an old logging road. Unfortunately, Highway 7B was now overgrown with brush and missing a bridge. Orderly retreat is the most difficult and dangerous of all military maneuvers, especially in the face of an aggressive enemy. But given the bleak circumstances and slim chance of American help, Thieu had no alternatives. Severely complicating the retreat, more than 200,000 civilian refugees jammed the roads to the eastern coastal enclaves as ARVN troops withdrew from Kontum and Pleiku, On March 18, NVA forces managed to block Highway 7B at Cheo Reo, cutting the retreating ARVN forces in half. Of eighteen ARVN battalions, only three made it to the coast.[209]

On March 19, a heavily armed NVA infantry and tank force smashed across the DMZ, forcing ARVN abandonment of Quang Tri and putting pressure on Hue. One million South Vietnamese civilian refugees fled to Da Nang on the coast.[210]

Because of long years of war, ARVN soldiers were allowed to house their families in nearby towns. Realizing that the U.S. had abandoned them and ammunition and supplies were running short, many ARVN battalions began to melt away as soldiers left to make sure their wives and children made it to safety. When Hue fell on March 25, two million civilian refugees crowded into Da Nang, resulting in a humanitarian crisis.[211] Under attack by 35,000 NVA troops, Da Nang fell on March 30. Within days the coastal cities of Qui Nhon, Tuy Hoa, and Nha Trang had to be abandoned. In less than a month, half of South Vietnam had fallen to the Communists.

On April 9, 40 miles northeast of Saigon, the ARVN 18th Division valiantly held off three NVA Divisions at Xuan Loc. This defense provided critical time for American efforts to evacuate more than 5,000 American civilians left in South Vietnam. In addition, the U.S. Navy and Air Force were able to airlift about 14,000 homeless children to the United States. Under heavy artillery attack, however, Xuan Loc fell on April 20.

Meanwhile, in Cambodia, the Khmer Rouge were firing artillery shells into civilian refugee camps. The U.S. Navy was able to evacuate the American Embassy staff and about 1,200 Cambodian civilians and their families on April 11-13. Upon parting, John Gunther Dean, the American Ambassador to Cambodia, offered General Sirik Matak, commander of the Cambodian Army, asylum in the United States. The general responded in writing:

> Dear Excellency and Friend,
>
> I thank you very sincerely for your letter and for your offer to transport me toward freedom. I cannot, alas, leave in such a cowardly fashion. As for you, and in particular your great country, I never believed for a moment that you would have this sentiment of abandoning a people which has chosen liberty. You have refused your protection, and we can do nothing about it. . .[212]

On April 16, the defenders of the Cambodian capital of Phnom Penh ran out of ammunition and were overrun the next day. The dogged but under-equipped Cambodian Army was forced to surrender. In Phnom Penh, two million civilians were marched out of their homes at gunpoint and taken to re-education camps. Execution of Cambodian leaders, government officials, army personnel, teachers, intellectuals, wealthy capitalists, and religious leaders began immediately. Among the first to be executed was General Sirik Matak. Thousands more would be shot or clubbed to death in the coming months.[213]

On April 10, President Ford asked Congress to approve an emergency fund of $722 million in military assistance and $250 million in humanitarian assistance for South Vietnam. Coming at such a late date, this probably would not have saved South Vietnam. However, it would have given them some leverage to negotiate better surrender terms including some assurances of safety for several hundred thousand South Vietnamese who had cooperated with U.S. forces over the past two decades. The safety of 5,000 American civilians still in

South Vietnam was also at stake. Considering the gravity of the situation, Ford asked for approval by April 19. Eight congressional committees debated it briefly, but in the end, the anti-war mentality of the majority was so entrenched that not a penny of military or humanitarian help was offered. The request never even came up for a vote on the House floor.[214]

Hanoi's leaders had declared that they would not negotiate with Thieu, and so, effective April 21, he resigned under pressure from those looking for a negotiated surrender. Once Thieu was out, however, Hanoi would not negotiate with his vice-president and successor, Tran Van Huong. General Duong Big Minh, who led the coup against Diem in 1964, was then put in charge to negotiate a surrender. Hanoi, however, had no intentions of negotiating anything.

President Thieu had been very reluctant to sign the 1973 peace agreement because it left 148,000 North Vietnamese troops in South Vietnam. He also had well-founded fears of North Vietnamese treachery. Nixon had to send General Alexander Haig to Saigon to convince him that such a drastic compromise was necessary because Congress was ready to vote the U.S. out of the war unless a peace agreement was signed within weeks.[215] On his last day in office, bitter that Congress would not even approve President Ford's largely humanitarian emergency relief proposal for South Vietnam, Thieu said: "There was a promise that if the Communists intruded and invaded again, there would be a reaction. But there has been no reaction. . . What does this amount to? This amounts to a breach of promise, injustice, lack of responsibility, and inhumanity toward an ally who had suffered continuously—the shirking of responsibility on the part of a great power."[216]

A BBC news program on Thieu's resignation reported that he had said, "But America did not keep its word. Is an American's word reliable these days?"[217]

The speech raised an uproar in Congress, but President Ford replied, "It is my judgment at the moment that the failure of Congress to appropriate the military aid requested . . . certainly raised doubts in the mind of President Thieu and his military that we would be supplying sufficient military hardware for them to adequately defend their various positions in South Vietnam. . . Now the lack of support certainly had an impact on the decision that President Thieu made to withdraw precipitously [from the Central Highlands]. I don't think he would have withdrawn if the support had been there."[218]

An NVA force of 150,000 men attacked Saigon on April 29. As NVA tanks rolled into the streets of Saigon, only 30,000 ARVN troops remained to defend it, and they had little ammunition. Continued South Vietnamese resistance would have been mad futility.[219] North Vietnamese flags began going up all over the city. South Vietnam had resisted Communist aggression for twenty-one years. It had successfully defended itself for two years, until the U.S. Congress cut its promised military aid so severely that capitulation was inevitable.

Many liberals in Congress blamed the fall of South Vietnam on its people's lack of determination to fight. None other than American labor leader, George Meany, President of the AFL-CIO, set them straight: "This may be—but should we not ask ourselves that, if it is true, could there be a connection between this loss of will on the part of the South Vietnamese and the complete and final refusal by the American Congress to provide them with the material resources needed to defend their country from Communist aggression?"[220]

On hearing of the fall of South Vietnam, U.S. Senator Hiram Fong (R-HI) stated, "There is no question but what we have betrayed the Cambodians, and we have betrayed the South Vietnamese. . . We have not lived up to our commitments."[221]

The end of the war did not bring peace. Millions died at the hands of the new Communist regimes.

President Thieu

Gerald Ford

Leonard M. Scruggs

CHAPTER 21

The Bloody Consequences of Communist Victory

On April 13, 1975, on the eve of the fall of Cambodia, *New York Times* columnist Sydney Schanberg posted an article headlined "Indochina Without Americans: For Most a Better Life."[222] The author's point—typical of liberal journalists during the Vietnam conflict and since—was that because of the possibility of civilian casualties from American bombing, most Cambodians would be better off under communism. But although there were occasionally some collateral casualties connected to American bombing in Cambodia, American bombers were bombing Khmer Rouge forces trying to overthrow the Cambodian capital of Phnom Penh, not Cambodian villages. In fact, U.S. policy emphatically stressed that the risk of collateral civilian casualties should be minimized. My own combat experiences in Southeast Asia confirmed that this policy was often stated and strictly enforced. Yet despite enormous evidence to the contrary, most liberal journalists convinced themselves and many of their readers that the Americans were the villains and that the North Vietnamese-supported Khmer Rouge guerillas were nationalist reformers who would stabilize Cambodia after a few scores were settled.

Governed by these distorted presuppositions, Schanberg and the *New York Times* found it difficult to imagine how the lives of ordinary people in Indochina "could be anything but better with the Americans gone." Schanberg even asserted that it would be "tendentious" (absurdly biased) to believe that "brutality and sadism" would be "a national policy under a Communist government once the war is over."[223] Events proved Schanberg, *The New York Times*, and their anti-war allies in Congress disastrously wrong. Following the fall of Cambodia on April 17 and of South Vietnam on April 30 of 1975, there occurred a bloodbath that rivals the Jewish Holocaust of World War II in numbers and brutality.

In Cambodia, more than 100,000 people suspected of being enemies of the new Communist order were rounded up and summarily executed by bludgeoning, stabbing, or shooting. Most were buried in mass graves. These included especially soldiers, teachers, intellectuals, government officials, religious leaders, prominent business people, and those who had some contact with the West.[224]

Pol Pot and Khieu Samphan, the leaders of the Khmer Rouge, wasted no time in implementing a plan to reconstruct Cambodian society into a doctrinal Maoist paradise. At gunpoint, three million people were abruptly herded from their city homes into the countryside and jungles. Soldiers opened fire on anyone who resisted or lingered. The sick and dying in hospitals were exterminated with ruthless indifference. In Siem Riep, more than 100 seriously ill patients were murdered in their beds with knives and clubs. Another 20,000 sick and wounded patients were carried into the jungle to almost certain death. At Mongkol Borei, 200 army officers were executed by being forced to walk through a carefully planted mine field. The Khmer Rouge cruelly beat a colonel, cut off his ears and nose, and then crucified him. The wives and children of these officers were then marched off to be killed.[225]

In all, more than four million city dwellers were dumped into desolate jungle tracts to carve out a new Communist society untainted by their former exposure to bourgeois living. Cambodia had been the rice bowl of Indochina, but the new residents of the jungle camps were given only 90 grams of rice per day, less than 15 percent of the minimum requirement for a normal worker.[226]

Malnutrition became rampant, and the usual ravages of disease followed. People resorted to eating leaves, snakes, worms, and termites to sustain themselves, but the areas around their campsites were quickly depleted of even these supplements. Complaining about the food was a capital offense. Married couples were forbidden to carry on prolonged conversations. The punishment on the second offense was death. People were executed for any suspected dissent or lingering, often after being forced to dig their own graves. Children were forced to watch as their parents were tortured, bludgeoned, decapitated or stabbed to death. In the first wave of terror during 1975 and 1976, more than 1.2 million Cambodians were executed or died of disease and starvation in the New Villages. By the end of 1978, approximately 2.4 million Cambodians had died at the hands of their Communist liberators—25 percent of the total population.[227]

In South Vietnam, the new Communist regime promptly executed over 100,000 potential political enemies. Another one million people, including virtually the entire South Vietnamese intelligentsia, were sent to prisons or concentration camps. Between 200,000 and 340,000 of these political prisoners were still being held in 1985. Yet another million South Vietnamese, considered disloyal to the new Communist regime, were sent to "New Economic Zones" to clear land and dig irrigation ditches. Malnutrition and disease took a high toll of these unfortunate South Vietnamese patriots. Somewhere between 200,000 and 500,000 died in these prisons and work camps.[228] In 1978, Hanoi decided to rid Vietnam of several hundred thousand ethnic Chinese. They were driven into the South China Sea where they attempted to escape on small boats. Hundreds of thousands more Vietnamese, fleeing Communist repression, also tried to leave by boat. A conservative estimate is that 600,000 drowned at sea. In addition, tens of thousands of South Vietnamese prisoners of war were never returned. Total South Vietnamese deaths under Communist rule probably exceeded 1.1 million.[229]

In addition, freedom of speech and the press ceased; religion was systematically suppressed; and government corruption became far more widespread than in the days of Diem. Before 1975 South Vietnam had had three TV stations, twenty radio stations, and twenty-seven daily newspapers. Following the fall of Saigon, the new Communist government allowed one TV station, two radio stations, and only two daily newspapers—all pumping out the same Communist propaganda.[230]

The terrible consequence of Communist victory was that more than 3.5 million Cambodian and South Vietnamese civilians were murdered, starved to death, or drowned in the South China Sea. Was this the "better life for most" that the *New York Times* predicted? Most anti-war liberals in the press and Congress pleaded ignorance. They claimed they did not know such a tragedy would result. This ignorance, however, is hardly excusable. The ruthless and bloody history of communism was clear to anyone who was not predisposed to deny it.

Shortly after Ho Chi Minh's victory over France in 1954, he had General Giap execute 50,000 political opponents. The Viet Cong assassinated over 35,000 government officials, school teachers, and village leaders during the early stages of their terrorism in South Vietnam.[231] Communist cadres brutally executed 3,000 civilians in Hue during the 1968 Tet offensive. NVA artillery barrages killed 25,000 civilian refugees fleeing Quang Tri Province in 1972.[232] Had no one noticed these Communist atrocities?

According to the *Black Book of Communism,* in the 20th century the two principal Communist regimes in the world—the Soviet Union and the People's Republic of China—murdered over 85 million of their own people.[233] The North Korean government murdered 50,000 political dissenters when it came into power after World War II and has since murdered close to 1.3 million of its own people to maintain its stranglehold on political power.[234]

R. J. Rummel's *Death by Government*, published in 1994, estimates that the Soviet Union murdered nearly 55 million of its own people and another ten million people of other nationalities in consolidating its evil empire. Stalin starved to death nearly 25 percent of the population of Ukraine in 1932 and

1933—a total of seven million people, including three million children. Rummel originally estimated that the People's Republic of China murdered 38 million of its own people in gaining and maintaining Communist power, but later raised his estimate to nearly 77 million to account for Mao's forced collectivization of small farms and the resulting severe famine during the 1958-1962 "Great Leap Forward." In addition, from 1945 to 1948, Polish Communists murdered over 1.5 million of the 15 million Germans still living in the former German Baltic states of Pomerania and East Prussia. The rest were deported. Nobody in the West called attention to this genocide.[235] In more recent history, 800,000 Tibetans have died in China's genocidal suppression of non-Communist culture, religion, and philosophy.[236]

Of the top ten murderers of all time, five were Communists. Stalin (with 43 million) and Mao Zedong (with 38 million) top the list, dwarfing Adolf Hitler's 20 million. Lenin makes the list with over 4 million from 1917 to 1924. Cambodian Communist, Pol Pot, is credited with at least 2.4 million. Yugoslav dictator Tito (Josip Braz) ranks tenth and was responsible for the death of nearly 1.2 million people. North Korea's Kim Il-Sung and North Vietnam's Ho Chi Minh also rank high in the annals of murder.[237]

Most of these Communist atrocities were well known long before Rummel and others collected the statistics. In the summer of 1974, journalist Max Friedman presented testimony to the U.S. House Committee on Foreign Affairs on the Khmer Rouge's utter brutality and their blueprint for the future of Cambodia. He also made himself available to as many others in Congress as would listen. But most did not want to listen. They remained in a state of willful ignorance.

In 1975, when the massacres following the fall of Cambodia and South Vietnam became known, some anti-war politicians and journalists repented, but most continued to plead ignorance. Many others in Congress and in academic circles made incredible rationalizations that somehow Nixon, the military, or the Republican right wing was responsible for the brutal behavior of Cambodian and North Vietnamese Communists. For a catalog of these absurd leftist myths see Michael Lind's *Vietnam: The Necessary War*, published in 1999.[238]

The bloody consequences of Communist rule in Cambodia and South Vietnam were easily predictable to those whose thinking was not shackled to left-liberal ideology. But millions of innocent people who desired to be free were abandoned to oppression or death by a Congress whose majority preferred willful ignorance and political expediency to responsibility and honor.

The human disasters that followed the Communist takeover of Cambodia and South Vietnam are an ugly chapter of American political history. Not surprisingly, the unconscionable betrayal and dreadful carnage of once free peoples have been largely swept clear of public memory. The political, media, and academic powers responsible for this human tragedy have generally tried to suppress or distort its embarrassing record. But burying or twisting truth is never honorable and will only lead to a debased national character incapable of discerning danger or acting with wisdom and rational courage.

Whoever covers his sins will not prosper, but he
who confesses and forsakes them will obtain mercy.

—Proverbs 28:3

Communist Cambodian
Leasder Pol Pot

CHAPTER 22

Lessons from Vietnam and Other Wars

Confederate General Robert E. Lee and Union General William Tecumseh Sherman had quite different philosophies on the conduct of war, but they had one opinion in common: war is terrible. But to say that war is terrible is not to say that all war is unjust or immoral. Whether a war is just and moral depends upon both its purposes and its conduct. When a nation's sovereignty, peace, and vital economic interests are threatened by armed aggression or invasion, it must destroy the aggressor's will to persist or see its cherished heritages and the rights and welfare of its people crushed or subdued. It is the solemn duty of a nation's leaders to assure the survival and prosperity of all that its people rightly hold dear. Peaceful intentions and talk are not enough to deter aggressors driven by imperialistic leaders or ideologies. History teaches us that peaceful nations must be prepared to defend themselves or be swallowed up by tyranny.

For most nations, the defense of liberty must often depend upon greater alliances ready to defend their membership against powerful aggressors. Indeed, the world has often seen that not even the largest nations are safe from the power of aggressive oppressors and totalitarian ideologies. Survival and liberty often depend upon magnifying their strength through armed alliances with the common objective of deterring or defeating violent expansion by aggressor nations. Isolationism and pacifism have proven unrealistic strategies for peace in the real world. They only allow aggressors to gobble up the friends of freedom one by one until either surrender or a desperate struggle for survival against the odds are the only remaining alternatives.

In a November 16, 1934, broadcast from London, Winston Churchill, speaking of the rising threat of totalitarian militarism in Europe, warned the British people of the foolishness of pacifism and isolationism:

> Many people think that the best way to escape war is to dwell upon its horrors, and to imprint them vividly upon the minds of the younger generation. They flaunt the grisly photographs before their eyes. They fill their ears with tales of carnage. They dilate upon the ineptitude of generals and admirals. They denounce the crime and insensate folly of human strife.

173

> All this teaching ought to be very useful in preventing us
> from attacking or invading another country, if anyone
> outside a madhouse wished to do so. But how would it
> help us if we were attacked or invaded ourselves? That is
> the question we have to ask. . .[239]

Beginning in 1932 and especially after Adolf Hitler was made Chancellor of Germany in 1933, Churchill began to warn the British people and the free world of the dangers of Germany's expanding territorial ambitions. In March 1938, Germany annexed Austria. The German threat to Czechoslovakia became more evident in August. On September 21, he warned, "The idea that safety can be purchased by throwing a small State to the wolves is a fatal delusion. . . If peace is to be preserved on a lasting basis, it can only be by a combination of all the Powers whose vital interests are opposed to Nazi domination."[240] In an October 16, 1938, broadcast to America, Churchill appealed to the United States to recognize the common danger of Nazi aggression: "The preponderant world forces are on our side; they have but to be combined to be obeyed. Britain must arm. America must arm."[241]

Britain would not have survived the National Socialist onslaught against it in World II had not the United States and other allies in the New World honored their commitments to defend and support each other. All of Western Europe would have been permanently lost to totalitarian regimes. How long would Western Europe have survived against Communism had it not been for the North Atlantic Treaty Organization, in which the United States played a substantial leadership role? Military alliances should not be entered into lightly, but they have been necessary for the survival of freedom. It is usually incumbent on the larger nations in an alliance to provide the leadership and much of the economic and logistical support for an alliance to successfully deter or defeat aggressor nations. It is also of utmost importance that the political leadership of the leading nations be firmly committed to the objectives of the alliance.

American opposition to Communist expansion in Southeast Asia was not dissimilar to the moral and political character of British, American, and Allied opposition to Nazi Germany during World War II. We committed ourselves to the defense of South Vietnam not only to preserve the freedom of a besieged allied nation, not only to halt the bloody expansion of Communism's oppressive and ruthless totalitarian ideology, but also, as President Kennedy said in his 1964 inauguration speech, "to assure the survival and success of liberty."[242]

Yet a constant drum-beat of the anti-war movement during the Vietnam War was that the war was "immoral." This charge was repeated over and over again by anti-war personalities and campus organizers. I heard it most often when I was in graduate school after leaving the Air Force in 1969. But these charges were seldom specified, and on the rare occasions when some specifics were stated, they were badly misinformed. I remember most vividly the shrill charges of campus organizers against Nixon in the spring of 1970, following the American and South Vietnamese incursion into Cambodia. The incursion was repeatedly described as "immoral" and an expansion of the war. Yet it was the North Vietnamese who had pushed aside Cambodia's sovereignty to occupy eastern Cambodia and build military bases there. Peace could not come to South Vietnam while the Communists were using Cambodia as a sanctuary from which to launch attacks against it. I still hear today absurdly exaggerated figures of civilian deaths from U.S. bombing. Any civilian deaths are regrettable, but the strictly enforced U.S. policy was to minimize the possibility of civilian casualties, while the North Vietnamese and Viet Cong inflicted civilian casualties as a deliberate policy of terrorism and intimidation. In addition, the North Vietnamese often placed antiaircraft guns, SAMs, and petroleum storage in or near populated areas to deter U.S. bombing attacks. Estimates of civilian deaths during the war are attended by much controversy, but the North Vietnamese estimated their civilian deaths from U.S. bombing at 65,000.[243] I suspect this figure is exaggerated, but it is only about one-fifteenth of the claim I once heard from a libertarian speaker relying on an anti-war internet source. South Vietnamese civilian war deaths are estimated at 300,000. Most of them were the result of Communist brutality and terror. North Vietnamese artillery barrages directed at fleeing South Vietnamese refugees killed 25,000 in the spring of 1972 alone.[244] As was pointed out in the previous chapter, extraordinary brutality was directed against Cambodian and South Vietnamese civilians following the Communist victories and occupation in 1975.

The Western concept of Just War is primarily derived from Biblical roots but has also been influenced by Greek, Roman, Celtic, and Germanic cultures. Augustine (354-430 AD) is generally recognized as the first writer to present a systematic treatment of Christian doctrine as it applies to a nation, its citizens, and its soldiers in time of war. First of all, Augustine recognized that war is often a necessity to defend a nation and its citizens from aggressive enemies and that Christians may justly bear arms in that defense. Although there are several pacifist traditions in Christianity, categorical pacifism cannot be justified biblically. It is also unrealistic and in many circumstances can even be seen as self-centered and unloving.

Augustine outlined three main criteria for a just war: it must be initiated by properly constituted authority (Congress, in the case of the United States), it must be for a just cause, and it must be conducted by just means. Properly constituted civil authorities must decide these issues on behalf of the citizenry, but Augustine emphasized that these authorities are also ultimately accountable to God and therefore the teachings of Scripture. Thomas Aquinas (1225-1274) and many others since have attempted to flesh out a more comprehensive Just War Theory, but the tragedy of war always generates many ethical loose ends.

Definitions of a just cause usually prescribe that a war must either be generally defensive or conducted to correct a grave wrong. Defensive war does not assume an isolationist perspective here. Reality acknowledges that defensive alliances are often essential to peace. Correcting a grave wrong could also involve a humanitarian crusade to prevent great slaughter or evil. However, violating the jurisdictional sovereignty of other nations is in itself a precarious moral endeavor with a slippery slope. In the face of an imminent attack or invasion by an enemy, even a preemptive war would be permissible in self-defense. A nation cannot remain irresolute in the face of impending attack. Confederate President Jefferson Davis once told an advisor that when you have a gun barrel pointed at your chest, it is not wise to allow an enemy to fire the first shot before resisting him.[245] However, the tendency of mankind to make perverse rationalizations for aggression makes preemptive war a morally exacting decision requiring rigorous critical evaluation of the reality and severity of the threat. In any case, reasonable attempts to resolve serious wrongs, grievances, and threats must be exhausted before resorting to war. Before initiating war, the chances of success must also be weighed against its costs. Finally, in accordance with Augustine's thoughts, the objective of war must be a just peace. (Therefore, allied nations should not be abandoned to slaughter or brutal tyranny.)

The concept of just conduct and means in war recognizes primarily that a distinction must be made between combatants and non-combatants. Non-combatants should never be deliberate or primary targets of military action. Senseless cruelty and wanton destruction are prohibited. Besides the lives and health of civilians, destruction of civilian properties that provide food, shelter, and medical attention should especially be avoided. Just conduct in war demands that prisoners of war must be treated humanely and respectfully. Torture of prisoners of war or non-combatants is prohibited. Additionally, the use of force must not be disproportionate to objectives, threats, or harm done. As much as prudence and realism will allow, the enemy must be treated in good faith to keep open the possibility of reconciliation.

These principles of just conduct and means in war are contained and expanded in the Geneva Conventions, the U.S. Law of Land Warfare, and the Uniform Code of Military Justice. Contrary to popular opinion and the ubiquitous residue of anti-war propaganda on the Vietnam conflict, the United States adhered to these more closely in Vietnam than in World War II. The

American record was by no means perfect in Vietnam. Not every bomb hit the right target, and our humanitarian record was severely marred in March 1968 by the massacre of approximately 347 unarmed civilians in a group of hamlets in the Son My district of Quang Ngai province, which are now generally referred to as My Lai. The My Lai incident (covered extensively in the appendix) undoubtedly damaged American moral credibility and contributed to the eventual Communist takeover of Indochina. But our failings in Vietnam pale in comparison to some in World War II. On February 13-15, 1945, at least 25,000 civilians were killed in the British and American bombing of Dresden,[246] and on March 9-10, 1945, the American fire-bombing of Tokyo resulted in at least 88,000 civilian deaths.[247] Granted the records of the Axis powers and of our Soviet allies in World War II were far more appalling in their enormity, but it would be a dangerous disservice to our posterity to whitewash the plain facts of our history.

Inadvertent civilian casualties are one of the great and common tragedies of war. Yet we cannot abandon the cause of freedom because war often begets such tragedies. We must seek to minimize these inhumanities without giving up on the cause of humanity.

Our principal objective in the Vietnam War was to prevent a Communist takeover of South Vietnam. This objective may have been too narrow strategically, but it was, nonetheless, a moral objective. Given especially the demonstrated aggressiveness, bloody history, and ruthless tyranny of Communism, attempting to rescue South Vietnam from such a fate was both a moral and compassionate objective. The results of the Communist victory in 1975 prove the justice of our intervention. Contrary to still popular anti-war myths, the Vietnam War was not an internal political struggle within South Vietnam. It was part of an aggressive North Vietnamese attempt to take over all of Indochina. Furthermore, it was encouraged and abetted by the Soviet Union and aided by the People's Republic of China. Halting the spread and influence of such hostile and dangerous enemies was not only in our national interest, it was in the interest of world peace and prosperity. Indeed, not to come to the aid of an ally in great jeopardy, though we had the power and means to do so, would have been reprehensible. As it was, the actions of Congress that abandoned South Vietnam and Cambodia to Communist invasion and takeover in 1975 was the real moral failure of the war.

Any reasonable interpretation of Just War Theory must conclude that our war against Communism in Indochina was a just war and was conducted, with a few regrettable and painful exceptions, in accordance with high ethical standards. The "rules of engagement" received frequent emphasis, and military forces—aircrews especially—often sacrificed effectiveness and exposed themselves to greater hazards to minimize any risk to civilians. This is not to excuse My Lai or any other moral failings, but by and large, the U.S. Armed Forces conducted combat operations at an exemplary level with respect to Just War Theory and the Geneva Conventions. Their just conduct and means in war would compare favorably with the military operations of any country in recent history.

There was, however, a technical flaw in adhering to the Just War requirement of initiating war by proper authority. It was that the August 1964 Gulf of Tonkin Resolution was not a full declaration of war as required by the U.S. Constitution. The Tonkin Resolution was not isolated from our foreign policy commitments, however. The United States had an obligation under the Southeast Asia Treaty Organization (SEATO) to defend South Vietnam. Moreover, in many circumstances of international conflict, full declarations of war are not always wise. Johnson and McNamara, who feared Chinese or Soviet intervention, were concerned that a full declaration of war against North Vietnam might cause the Soviet Union and China to react with more aggressive support for their ally. Of course, in the nuclear age, military response cannot always await a formal declaration of war.

Although the incident in which the North Vietnamese fired on two U.S. destroyers conducting electronic intelligence missions in the Gulf of Tonkin was undoubtedly real, there is no question that Johnson used it to bolster Congressional support for the war. But this was in the same period during which North Vietnam was rapidly and aggressively escalating its war against South Vietnam, and South Vietnam was in serious danger. Johnson would have been remiss in not calling on Congress to allow him to expand his options to defend Southeast Asia. As a former intelligence officer, I have always thought that the destroyers may have purposely been sent close enough to North Vietnamese territory to draw fire, just as Lincoln contrived to draw Confederate fire on Fort Sumter and Union ships in Charleston harbor in order to rally Northern public support for an invasion of seceding states.[248]

In retrospect, a declaration of war would have been much more useful in the longer run both for Johnson and Nixon. The lack of a formal declaration may have doomed effective prosecution of the war. Johnson needed to rally both Congressional and public support for a long war. The Tonkin Resolution got him the immediate results he wanted, but it did not fully mobilize public and Congressional sentiment for the national pain that would come. Nor did it give him the powers to deal with subversion that a declaration of war would have given him. Nixon inherited a legitimate Congressional concern with Presidential War Powers. However legitimate, this concern became exaggerated and severely handicapped his conduct of the war and the Allied cause. The issue of War Powers is complex, but as a nation we should be extremely wary of eroding respect for the Constitution. Could Johnson have gotten a declaration of war? The Tonkin Gulf Resolution passed the U.S. House by a vote of 416 to 0 and was approved by the Senate 88 to 2.[249]

A declaration of war would have certainly distracted Congress and the public from passing Johnson's Great Society programs—which might have been a cheerful result in itself. It would also have made a critical difference in gaining and sustaining public support for the war—a *sine qua non* for democratic governments during protracted and costly conflicts. Perhaps it would even have deterred the Soviet Union and China from providing substantial support for North Vietnam. Soon after taking office in 1953, President Eisenhower sent a diplomatic message to the Soviet Union and China through Indian diplomats that North Korea had better start serious peace negotiations or he would consider a geographical expansion of American action to halt North Korean aggression. It worked, and the Korean War ended.[250]

The first great mistake of the Vietnam War was that we failed to comprehend its full military and geographical scope. Consequently, our objective was both too narrow and too passive. Hanoi's objective was to defeat us and take not only South Vietnam but also Laos and Cambodia. Our objective was simply to stop them from taking South Vietnam. Once Hanoi's aggressive actions were evident, our objective should have been to challenge and destroy their military capabilities in every part of Indochina and cut off their war materials from the Soviet Union and China. Nixon finally did this in 1972, but his victory was thrown away by a war-weary Congress.

We also made the initial mistake of assuming North Vietnam's threat to South Vietnam consisted principally in guerilla warfare against the Saigon regime. Their insurgency, however, was only the first phase of an aggressive invasion in which a modern and well-equipped North Vietnamese Army would supply at least 80 percent of the manpower.[251] The training and equipment we supplied to the South Vietnamese Army (ARVN) were thus at first inadequate to successfully challenge the superiority in equipment and fire-power of an invading North Vietnamese Army. Even the Viet Cong were better equipped than the ARVN at first. It took precious time to remedy this imbalance.

Even as late as the spring of 1972, when the NVA rolled into the northern provinces of South Vietnam with over 500 modern Soviet tanks, the ARVN had few anti-tank weapons to halt the surprising NVA blitzkrieg. Bloody and precarious weeks passed before they were adequately supplied with anti-tank weapons and more tanks of their own. It required fierce ARVN resistance and concentrated U.S. airpower to slow the NVA assault during those weeks.

Undoubtedly, the most disastrous political mistake during the war was President Kennedy's encouragement and support for a regime change in South Vietnam in late 1963. This coup resulted in the death of South Vietnamese President Ngo Dinh Diem and the political destabilization of the country for two years. The North Vietnamese reacted by stepping up their invasion of South Vietnam. Although the political crisis ostensibly involved Buddhist protests over alleged discrimination, the real precipitating cause was unfavorable and distorted U.S. press coverage of the Diem regime. Seeking to disassociate U.S policy from Diem and to avoid any political damage to himself, Kennedy began to promote the idea of regime change.[252] Underlying this was a common American mindset typical of journalists and politicians who are more inclined to abstract idealism than concrete realism. Some have called this mindset "liberal perfectionism." It tends to impose standards in politics, personality, and leadership styles on foreign leaders whose cultural environment and political circumstances and demands are not comparable to those in the United States or Western Europe. The issue is frequently a more autocratic leadership style than Americans would like. In South Vietnam, we got rid of Diem and got chaos. In Iran, we helped ease out the Shaw and got a nightmare Ayatollah. The United States needs to resist imposing unreasonable tests of American similitude on allied leaders. Imposing regime changes on allied nations should be out of the question.

In one of the strange ironies of history, President Kennedy was assassinated on November 22, 1963, just twenty days after the death of Diem. Lyndon Johnson (who did not support the coup) assumed the presidency the same day. Johnson embraced Kennedy's objective of preventing a Communist takeover of South Vietnam, but as Hanoi escalated its invasion of South Vietnam in 1964, Johnson took counsel of his fears rather than his generals. Johnson and Secretary of Defense McNamara both had a fear of direct Chinese or Soviet intervention. This was not an unreasonable concern, since the Chinese had intervened in the Korean War in November 1950, after the North Korean Army had been routed by MacArthur. Unfortunately, Johnson and McNamara allowed their fear of direct confrontation with the Soviet Union or China to overshadow experienced military judgment and to have an inordinate influence on shaping strategic, and even tactical, war policies. The overall result was what Admiral U.S. Grant Sharp, the supreme U.S. commander in the Pacific, later called "a strategy for defeat."[253]

Another outrageous and self-defeating policy of the Johnson Administration was to allow the North Vietnamese Army (NVA) to operate out of sanctuaries in Cambodia and Laos as well as North Vietnam. President

Kennedy had agreed to the neutralization of Laos in July of 1962. North Vietnam, of course, did not honor Laotian neutrality and within months there were 80,000 North Vietnamese troops in eastern Laos, building supply lines and bases from which to strike South Vietnam. The supply and communication lines, begun in 1959 by NVA General Vo Bam, became the famous Ho Chi Minh Trail. From there the supply lines were extended into eastern Cambodia from where four NVA divisions and their Viet Cong allies could strike at the very heart of South Vietnam. At least one of fourteen NVA bases there was within thirty miles of Saigon.[254] North Vietnam also supplied the Viet Cong by sea until the U.S. Navy successfully blockaded the South Vietnamese coast to enemy traffic in 1965. Cambodian sanctuaries were also supplied by sea through the port of Kompong Som until Nixon's incursion and bombing of Cambodian sanctuaries in 1970.

Kennedy's second error, continued by Johnson, was not to contest North Vietnam's violation of the neutrality agreement on Laos. There is a general rule of contract law that if one party violates a contract, the other party is freed from its contractual obligations. But timidly and foolishly, the United States abandoned eastern Laos to Hanoi. By 1965, the U.S. was bombing the Laotian part of the Trail, but bases there remained inviolate to ground attack by Allied forces.

From these sanctuaries, Communist forces could strike South Vietnam at will but could then retreat into the safety of their sanctuaries without fear of reprisal by Allied forces. This was an enormous advantage to the Communists and a considerable and frustrating burden to U.S. and ARVN forces. This allowed the enemy complete initiative and left Allied forces only able to react until the NVA slipped back across the border. In addition, there could be no Allied flanking movement to cut off enemy supply and communication lines. There could be no surprise amphibious assault on the coast of North Vietnam, cutting off half the enemy's army, which could compare to MacArthur's brilliant assault and flanking of the North Korean Army at Inchon during the Korean War. The U.S. was left without any option but to use its immense firepower in search and destroy missions, but they had to stop at the Cambodian or Laotian border.

The Cambodian and Laotian sanctuaries also meant that the ARVN had to defend 640 miles of border rather than just the narrow 40 miles across the DMZ. This required a huge commitment of manpower which the NVA did not have to match. Johnson's airwar policies allowed North Vietnam many sanctuaries where U.S. bombing was prohibited or severely restricted.

Nixon finally ended the safe-haven status of NVA bases in Cambodia in 1970. This allowed for the Vietnamization of the war and the eventual safe withdrawal of American troops. But U.S. and South Vietnamese destruction of Cambodian sanctuaries in 1970 raised a great howl in the anti-war movement and in Congress. In December 1970, Congress prohibited further use of American combat forces and advisors on the ground in Cambodia and Laos, thus encouraging the NVA to re-establish its sanctuary bases and hindering the defense of South Vietnam.

Allowing the enemy safe havens is no way to break his will for aggression. It is rather a policy that erodes the hope and morale of those charged to defeat him. Prussian military theorist Carl von Clausewitz (1780-1831) would have been appalled.

Clausewitz would have been equally appalled at the Johnson-McNamara policy of gradualism (or graduated escalation) in regard to the use of American airpower. He would have been aghast at McNamara's announcement in the spring of 1965 that America's most powerful tool of military superiority would primarily be used for the tactical support of Allied ground forces rather than to cut off the enemy's means of making war and breaking the will of Hanoi's leaders to continue the war. He would have been astonished at Johnson's micromanagement of the airwar and the limits and restrictions placed upon strategic targeting in North Vietnam. He would have been horrified to see much of our Air Force wasted attacking secondary targets in North Vietnam, while its leaders, its most important strategic targets, and the primary entry points for Soviet and Chinese arms were given the security of sanctuary. Rather than interdicting enemy arms and supplies where they were most concentrated and vulnerable, USAF and Navy fighter-bombers were forced to hunt them down after they had already been disbursed. This was a marginally effective and extremely inefficient way to prevent the buildup of enemy forces in Laos, Cambodia, and South Vietnam. It maximized our costs rather than his.

This policy of gradualism, the brainchild of McNamara and his Harvard academics in the Defense Department, was imposed upon the Joint Chiefs of Staff and the Pacific Area Commanders despite their strong objections. The cautious and measured pace of McNamara's gradualism allowed North Vietnam to build its military capabilities with only limited danger of harassment. Most importantly, it allowed the North Vietnamese to build one of the most formidable antiaircraft systems in history, making attacks on North Vietnam increasingly costly. The slow and measured pace of gradualism also allowed the North Vietnamese to predict, at least roughly, which targets and types of targets would be hit next and to make sure they were adequately protected before American bombers arrived to meet a hail of antiaircraft fire and SAMs. Gradualism also meant that North Vietnam's leaders could direct their war against South Vietnam in safety.

The policies of gradualism, severely restricted use of strategic airpower, and toleration of enemy sanctuaries on South Vietnam's borders forced the United States to rely on a huge commitment of ground forces to defend South Vietnam. This also drastically limited their tactical options. The number of U.S. military personnel in Vietnam peaked at 543,000 in April 1969.[255] South Vietnam could have been successfully defended with far fewer men and we would have suffered fewer casualties, if only we had rejected these insane impositions on military tactics and strategy and had courageously embraced more prudent policies based on the accumulated wisdom of political and military history.

The Johnson Administration failed to learn one of the lessons of the Korean War: Communists do not negotiate in good faith. They regard any action that advances their cause as just and any lie that advances it as truth. They understand power and commitment to use it alone. This was also true of the Nazis in World War II and is probably true of every totalitarian ideology, including the one that now advances terrorism in the world.

Johnson initiated sixteen bombing halts to encourage North Vietnam to negotiate a peaceful settlement of the war. They abused each one by frantically using every hour to strengthen their positions, bolster their munitions, and maneuver for military advantage. They regarded every bombing halt, peaceful gesture, and American concession as a sign of weakness and lack of American commitment. Yet Johnson eagerly made concessions in hopes of a negotiating "breakthrough." None ever came. In his final months in office, he halted all bombing of North Vietnam and placed all his hopes for peace on negotiations. The North Vietnamese only demanded surrender and frequently used negotiations as a propaganda platform. Johnson seemed to have a naïve faith in negotiations, as if negotiation were simply a matter of friendly agreement unconnected to long-standing national ambitions and unaffected by human depravity, the lust for power, and disparate philosophies of truth and justice. Such unrealistic idealism is especially dangerous when dealing with brutal tyrants. Americans need to learn the difference between negotiating a just peace and negotiating a gullible surrender.

After learning a few lessons of his own on the futility of negotiating with Communists, Nixon finally had to bomb them to the negotiating table in late 1972. One of the lessons we learned in Korea is that more and constant pressure—not less and intermittent pressure—is what brings Communists and other totalitarians to the negotiating table and gets results.

We should have also remembered how the Communists defeated the French in Indochina in 1954. Dien Bien Phu was a spectacular Communist military victory, but it was in itself not sufficient to drive the French out of Indochina. Ho Chi Minh and the Communist leaders of the Viet Minh had a two-pronged strategy, one military and the other political. They knew that, to drive the French out of Indochina, they must break the will of the already war-weary French people to support the war. This they did through propaganda and organized protest.

They had a similar strategy to drive the United States out of Vietnam. The Communist regime in Hanoi knew that it could not match American soldiers and fire-power on the battlefield. It was necessary to undermine the will of the American people—and especially of the Congress—to support the war. The Communists did this through both propaganda and organized protest. Their propaganda depicted the war as a nationalist insurgency to uproot the corrupt vestiges of French colonialism and defeat American interference and imperialism. It continually attempted to obscure North Vietnam's connection to the Soviet Union, the People's Republic of China, and even to Communism. It continually tried to portray American objectives as self-serving and unjust, and its purposes and actions as immoral. Wherever possible it exploited racial and social grievances.

Relatively small cadres of New Left radicals, some of them actually members of the Communist Party or its front organizations, were able to orchestrate waves of anti-war demonstrations involving organizations and participants of divergent interests and views—the radical left, isolationists, pacifists, civil rights activists, socialists, students and parents concerned about the draft, Libertarians concerned about the draft and Constitutional issues, even the simply curious. These rallies and teach-ins generally broadcast a heavy dose of Soviet- and North Vietnamese-generated propaganda.

College students were probably by far the most numerous rank-and-file participants and were particularly vulnerable to anti-war propaganda because of the draft. Anti-draft organizing was generally the most successful. Naturally, student interest spilled over into college faculties and a huge slice of academia.

Although draft deferments were numerous, they actually made the draft more controversial by raising the specters of privilege and unequal burdens. General Westmoreland also believed that the policy of draft deferments "contributed to anti-war militancy on college campuses in that young men feeling twinges of conscience because they sat out a war while others fought could appease their conscience if they convinced themselves the war was immoral."[256] Allowing student draft deferments, not calling up the reserves, and not formally declaring war were all part of a deliberate policy to reduce public concern about the war. But this is just the opposite of what should have been done. In a democracy, it is necessary for leaders to lead. In war, they must rally the public will to endure hardship and defeat the enemy. Citing Clausewitz, Harry Summers, former Colonel of Infantry and retired faculty member of the Army War College, believed that "Presidential failure to invoke the national will to victory was one of the major strategic failures of the Vietnam War."[257] Certainly, it helped produce a strategic vulnerability that our enemies on the left had great expertise in exploiting.

The draft has always been problematic. Modern technology and weapons have reduced the need for the large land armies seen in World War II. Neither would a prudent strategy in Vietnam have required more than a half million American servicemen. Modern military organizations require intelligent, well-educated, principled, and highly motivated soldiers. America will be far more secure in the future, if we are more selective and attract high-quality applicants through high pay and generous benefits that recognize not only education and skills but also the dangers and hardships of military life. Service in the National Guard and Reserves should also recognize these factors. We must also recognize our special responsibility to seriously disabled veterans and their families. The draft should be a last resort and meticulously fair and non-political.

The American people never identified with the anti-war movement or the New Left, but anti-war sentiment and left-wing influence were strong in the media and in the Democratic Party, especially as the public grew weary of a protracted war. Anti-war pressures in Congress forced Nixon to compromise the provisions of the 1973 peace agreement that had resulted from his aggressive strategic bombing of North Vietnam in December 1972. In accordance with the terms of the peace, the few remaining American troops in South Vietnam were withdrawn, and Hanoi released its 591 prisoners of war. The war had essentially been won, and the peace accords, though compromised, would have brought a workable peace to Vietnam—if only Congress had had the will to enforce its terms.

In the wake of the Watergate scandal, Nixon was forced to resign in August 1974. This resulted in a huge Democratic majority in Congress in November 1974. When North Vietnam again launched an invasion of South Vietnam in December 1974, Congress turned its back on South Vietnam and Cambodia and refused to honor its obligation to enforce the terms of the peace accords. Nixon's Vietnamization plan had built the South Vietnamese Armed Forces to strength of 1.1 million.[258] The South Vietnamese Army's battle worthiness had been proved during the 1968 Tet offensive and North Vietnam's Easter 1972 offensive. But Congress reduced its budget for the support of South Vietnam by more than two-thirds from 1973 to 1975.[259] As the South Vietnamese ran out of ammunition and equipment, the NVA swept over them in battle after battle. By the end of April 1975, both Cambodia and South Vietnam had fallen into Communists hands. The terrible consequence of the Communist victory was that more than 3.5 million Cambodian and South Vietnamese civilians were murdered, starved to death, or drowned in the South China Sea.

The United States suffered over 47,000 combat deaths in Vietnam. Another 10,000 died from other causes. In addition, South Korea suffered just over 4,400 battle deaths; Australia and New Zealand suffered 469 battle deaths; and Thailand suffered 351 battle deaths. The South Vietnamese had suffered 224,000 battle deaths before North Vietnam's 1975 offensive.[260]

We made many mistakes in Vietnam, but the cause and our means were just. The war could have been won easily in 1965, before North Vietnam became a hornet's nest of antiaircraft guns and SAMs. We were beginning to win it in 1967, and could surely have won it following the devastating defeats suffered by the NVA and VC during their 1968 Tet offensive. Nixon did win it in December 1972, but a defeatist Congress threw victory away. The great moral tragedy of the Vietnam War was that Congress did not have the political backbone and moral courage to persevere in a just cause. Thousands of Allied soldiers had died for that cause, yet South Vietnam and Cambodia were abandoned to slaughter and ruthless despotism.

APPENDIX 1

The Moral and Political Tragedy of My Lai

The soldier, be he friend or foe, is charged with the
protection of the weak and the unarmed. It is the very
essence and reason for his being.[261]

—*Gen. Douglas MacArthur, 1946*

In February 1968, Major General Samuel W. Koster, commander of the American Division, whose troops were engaging Communist forces in Quang Ngai Province near the coast of central South Vietnam, became concerned by reports that some troops under his command had been accused of looting, brutality, and rape. He issued a memorandum to all officers under his command entitled "Acts of Discourtesy Toward Vietnamese People," reminding them that such acts are "destructive to our mission and to the image of our great nation" and would not be tolerated. A portion of the memorandum made these points: ". . . Every time a Vietnamese female is insulted by word, gesture, or touch, the name of the United States is insulted. Every time we carelessly call the Vietnamese people childish and crude nicknames, we heap criticism on the United States. . ."[262]

American Division records show that eleven men were court-martialed on such charges from September 1967 to June 1968. Several were acquitted; several were fined and reduced in rank; and three were sentenced to prison terms of two to twenty years. Yet the same division records did not even hint that one of the greatest civilian massacres ever attributed to U.S. forces was perpetrated by an American Division task force in Quang Ngai Province during that same period.[263]

On March 16, 1968, approximately 347 unarmed civilians—mostly women, children, and elderly men—were killed by two companies of a task force of the 11th Brigade of the American Division while sweeping through several hamlets in the administrative area called Son My.[264] Some Vietnamese estimates, however, place the death toll at over 500. This toll included approximately twenty women and young girls aged from ten to forty-five who were raped and then killed. Most of the deaths occurred as a result of the systematic slaughter of civilian detainees at a hamlet called My Lai 4 on U.S. Army maps.[265] Approximately 87 deaths occurred at a nearby hamlet designated as My Khe 4.[266] Because of cover-ups within the American Division, the incident remained unknown to higher military command levels and the American public until September 1969.

Following investigations by the Army Criminal Investigation Division (CID) and the Peers Commission (appointed by the Secretary of the Army Stanley Resor and headed by Lt. Gen. W. R. Peers), four officers and nine enlisted soldiers were initially charged with war crimes. In addition, the Peers Commission brought charges against twelve officers for covering up war crimes or dereliction of their duty to prevent or report war crimes.[267] Four more officers, including Lt. Col. Frank Barker, the task force commander; Capt. Earl Michles, commander of B Company; 2LT Michael Lewis, second platoon leader, B Company; and 2LT Steven Brooks, second platoon leader, C Company, were heavily involved in Son My operations but had been killed in action before the investigations. (Michles was known to be a conscientious officer who strongly opposed mistreatment of civilians and prisoners, but a number of his men either purposely or negligently killed Vietnamese civilians at My Khe. Lewis was killed during the assault on My Khe.) In addition, there were twenty-five enlisted men who were implicated in the Son My war crimes, but who had left the service and could not, according to U.S law, be prosecuted by the Army.[268] In the U.S. Congress, the House Armed Services Committee also held hearings on the alleged war crimes. Thereafter raged a military and political controversy that substantially weakened public and Congressional support for resisting Communist aggression in Southeast Asia.

At the center of the My Lai atrocity controversy were Lt. Col. Barker, the Task Force Commander (killed in action June 1968), Captain Ernest Medina, commander of "Charlie" Company, and especially his first platoon leader, 2LT William Calley. Task Force (TF) "Barker" was a temporary organization put together to destroy the Viet Cong (VC) 48th Local Force Battalion which was believed to have its headquarters in Son My. Barker's task force consisted of three infantry companies and an artillery battery from the 11th Brigade of the Americal (23rd Infantry) Division.

Quang Ngai and neighboring Binh Dinh provinces were among the most dangerous areas of South Vietnam. Quang Ngai is part of a narrow coastal plain lying between the sandy beaches of the South China Sea and the rugged Annamese mountain range to the west. Most of its farming hamlets were built in the shade of huge bamboo and banana trees. The rural areas of Quang Ngai Province were a Viet Minh stronghold during French rule and remained under Communist domination after the partition of Vietnam in 1954. Only the provincial capital, Quang Ngai City, was relatively secure to the Saigon government. The more rural hamlets had been under the effective control of the National Liberation Front and their Viet Cong militias for more than a generation. The area's 48th Local Force Battalion had proved itself to be a deadly force of 350 to 400 experienced guerilla fighters.

Following the 1968 Tet Offensive, which lasted from late January to the end of February, Allied Forces lost contact with the 48th VC Battalion. Later intelligence reports consolidated at higher Allied command levels revealed that the VC had suffered enormous casualties during Tet. Most of the 48th Battalion was recuperating in the Annamese Mountains. Its commander had been killed, and the battalion's effective fighting strength had been reduced to between 30 and 100 combatants. A few of them, however, had begun to infiltrate back into the Son My area.

"Charlie" Company of the 1st Battalion, 20th Regiment of the Americal Division, did not arrive in Quang Ngai Province until late December of 1967. They had been training in Hawaii. Little did they know that they would be walking right into the 1968 Tet Offensive in one of the hottest VC areas in Vietnam. Charlie Company's commander, Captain Ernest Medina, was a stocky Mexican-American who had graduated in the top five of his Officer Candidate School (OCS) class in March 1964. He had enlisted in the Army in 1956 and proved his leadership skills as an NCO. He had spent much of his Army career in Germany and married a German woman. In Germany, he had also taken a few college courses which gave him the confidence to try for OCS. Medina was well regarded by superiors and the vast majority of his subordinates. He also had a knack for winning company competitions and somehow earned the sobriquet "Mad Dog Medina." His company was usually rated the best in the battalion. His main problem as a company commander was the high turnover of personnel. In Hawaii, there had been a mass exodus of reassignments and soldiers whose enlistment tours were expiring. In addition, his young platoon leaders were inexperienced. At 32, Medina was ten to twelve years older than most of his men and enjoyed a natural as well as an official leadership role. He could sometimes be abrasive, but he was regarded by most of his men as competent and tough but fair. Medina had some leadership failings, however, that would not serve him well.

Medina regarded his new first platoon leader, 2LT William Calley, as an incompetent. Furthermore, he often showed his disregard for Calley by ridiculing him in front of his men. He frequently addressed Calley as "sweetheart" and referred to him as "Lt. Shithead." It is not surprising then that Calley's men also thought of him as incompetent and a joke. Yet Calley practically worshiped Medina and thought of him as the ideal officer.

Following the My Lai investigations, General Westmoreland remarked that Calley should never have been made an officer. This is the opinion of almost everyone familiar with Calley's record prior to his commissioning in September 1967. Calley failed the 7th grade for cheating—for giving other classmates answers during a test. One of Calley's personal characteristics was that he was a people pleaser. This would enhance his admission to OCS later but probably contributed to his leadership failure in Vietnam. Calley, however, was generally a poor student. After being expelled from a junior high school in Miami for arguing with a teacher, his parents placed him in Florida Military Academy, where he did better. He attended Georgia Military Academy near Atlanta in the 10th grade and returned to public schools in Florida for his last two years of high school. He graduated from Miami Edison High School number 666th in a class of 731—in the bottom 10 percent of his high school graduating class. Nevertheless, he attended some college courses at Palm Beach Junior College for a while, where he made two Cs and several Ds and Fs.[269]

Calley then tried to enlist in the Army but was rejected for being tone deaf and received a 1-Y draft classification. He then worked at several jobs but was called up by his Miami Draft Board. Rather than be drafted, he enlisted in the Army to get his choice of assignments—in this case, Clerk Typist School, where he did well and graduated in the top half of his class. His career as an Army clerk typist was going well and it might have gone well for Calley and the Army thereafter had not someone noticed that he had two years of military school and might be officer potential. This may be related to Calley's skill as a people pleaser as well as a clerk typist.

Calley went through OCS when the demand for junior officers was greatest, and the standards were at their lowest. About 75 percent of OCS candidates were college graduates the year before and the year after Calley's admission. Only 25 percent of OCS graduates in 1967 were college graduates, and the attrition rate dropped from 42 percent to 28 percent. Calley ranked in the bottom quarter of his class. In addition to his difficulty with map reading—an absolute essential for infantry officers—Calley, at five-foot-three, did not have an imposing physical presence or a commanding voice.[270]

Medina was right about Calley being an incompetent. Calley was enthusiastic and eager to please, but he did not have the mental aptitude or necessary critical judgment to function as an officer. In fact, his enthusiasm and inordinate desire to please, combined with marginal analytical judgment, made him a potentially dangerous officer. One of Calley's men summed it up aptly: "Calley is just gung-ho and has no common sense."[271] Calley's many appalling statements about blind obedience to orders and his subsequent callous disregard for the lives of Vietnamese civilians reflect both poor analytical judgment and poor moral judgment. His excuse for killing babies was that they would grow up to be Viet Cong. But Medina's derisive treatment of Calley may have helped turn a dangerous potential into a dangerous reality.[272]

Medina also had a critical weakness that was noticed by only a few until too late. Although he had a reputation as a strict disciplinarian, he was actually extremely lax in matters of moral discipline within his company. It was common knowledge that there were half a dozen soldiers in his company who regularly committed acts of rape and forced sodomy on Vietnamese women, but he took no action against these men. On such issues, he was their buddy rather than their captain. This style of leadership also became notable in two of his platoon leaders, lieutenants Calley and Brooks. One subordinate described Calley as yelling and screaming and telling everybody he was the boss one day and then turning around to be your buddy the next day. Neither approach gained him any respect. Whether from predilection or necessity, Medina also tended to be a one-man leadership show. Hence his lieutenants had little authority of their own among their men.

Charlie Company had been in Quang Ngai Province for almost three months before the My Lai tragedy but had had little direct contact with the enemy. With only 132 men on arrival, the company was under strength to start and had already suffered 27 casualties from snipers, booby traps, and land mines. Seven men were dead, one by a sniper bullet, and the others ripped apart by land mines and booby traps. Several of the wounded had lost arms, legs, and eyes from land mines. Yet they had never seen the enemy. Bravo Company had experienced similar frustration. Hence the men began to turn unfriendly to the Vietnamese civilians they saw during their patrols. They blamed them for not warning them about the mines and booby traps.

Both the North Vietnamese and the VC knew that American policy was strongly adverse to endangering civilians, and they took maximum advantage of it. In North Vietnam, anti-aircraft guns and petroleum storage were often placed near civilian concentration centers to deter American attacks. The VC often used civilians as cover and frequently used women and children for retrieving weapons, placing explosives near American troops, or acting as decoys. This was the cause of many ambiguities in judging whether someone was a friend or foe. Charlie Company was also instructed by an Australian advisor on the many ingenious deceptions practiced by the VC and their sympathizers. Consequently, the men of Charlie Company were afraid to trust any Vietnamese whose loyalties were not known.

On the morning of February 25, Medina led a patrol that ran into a minefield. A huge explosion was followed by screams and more explosions. Anyone who moved to help someone just got blown up himself. Medina shouted "Freeze!" but several men panicked and ran, setting off more explosions. Yet Medina kept his head and eventually got his men out of the minefield. He was subsequently awarded the Silver Star for his "courage, professional actions, and unselfish concern for his men."

He later described the terror of seeing people blown apart—one man "split from his crotch all the way up to his chest cavity... Everybody was shaken. Three men were dead. Another twelve suffered ghastly injuries. Few could forget their own fear or the screams of the wounded, or the gruesome task of loading the medevac helicopters."[273]

Calley had been on leave during this patrol and observed a change in the mood of the men when he returned. His men no longer gave candy to Vietnamese children. He noticed with satisfaction that they kicked the kids aside—even the nice, sweet kids. He could hardly refrain from telling them, "Well, I told you so." As for Medina, he was openly hostile to the Vietnamese and was harsh to any of his men who showed kindness or consideration to them. Sergeant Kenneth Hodges, a second platoon squad leader, described the sentiment of his men: "Feelings of revenge extended to all the people in the village, because we felt that all of them, whether they were female, military-age male, old men, or kids, they were all part of the problem."[274] Hodges, however, was one of the NCOs whom the Army CID charged with a war crime—assault and suspected rape on a female at My Lai. The charges were dropped, but he was recommended for discharge and barred from future enlistment.

Two days before Task Force Barker's planned assault on the 48th VC Battalion, which was believed to be headquartered near My Lai 4, Sergeant George Cox and his third platoon squad were patrolling near the Task Force helicopter landing zone. The popular and thoughtful sergeant unfortunately stopped to examine what he thought was a 155-mm artillery round. It was booby trapped and blew him apart and hideously wounded two of his men. One was blinded and lost an arm and a leg. Another lost both legs. Charlie Company was now down to 105 men.

Returning to camp, some of the men were crying and others were furious. Michael Terry reported that some of them brutally killed a Vietnamese woman. Medina had to deal with angry villagers but managed to keep it quiet. Calley remarked that Medina was not about to lose men just because they "kicked a Vietnamese kid or killed a damn innocent woman. . . He had to keep a combat effective unit."[275]

The next day briefings began for TF Barker's assault on My Lai 4 and nearby hamlets. The assault would start with armed reconnaissance by helicopter gunships nicknamed "Sharks." TF Barker's artillery would then soften up the landing zone and the outskirts of My Lai 4. Then the infantry companies would be transported to Landing Zone "Uptight" by transport helicopters nicknamed "Dolphins." From there the infantry would assault and clear My Lai 4 and surrounding hamlets of enemy soldiers, weapons, and supplies. The operation would also be monitored from the air by Barker; Col. Oran Henderson, the new 11th Brigade Commander; and Major General Koster and several staff officers.

Before the briefing by Barker, Henderson arrived to encourage aggressive action and success. The mission was to smash the troublesome 48th VC Battalion. While Henderson was still at the briefing, Captain Carl Creswell, the division's artillery chaplain, joined them. He recalled that a major there (undoubtedly Major Charles Calhoun) had said, "We're going in there, and if we get one round out of there, we're going to level it."

Creswell had looked at him and said, "You know, I really didn't think we made war that way."

His response was, "It's a tough war, Chaplain."

Creswell left the briefing shortly thereafter.[276]

The briefing was led by Lt. Col. Barker; Major Calhoun, the TF operations officer; and Captain Eugene Kotouc, the TF intelligence officer. It was a disorganized briefing with Barker leaving and coming back several times. The briefing included an illegal order to burn the hamlets, kill all the livestock, destroy all food supplies, and poison the wells. Such actions against civilian populations are prohibited by the U.S. Law of Land Warfare, the Geneva Convention, and the Uniform Code of Military Justice. No order was given to kill civilians, but no plans were specified on locations and procedures to handle civilians or prisoners.

In addition, Captain Kotouc either deliberately or negligently led the company commanders to believe that 250 to 280 enemy combatants would be in My Lai 4 and by 0730 in the morning, *all* the innocent civilians would be away at the market. This was either deliberate misrepresentation of the facts or a ridiculous assumption by an inexperienced intelligence officer with just enough Vietnamese cultural education to make him dangerous. Koutoc also told them that the entire population of My Lai 4 consisted of active VC sympathizers. Task Force officers left the briefing with the clear impression that all the houses, dwellings, and livestock around My Lai 4 were to be destroyed.

That afternoon an emotional funeral service was given for Sergeant Cox. At the close of the service, Captain Medina told his men that the next day would be their chance to revenge their fallen and mutilated comrades. He repeated what he had learned at Barker's briefing. Charlie Company would be outnumbered two-to-one by 250 to 280 VC combatants, but they would be supported by helicopter gunships. He told them to expect "a hell of a good fight." He repeated the contention that all the innocent civilians would be gone by 0730 in the morning. He told them that Barker had received permission from the South Vietnamese Army to destroy the village, since it was a VC stronghold. He told them to burn the houses, kill the livestock, destroy the crops, and cave in the wells.[277]

Army investigators and the Peers Commission later determined that Medina did not give any order to kill women, children, and old men, or "everything that moves," as one of his men later said. But twenty-one members of Charlie Company testified at Lt. Calley's trial that Medina had said to "kill everything in the village." The Army CID, however, pointed out that Calley and his twenty-one other accusers had all been implicated in war crimes.[278]

Those who were not charged or implicated in war crimes remembered no such order. Greg Olsen, a devout young Mormon, wrote his father that:

> There clearly, absolutely, wasn't an order to go in and kill everybody in the village and anybody that says so is a liar. Medina said that the villagers would be rounded up and airlifted to refugee camps. That was specifically addressed in the meeting. If I thought I was going to get on a helicopter that morning with clear orders that I was to slaughter every living breathing human being in that village, I'm sure to God, it would have been so appalling and unthinkable. I mean, I'm not stupid. I know they couldn't have forced me to do something like that."[279]

But some, like Sergeant Michael Bernhardt said, "He didn't actually say to kill every man, woman, and child in My Lai. He stopped short of saying that. He gave every other indication that that's what he expected."[280]

Just before 0730 on March 16, four 105-mm guns from TF Barker's artillery battery fired 120 rounds into Landing Zone (LZ) Uptight, the target area for disembarking the infantry. They also fired into possible VC defensive positions just beyond the hamlet. The terrified residents fled to underground tunnels and crude bomb shelters dug under their homes. The Sharks blasted the surrounding area with machine guns, grenade launchers, and rockets. Then the small bubble-cockpit "Warlord" aero-scout choppers arrived on the scene and began chasing some fleeing VC. Shortly thereafter, the Dolphin liftships were dropping down through the smoke to the LZ. Then the liftship door gunners poured a fusillade of machine gun fire and tracers into the zone as they landed to disembark their infantry cargo. Little, if any, enemy fire had been returned. At about 0800 the infantry assault on My Lai 4 began with three squads of Calley's first platoon of Charlie Company advancing from the west into the southern portion of My Lai 4.

Many of them began to fire at anything that moved, but others, refusing to fire at possible civilians, just shot above their heads. Many civilians—almost all women, children, and elderly men—were killed before several groups of them were rounded up and escorted to two different locations. Meanwhile, troops threw grenades into houses and bunkers, sometimes without giving the people a chance to come out. Sometimes the people who came out were gunned down.

About seventy to eighty Vietnamese were taken to a large ditch east of My Lai. Calley ordered that they be shot, but three of the four men guarding the detainees, Robert Maples, Herbert Carter, and James Dursi, refused to fire on them. Maples, an M-60 machine gunner, directly refused an order to load his machine gun and shoot them, and refused to let Calley have the gun. He flatly told Calley, "I'm not going to do that." Calley turned his M-16 on him as if to shoot him, but other soldiers arrived and Calley lowered his gun. A fourth man, Paul Meadlo, began firing into the ditch with Calley, but began to cry hysterically. Later, a helicopter crew commanded by Warrant Officer Hugh Thompson landed and rescued a small boy who had somehow survived— probably protected by the body of his mother.[281]

Another group of twenty to fifty was to taken to a trail south of the hamlet and then shot. The second platoon killed at least sixty to seventy Vietnamese women and children as they swept through the northern half of My Lai 4 and Binh Tay.

The third platoon then swept through and burned or destroyed the remaining buildings and killed the remaining livestock. Several members gathered and shot seven to twelve women and children.

By the time Charlie Company had moved through My Lai 4, approximately 175- 200 civilians had been killed. Yet many soldiers refused to participate in the killing. Herbert Carter even shot himself in the foot to get out of the situation. The Army charged Calley with at least 22 murders in 1970, but it is estimated that he personally killed over 100 Vietnamese men, women, and children.[282]

Bravo Company landed at 0815. Little resistance was encountered, but the second platoon suffered one killed (Lt. Lewis) and seven wounded from mines and booby traps. The first platoon opened fire on the subhamlet of My Khe 4 with an M-60 machinegun and M-16 automatic rifles for five minutes before entering it. Thereafter, ten soldiers hurled grenades into homes and buildings without warning. In all, an estimated eighty to ninety people were killed. It is believed that only about ten men were responsible for these deaths.

In addition to the killing, several soldiers and small groups of soldiers raped and sodomized Vietnamese women and girls, much to the shock and disgust of many of their comrades. But no one intervened. That was hard on Harry Stanley who noted that this type of behavior seemed to be a pattern that had repeated itself on several previous patrols.[283] He was personally revolted and frustrated that nothing was done to the perpetrators: "You feel this is not right, but there's nothing you can do about it."[284] He also refused to fire on civilians. During the next few days, Medina and several others were also involved in brutal interrogations and torture of suspected VC.

Orders to stop the killing were issued two or three times during the morning. Charlie Company's second platoon received the order at 0920 and immediately complied. Calley's first platoon continued the killing until around 1030. These orders may have come from Col. Henderson who had observed a number of civilian dead from his helicopter. Several reports of the killings came from helicopter pilots. The most notable was from Warrant Officer Hugh Thompson who landed his aero-scout copter several times to rescue women and children and intervene in Charlie Company's killing spree. He personally confronted Calley, and perhaps Brooks, and at one point had his door gunner and crew chief aim their weapons at Charlie Company soldiers who were threatening to kill women and children. He also enlisted the aid of gunships to carry civilians out of danger. Thompson immediately reported his observations to his superior officer and Chaplain Creswell on landing, but by that time the killing was largely over. Unfortunately, due to the later cover-up within the Americal Division and the political controversies that emerged from the My Lai affair, Thompson's heroism, moral courage, compassion, and integrity and that of his two crewmembers, Larry Coburn and Glenn Andreotta, were not recognized until thirty years later, when they received the Soldier's Medal on March 6, 1998. Glenn Andreotta's medal was awarded posthumously. He was killed in action just weeks after My Lai.

According to Lt. Dennis Johnson, an 11th Brigade Intelligence officer, and his ARVN interpreter, Sergeant Duong Minh, who gathered intelligence on the ground at My Lai 4, there had been about thirty VC in the hamlet early in the morning, but they fled as the Sharks arrived. A few were gunned down by the Sharks, but there was no resistance from within My Lai 4. It is estimated than no more than half a dozen of the civilians gunned down by Calley's men were military-age male VC. Minh, whose family had barely escaped a VC reign of terror in Duc Pho where thousands were killed, was very upset to see Americans killing Vietnamese civilians.[285]

Knowledge of the Son My massacres did not become public until 1969. In April 1968, Ron Ridenhour, a former member of the 11th Brigade was told by friends about the ghastly events of March 1968. He was sickened and eventually made it his business to see that justice was served and the honor and integrity of his country preserved. After interviewing other friends who were members of Charlie Company during the Son My massacres, he was determined to take action. Ridenhour was encouraged and assisted in this by Sergeant Michael Bernhardt, a member of Charlie Company who had refused to participate in the massacre. Bernhardt was threatened by Medina not to write his congressman about the event and was allegedly given more dangerous duties thereafter. On March 29, 1969, Ridenhour composed a long letter to the Secretary of the Army, his congressman, Representative Morris Udall (D-AZ), and thirty other congressmen, outlining the terrible tragedy of March 1968. In the latter part of his letter he quoted Winston Churchill: "A country without a conscience is a country without a soul, and a country without a soul is a country that cannot survive."

On September 6, 1969, William Calley was placed under arrest at Fort Benning, Georgia, and initially charged with 109 murders of Vietnamese civilians. By late October, free-lance reporter Seymour Hersh, who covered the Pentagon for the Associated Press, had picked up the story. On November 13, his stories on the My Lai massacre began to appear in several large newspapers in the United States and Europe. On November 20, *the Cleveland Plain Dealer* published personal and Army photographs taken by Army photographer, Ron Haeberle, during the massacre. The next evening they were shown on Walter Cronkite's CBS News. On November 24, Paul Meadlo was interviewed by Mike Wallace on his CBS show. CBS bragged that it had not paid Meadlo a dime for his public confession. However, it had paid Hersh $10,000 dollars to get him there. Haeberle also tried to cash in and received $35,000 from several publishers. He was later charged by the Peers Commission with failing to report war crimes. Neither Army prosecutors nor defense attorneys were pleased with the media explosion. As the public and Congress began to take sides, it jeopardized any appearance of a fair trial for Calley and others. Both the American Civil Union and Secretary of Defense Melvin Laird called for dismissal of the charges against Calley because press coverage had made it impossible for him to get a fair trial.

The anti-war movement immediately latched onto the My Lai story in an effort to discredit the war. In fact, Hersh had been connected to the anti-war movement as press secretary for anti-war presidential candidate Eugene McCarthy in 1968. The media frenzy over My Lai was also juicy ammunition for anti-war leaders in Congress. The Nixon Administration naturally became concerned that My Lai publicity would undermine public and Congressional support for administration strategies to halt Communist aggression in Southeast Asia. On the very day of Mike Wallace's interview with Paul Meadlo, Mendel Rivers (D-SC), the conservative and hawkish chairman of the powerful House Armed Forces Committee, announced that a subcommittee chaired by equally conservative and hawkish H. Edward Hebert (D-LA) would hold hearings on My Lai. Also the same day, Secretary of the Army Stanley Resor disclosed creation of the Peers Commission.

The House Armed Service subcommittee on My Lai interviewed over 150 witnesses. Then it refused to let the Army use the testimonies to prosecute those charged with war crimes. This seriously undermined the Army's ability to prosecute the cases. With much of the evidence denied to both prosecutors and defense attorneys by Congress, the Army began dismissing cases one by one and had difficulty prosecuting the cases that came to trial. They were also prohibited from charging 25 enlisted men who had returned to civilian life with war crimes. In the end, only four officers and two enlisted men were tried. Only Calley was convicted. The Army, however, took administrative action against eight officers, including the commanding officer of the Americal Division, Major General Samuel Koster, and his deputy, Brigadier General George Young. Captain Medina was among those tried and found not guilty, although the stain on his leadership record caused him to resign from the Army.

The left continually tried to portray My Lai as one of the many symptoms of a systematically evil American policy in Southeast Asia. The right generally condemned the massacre as an aberrant tragedy, although some shrugged it off with Union General William T. Sherman's famous quote, "War is hell." But among the public, both hawks and doves believed Calley was a scapegoat. The scapegoat suspicion was particularly prevalent in the public mind because they were not aware of other prosecutions and administrative actions in progress. They were also not aware of how Congress had hamstrung Army prosecutors, and they knew little of the facts or the complex issues of the case against Calley.

On March 29, 1971, an Army court-martial found Calley guilty of the murder of at least twenty-two Vietnamese civilians and sentenced him to life imprisonment. There was an immediate and enormous public outcry against the decision. Congress and the White House were flooded with tens of thousands of protest letters. President Nixon promised to make a final review of the case once it had gone through the appeals procedure.

For a while, Calley, the suspected scapegoat, was a national celebrity with many public speaking offers. Calley was allowed to stay in his quarters during most of the appeal process. After several appeals, the Army finally reduced Calley's sentence to ten years.

Largely due to the interventions of a U.S. District Judge and pressure from Congress, the Army paroled Calley in September 1975. He now manages his father-in-law's jewelry store in Columbus, Georgia. Most military officers who knew the facts and issues, however, regarded Calley as worthy of hanging. He had not only committed heinous crimes; he had disgraced the whole officer corps of the United States.

On September 22, 1971, Captain Medina, who was defended in court by the famous F. Lee Bailey, was found not guilty on all charges. He resigned from the Army three weeks later. Army prosecutors and the Peers Commission believed that Medina let his men get out of control and declined to rein them in until being ordered to stop the killing by higher command levels.

Eight officers received administrative discipline as a result of attempts to cover up or minimize civilian deaths, or for dereliction of duty in preventing civilian deaths and unlawful acts of war against civilians. Major General Samuel Koster was reduced in rank to Brigadier General and forced to relinquish his Distinguished Service Medal. He had been a promising officer and was Superintendent of the U.S. Military Academy at West Point at the time of the charges. He requested to be relieved of that command so as not to embarrass the institution or the Army. According to Col. Harry G. Summers, Koster was such a hard-nose that his staff was terrified of him and afraid to approach him with a problem or bad news. When the results of the assault at My Lai 4 began to come into focus, they thought, "My God, the last thing we want to do is to have the old man find out about it." According to Summers, "In keeping it from him—almost with poetic justice—they destroyed him."[286]

Koster's deputy commander, Brig. General George Young received a formal letter of censure from the Secretary of the Army, essentially ending his career. He, too, was forced to give up his Distinguished Service Cross. Army administrative boards similarly abbreviated the careers of several other officers and forced several NCOs out of the service. Col. Henderson, Major Calhoun, Captain Koutoc, and Lt. Thomas Willingham (Bravo Company) were among those receiving administrative discipline.

Undoubtedly, there should have been more war crime convictions, but due to political pressures—especially from the House Armed Services Committee—Army JAG prosecutors were handicapped in bringing convictions according to the rules of evidence.

Several cases had to be dropped because the evidence withheld by Congress handicapped the defense attorneys, denying the defendants a fair trial. But it should be known that General Westmoreland, Secretary of the Army Resor, and General Peers fought hard against the restrictions Congress placed on prosecuting war crimes. The Army was able to apply administrative discipline in some war crimes cases that could not be successfully prosecuted in courts-martial.

The Peers Commission noted several significant factors that contributed to the My Lai (Son My) tragedy:

1. Although there was no order to kill civilians in TF Barker's operations plan, crucial errors and omissions in the plan were

powerful factors leading to wanton killing of civilians and unlawful destruction of civilian property. The order to destroy the hamlet and its livestock was clearly illegal and a serious violation of the standards of U.S. military conduct. In addition, no provisions had been made to handle civilian detainees and prisoners of war. Communication of the plan was imprecise and haphazard and was embellished at the company and platoon level. Officers at the Brigade and Division level had failed to exercise proper oversight in this planning.

2. There seemed to be little emphasis or regard for the rules of engagement at the Task Force command level. The Rules of Land Warfare, the Geneva Convention, and procedures for handling and safeguarding noncombatants received too little time and emphasis in training and thereafter. There is evidence that Lt. Calley projected a mocking attitude on these subjects to his men.

3. TF Barker had some men who had been law violators and hoodlums during civilian life. These men continued to exercise these traits yet were not disciplined.

4. Heavy personnel losses from mines and booby traps resulted in extreme frustration among the troops and several officers.

5. Excessive demands on a small TF staff resulted in poor planning and oversight.

6. Lt. Col. Barker did not have a close personal relationship with his company commanders. He seldom visited them in the field. There were no field-grade officers on the ground to coordinate communications with the company commanders during the My Lai incident. None of the company first sergeants were in the field at the time, thus forfeiting badly needed experienced and mature leadership.

7. The South Vietnamese government considered the people of Son My to be of little consequence because of their generally Communist loyalties.

8. The Son My area was principally peopled by VC and VC sympathizers and this caused a distortion of the classic distinction between combatants and noncombatants. It was very difficult to tell friend from foe. Many VC women bore arms and killed U.S. soldiers. Children were often used to retrieve weapons and were used as booby trap specialists and assassins. Knowing the American reluctance to risk civilian casualties, the VC and NVA deliberately put civilians at risk to act as cover for weapons or logistics concentrations as a matter of tactical policy.

9. A permissive attitude toward mistreatment of Vietnamese civilians and prisoners of war existed at the Task Force command and staff level. This was also true of Captain Medina, two of his platoon leaders (Brooks and Calley), and several NCOs.

10. Leadership failures: The Brigade commander, Col. Henderson, should have gone over Lt. Col. Barker's plans in detail but failed to do so. Henderson was also a key player in the cover-up and attempted minimization of the My Lai massacre. Lt. Col. Barker's assumptions, plans, decisions, and orders reflected a degree of incompetence, including an inability to make the kind of distinctions required of a successful combat commander. Both Henderson and Barker were relatively new to command positions at the field-grade level. Though Captain Medina was known as a strict disciplinarian, he exercised no control over his men in regard to moral issues and the treatment of Vietnamese civilians. His style of leadership over his inexperienced platoon leaders undermined their authority and their self-confidence. Both Lt. Col. Barker and Captain Medina were guilty of ambiguous communications.

11. Psychological buildup: Captain Medina's exhortation to revenge was undoubtedly a key factor in the massacre.

Col. Harry Summers has also pointed out the corrosive effect of using body-count as a measure of military success. During the My Lai massacre, there were several reports from the field of body-count. These were eagerly awaited at higher levels. But, of course, the body-count was a complete fabrication. It was civilians and not military-age males and armed VC who were being killed. Elsewhere during the war, the emphasis on body-count resulted in considerable exaggeration and outright lying to make combat reports look favorable.

Summers best articulates the problems of using body-count: "It had an effect beyond belief in terms of lowering the ethical standards of everybody involved, because if you didn't have body-count, God help you. It really began to undermine the entire integrity of the force. We saw the result of that when somebody asked General Schwarzkopf in the Gulf War about body-count and he went up like a sky rocket."[287]

The Peers Commission also took some time to study the composition of TF Barker. Almost half of Charlie Company's soldiers were black, and a total of all minorities were probably in a slight majority. This was not considered an unusual demographic for infantry companies in Vietnam, but it may have seemed an intimidating challenge to many of the young and inexperienced platoon leaders. Three of Calley's top NCOs were black. He liked them and got along well with them, but they had little respect for him. Robert Maples, the machine gunner who courageously refused Calley's orders to kill civilians, was one of the blacks in his platoon. The TF Barker companies were not marginal units. They were above average in many ways, including the number of high school graduates and college graduates among them. As we have already stated, however, there were groups of hoodlums who had carried their behavior from civilian to military life and were insufficiently restrained by Medina and his lieutenants.

In addition, about 10 percent of Charlie Company's 130 men were Project 100,000 enlistments. This was a Lyndon Johnson Great Society Plan to give Category IV men (at intelligence levels in the bottom 25 percent of the population) an opportunity to improve their lives in the military. Project 100,000 was an absolute disaster. According to Summers, "We found a 100 percent correlation between these IQ levels and indiscipline, AWOL, drug use, and right down the scale. Project 100,000 was a disaster both for the people involved and for the military."[288]

Reading over the biographies of many of the soldiers involved in My Lai, one can detect some relationship between intelligence and the war crimes committed. Those with poor intellectual judgment were more likely to make poor moral judgments. At the officer level, this is certainly true of Calley. In addition, those who resisted participation in the killing were more likely to have strong religious values and backgrounds, for example Greg Olsen, Michael Bernhardt, Harry Stanley, and Hugh Thompson. I have already cited Thompson's courage in actively opposing and then reporting what went on at My Lai. Although many soldiers avoided direct participation in the massacre, only a few had the courage to actively oppose it.

Among the other charges against Captains Medina and Koutoc, were charges of torturing prisoners and detainees to get intelligence information. One wonders what information they could have gained that could possibly justify the risk their actions posed to the moral credibility of their country and the overall success of U.S. policy in Vietnam. What possible advantage could have been gained in comparison to the inevitable results—fueling anti-war sentiment in the public and Congress. In the end, they helped to bolster the domestic political forces that eventually caused the U.S. to abandon South Vietnam and Cambodia to the Communists. Torture is effective in getting some people to talk or to sign worthless coerced confessions. It is not very effective in getting people to reveal information that is both valuable and accurate. Aside from its pragmatic failures, it is a violation of the Christian Principles of Just War, the Geneva Convention, and U.S. military policy. It is beneath the dignity of honorable soldiers and a great nation.

The Peers Commission did not believe that the atrocities committed at My Lai were anything close to being representative of normal combat operations in Vietnam. Nor was there any credible evidence that atrocities and war crimes were commonly committed by U.S. troops. Aside from My Lai, the Army formerly charged 203 other soldiers for war crimes involving fewer than 200 civilian or enemy POW deaths during the Vietnam War.[289] None of these incidents was even close in scale to what went on at My Lai. There were undoubtedly many more small-scale war crimes that went undetected, but the Army CID and most unit commanders were quick to investigate and punish convicted perpetrators. Notwithstanding the fraudulent claims of the "Vietnam Veterans against the War," American war crimes were relatively infrequent in Vietnam. Nevertheless, an honorable nation should have zero tolerance for war crimes. The Communists, however, perpetrated numerous atrocities as a matter of policy.

Moral leadership is important at every level, but it is particularly important at command levels. Having a thick book of regulations and some training on the principles of the Geneva Convention does not mean much unless you have commanders who will stand up under military and political pressures and say, "No! We're not going tolerate any deliberate mistreatment of civilians or prisoners of war." This attitude must prevail for all command levels right down to platoon leaders and squad leaders.

My Lai was a great human tragedy and a great moral tragedy, and such infractions of human decency and moral sensibility should be severely punished, even in war. But we must not draw an even more tragic conclusion from it. We cannot abandon the cause of freedom because war often begets such tragedies. We must seek to minimize these inhumanities without giving up on the cause of humanity. Millions of South Vietnamese and Cambodian civilians died when the Communists took over their countries in 1975. Terrorism and atrocity were Communist policy in Vietnam and Cambodia.

The tragedy of My Lai contributed to Communist victory in Southeast Asia by undermining the moral credibility of U.S. conduct in the war. This in turn undermined confidence in American objectives and resolve to prevent a Communist takeover of South Vietnam and Cambodia. The consequences were disastrous. Freedom was eclipsed in Indochina, and more than 3.5 million Cambodian and South Vietnamese civilians were murdered, starved to death, or drowned in the South China Sea by their Communist liberators.[290]

There are two lessons here: We must not tolerate war crimes against civilians or captured enemy soldiers, and we must never abandon the cause of humanity and freedom because of the tragic ambiguities of war.

Whoever covers his sins will not prosper, but he
who confesses and forsakes them will obtain mercy.

—Proverbs 28:3

Lt. William Calley

Lt. Gen. William Peers

WO1 Hugh Thompson, Jr.

APPENDIX 2

The American Prisoner of War Experience in Vietnam

On February 12, 1973, an anxiously awaited Air Force C-141 landed at Clark Air Base in the Philippines. Aboard were the first 40 of 591 prisoners of war returned by their North Vietnamese captors. The first man to deplane was Navy Captain Jeremiah Denton, the senior officer among the first group of returning POWs. Denton saluted the Admiral and General in charge, shook their hands, exchanged a few words, and proceeded to a set of microphones waiting for his brief message: "We are honored to have had the opportunity to serve our country under difficult circumstances. We are profoundly grateful to our Commander-in-Chief and to our nation for this day. God bless America."[291]

By the end of March, all 591 of the surviving American POWs were safe at home. Thus ended the longest captivity ever endured by American POWs. Some had spent nearly a decade in confinement. Many had suffered enormous pain and deprivation for years, but their return was a time of joy, and Americans made it a heroic return—and justly so, for these men had demonstrated much more than the courage of battle. They had demonstrated the rarer and more important virtue of moral courage, which must persevere through many physical, psychological, and spiritual struggles over long periods of time. And it is moral courage that is the *sine qua non* of the survival of peoples and nations and of liberty and freedom.

Another 67 POWs had previously been returned to U.S. military control, bringing the total of safely returned to 658. Another 113—more than 17 percent—died in captivity. In the twentieth century, only the Korean War had a higher death rate for American POWs, when 2,701 of 7,140 U.S. POWs— almost 38 percent—died in the captivity of North Korea's Communist regime.[292]

The treatment of American POWs in both wars proved the brutality of the Communist ideology. From its extensive debriefing of returning prisoners from North Vietnam, the U.S. military learned that over 95 percent of the men underwent torture of one kind or another. Many excruciatingly painful torture methods were used and repeated again and again. They often threatened life and permanent disabilities. Some men were driven insane.[293]

Following capture, most men were interrogated for military information. Most of the military information the captors extracted, even under torture, was already known, misleading, false, or a ridiculous joke. One downed airman, Air Force Captain Kile Berg, succeeded in convincing his North Vietnamese interrogators that Batman and Robin were real and would soon be a serious threat to Hanoi. But probing for military information was not the primary objective of their Communist captors. What the Communists really wanted were confessions of war crimes, American conspiracies to dominate Asia, or anything that made good international or domestic American propaganda. They wanted anything that could be used to humiliate the U.S., manipulate the American press, or fuel public or Congressional anti-war sentiment. Of course, the truth mattered not at all to Hanoi's leaders. They wanted to force American prisoners into signing statements, making broadcasts, or participating in films that would damage the Allied cause in Vietnam. The Communists were never really successful on the battlefield against American forces. Their propaganda, however, which was directed at undermining American public and Congressional support for the war, was very successful. South Vietnam and Cambodia fell in 1975 because Congress refused to honor the American commitment to supply South Vietnam with the arms and supplies needed to meet a renewed North Vietnamese invasion.

Most of the POWs from the Vietnam War were aviators, especially Air Force and Navy, who usually had to eject or bail-out over enemy territory. In the ground warfare of South Vietnam, the Viet Cong had a general policy of executing captured Marines. Nor did many Army personnel survive Viet Cong capture. For airmen, one's chances of rescue or survival as a POW varied greatly with the area. Only 45 percent of airmen survived being shot down over North Vietnam. Rescuing downed flyers in North Vietnam was extremely difficult. On the other hand, the chances of surviving prison in North Vietnam were about 90 percent, despite the torture.[294]

Laos was a different and horrifying story. One's chances of being picked up alive by Air Rescue in Laos were fairly good—61 percent. Air Rescue bases in Thailand and South Vietnam were nearby, and the antiaircraft environment was not so terrible until late in the war. But of the 300 flyers who were lost in Laos, only nine wound up in North Vietnamese prison camps and survived. The Laotian terrain, with its many jagged karst mountains and thick jungles, was generally more dangerous, but the main danger was the barbarous Pathet Lao (Laotian Communist guerillas). They were known to skin captured airmen alive. Others were simply shot while hanging in their parachutes from jungle trees. Disease and filth were rampant in the Laotian camps, and the trek to North Vietnam was extremely arduous. It is only because Navy Lt. Dieter Dengler managed to escape from the Pathet Lao that we know much about conditions for POWs there. What he described to Navy debriefers leaves little hope that any of the POWs that were seen in Laos after their capture would be seen alive again.[295] That is why I always had an eerie and uneasy feeling flying over Laos.

Prior to October 1965, there were only sporadic instances of mistreatment of American POWs and no documentation of outright torture. Until that time, persuasion, harassment, verbal threats, and some deprivations had been used to manipulate prisoners into compromising statements. But all they got from the American prisoners was the "big four": name, rank, serial number, and date of birth. With the U.S. beginning to bomb some targets in North Vietnam and the POWs seemingly unmoved by early interrogation tactics, the Communists decided to get tough and employ more traditional Red Chinese and North Korean torture methods.

Most American POWs had to make some compromises with the unrealistically strict 1955 Code of Conduct to survive without suffering death or serious permanent maiming. To encourage frankness, returnees were promised that their official debriefings would always be held in strictest confidence and that researchers would only be granted restricted access. No individual's debriefing would ever be released to the public or even another POW. This pledge continues to be honored. The vast majority of Vietnam POWs endured the hardships of torture and confinement honorably and heroically. Despite extreme techniques of coercion, their Communist captors were never able to gather enough credible propaganda from the POWs to be effective. In the end, their attempts to score propaganda victories with coerced POW confessions, broadcasts, and films did Hanoi more harm than good. Our military men were made of sterner stuff than the anti-war majority in the 1975 Congress.

On October 17, 1965, Navy Lt. Rodney Knutson, a radar intercept operator, was captured along with his pilot, Ralph Gaither, when their F-4 Phantom went down. After parachuting to the ground, he had been forced to shoot it out with local militia and killed two of them before he himself was wounded. He was taken to Hanoi and would not see Gaither again for several years. At the direction of their superiors, his North Vietnamese guards locked him in ankle straps and bound his arms so tightly behind his back that they lost circulation. He was denied food and water until he apologized. When this was not forthcoming, they punched him with their fists until his nose was broken, several teeth were shattered, and his eyes were swollen shut. They left him in the stocks for three days, meanwhile beating his back and buttocks with bamboo clubs until they were bruised and bloody. When they released his bonds, he was in intense pain as the blood re-circulated into his forearms and hands and turned them black.

On October 25, his captors administered the "rope torture": guards forced him face down on his bunk and placed his ankles in stocks. Then they bound his arms behind his back tightly at the elbows with a rope. They bound his wrists together, and the long end of the rope was pulled through a hook in the ceiling. He was then hoisted off the bunk so that he could not relieve any of his weight. This produced incredible pain, and it seemed to him that his arms would be torn out their sockets. His breathing was terribly restricted. Screaming in pain, Knutson finally agreed to talk. There were several variations of the rope torture, and it became a standard and usually successful method of breaking down POW resistance. A gag was sometimes forced down a prisoner's throat with an iron bar, shattering teeth in the process. Air Force Captain Konrad Trautman was subjected to the rope treatment on twelve separate occasions.

Ejection and parachuting injuries like broken legs were often twisted or aggravated to cause great pain. Navy Lt. Cdr. John McCain (now a U.S Senator) was shot down in October 1967 and was one of the most badly injured men to arrive in the North Vietnamese POW camps. He was forced to eject from his A-4 Skyhawk upside down and at high speed, breaking his right leg, his right arm in three places, and his left arm. Nevertheless, he was worked over during his interrogation. In September 1968, McCain was subjected to four days on intense torture. His left arm was rebroken, and he had to endure the excruciating pain of the rope torture. They also beat him every two to three hours. Although McCain had gained a reputation as a fervent resister, he admitted that this broke him—as it did most men.

Another common method of torture was the use of wrist and ankle cuffs that could be ratcheted so tightly that the wrist and ankle bones were penetrated. A favorite beating weapon was a fan belt. Men were often hit with rifle butts or kicked in the groin, face, or ribs. Various straps, bars, and chains were used for beating or to apply painful pressures to various body parts. Prisoners were frequently forced to kneel or sit for long periods without food or sleep. They often had to kneel on concrete floors for hours or days, often with their hands raised over their heads for long periods. Sometimes a pencil or pebble was placed under a knee to increase the pain. Prisoners were often beaten-up for minor reasons or at random. More than 94 percent of prisoners suffered the isolation of solitary confinement one or more times, sometimes for as long as two years.[296]

As early as September 1965, Hanoi was making plans to conduct public show-trials for the POWs as war criminals. On July 6, 1966, captors cleaned up fifty-two prisoners, gave them clean shirts and trousers, and boarded them on trucks. Upon their arrival in Hanoi, the prisoners were marched two miles through the streets toward a stadium. As they marched through the streets, many of the prisoners tried to hold their heads up proudly. But this demonstration of POW defiance was much to the displeasure of the guards and prison officers who always made a great issue of making prisoners bow. Many were pummeled by their guards. The streets became crowded with hostile spectators, as many as ten deep on each side. Meanwhile, the hostility of the crowds was further worked-up by blaring loudspeakers, and spectators began to throw bottles and garbage at them. Many of the POWs were hit with fists or sticks by screaming and spitting onlookers who began to close in toward them. The crowd became frenzied as they marched by the Soviet and Chinese embassies and began to get so out of control that even the guards and political officials became frightened. As the procession came within fifty yards of the stadium gate, both prisoners and guards had to force their way through the hysterical crowd to sanctuary.

Nearly every prisoner was injured during the march. A blow to Denton's groin caused a partial hernia. Others had broken noses, blackened eyes, lacerations, terrible bruises, and loosened teeth. Although they were safely in the gates, loudspeakers announced to the outside crowd that the Americans had experienced the just wrath of the Vietnamese people. After the crowd had dispersed, the prisoners were transported back to their camps where their Communist captors continued the next day with their routine of interrogation, torture, and beatings. Hanoi's leaders, however, quietly abandoned serious plans for public show-trials.

POW resistance to frequent torture was often courageous and sometimes ingenious, but the North Vietnamese managed to coerce some compromising statements from about 80 percent of their prisoners. Even Medal of Honor winner, James Stockdale; Navy Cross winner, Jeremiah Denton; and Air Force Cross winner, Robbie Risner, were tortured into some compromises. Denton made a film, but blinked his eyes in Morse code to spell "T-O-R-T-U-R-E."

The anguish and regret that men felt after surrendering to torture were in themselves torture. Thanks to the leadership of the senior-ranking POWs, however, new and more flexible rules were informally sanctioned. Men were asked to endure the torture as long as they could without endangering their lives or being permanently maimed or impaired. Then they would give their Communist captors as little as possible. Like Captain Troutman, many had to endure periodic interrogation and torture.

Conditions in most POW camps were filthy, and diarrhea, infections, and other ailments were a frequent problem. Their Communist overseers often deliberately exacerbated the unsanitary environment to humiliate and debilitate noncompliant prisoners. At one point, Denton was kept blindfolded and was allowed no waste bucket. He had to defecate on the floor of his cell. Disease hindered and debilitated POWs at every turn.

In addition, the men endured the many mental hazards of POW life: despair, separation from family, loneliness, self-doubts, fear of wasting their prime years, the continuous propaganda of their captors, and especially, uncertainty. Many were angry about statements made by anti-war politicians, especially those of senators Mansfield, Fulbright, and McGovern. They were furious with anti-war celebrities like Jane Fonda, Tom Hayden, and Pete Seeger. There was much frustration over American pilots risking their lives and wasting aircraft and firepower on "junk targets" during the Johnson Administration. Their captors let them have all the latest news items featuring anti-war activities on campuses and pronouncements by anti-war Congressmen and entertainment celebrities. All this kept them shaken and bewildered.

More than any other factor, men relied on their faith to pull them through the ordeals of POW life. It was not faith in America, or faith in the flag, or the American people or democracy; it was faith in God. According to the Naval Institute, there is not a single personal account in Vietnam POW literature that does not contain some reference to a transforming spiritual episode. Denton later explained, "Those not subjected to the prisoner-of-war experience may have trouble understanding how real was the presence of God to most of us."[297]

The sign-off on the POW Morse code-tapping communication system was G-B-U for "God Bless You." Many men, such as Red McDaniel, shared their religious faith with gravely injured comrades. Many sick, wounded, or tortured prisoners were nursed, coached, and brought back to physical and mental health by their cell mates. Some were able to hold make-shift religious services. Past memories of Bible verses and liturgy were memorized. There was open and sympathetic conversation among many different religious denominations.

Simple love of country and a generally common moral code also held them together. Family remembrances were also important, although some had to endure divorce and family losses that made prison life more unbearable. Fellowship with other prisoners was critically important, and that was part of what made solitary confinement so mentally devastating. In addition, humor was important in keeping up morale. The prisoners had nicknames for guards, like "Lump," "Rabbit," and "Magoo," and reveled in sly deceptions that befuddled them. Those in the Hanoi Hilton named their bleak quarters after Las Vegas casinos.

"The Hanoi Hilton" was the best known of North Vietnam's POW camps. It was a nickname the POWs gave to Hoa Lo Prison Camp in central Hanoi. There were fourteen others. Cu Loc Prison Camp, colloquially referred to by the prisoners as "the Zoo, "had a reputation for harsh treatment of POWs. There were 120 Americans and a few Thais there in early 1967. The two senior POWs there, Majors Larry Guarino and Ron Byrne, took some of the worst beatings. In the heat of August 1967, they were taken to a small building and locked in cuffs and irons for a month. They were beaten by day and attacked by squadrons of mosquitoes at night. They went sixteen days without sleep, and their faces were terribly bruised from continual beatings. Guarino was trussed in ropes and one of the guards (nicknamed Dum Dum) stuck the barrel of a pistol in his mouth and threatened to shoot him if he did not confess to war crimes. Guarino just muttered, "Please, do me a favor, will you?" Byrne was also given the rope torture. Guarino was left clamped in leg irons for another six months.

In the fall of 1967, two expert Cuban interrogators arrived at the Zoo to experiment with the prisoners and determine the most successful methods for breaking them. Their overall objective was to improve the results of interrogation in terms useful information, war crime confessions, and important propaganda. They would frequently beat one prisoner while forcing another to watch. They seemed to especially enjoy kicking prisoners with their paratrooper boots and bashing them directly in the face. With some of the more resistant POWs they used the "water torture," gagging their mouths and pouring water into their noses. This resulted in breaking ten prisoners by Christmas. One resistant prisoner, Captain Earl Cabeil, was beaten and tortured so often that all feared he had lost his senses. One day, the guards beat him seventy-eight times. Before the Cubans were finished, he was catatonic. He was sent to "electric shock treatment" at the hospital but never regained his senses. Amazingly, he survived another two years. The Cuban leader, a huge fellow the POW's nicknamed Fidel, also beat Major James Kasler into a semi-coma, rupturing an eardrum, and fracturing a rib. He had battered Kasler's face and busted so many of his teeth that he could not open his mouth. Kasler, an Air Force Ace, however, recovered. Had not the "Cuban Program" at the Zoo been phased out, Fidel might have eventually killed him.

In the fall of 1968, Bud Day conducted a mock presidential election at the Zoo. The POWs registered their disgust with the Democrats' "No-Win" policy in Indochina, and thirty-three out of thirty-six voted for Nixon. They were particularly angry at Johnson because he had just ordered a bombing halt of North Vietnam. The camp propaganda radio lauded Humphrey and some aspects of the Democratic Party platform, but the staff became uneasy when Nixon won.

Xom Ap Lo Prison Camp, thirty-five miles west of Hanoi, was called "the Briarpatch" by the POWs because of a special routine torture there: men were forced to run barefoot through rough evacuation trenches—usually dragged by ropes around their necks. The combination of bloodied toes and ankles and poor diet produced a painful beriberi-like condition that came to be called "Briarpatch feet."

All the camps had an almost unbearable stench, but Briarpatch had the reputation of being the worst smelling of the lot. Navy Lt. Everett Alvarez, who had been in captivity since August 1964 described it:

> The stench was with us all the time. We had long since accepted as normal having to sit a few feet away from each other when one of us had a bowel movement, which was often because we always seemed to come down with diarrhea. There was never enough water to wash the odor off your hands. And though we took daily turns dumping the bucket and swishing the inside with sticks and straw brushes at the bottom of a hill, they never supplied us with disinfectant. As the tin buckets were not replaced, they developed a hard coating of crap that no amount of cleaning could remove. Though it was a source of interminable smell, we had to live with the bucket in our sealed quarters day in and day out.[298]

The camp commander at Briarpatch, whom the prisoners nicknamed "Frenchy," implemented a new program called "Make Your Choice" in July 1966. It was administered by a political commissar nicknamed "Doc" and a torture specialist who earned the name "Louie the Rat." Prisoners were given a blank sheet of paper and asked to write on one of two topics: "Follow the Way of Ho Chi Minh" or "Follow the Way of LBJ." Most prisoners originally refused to write anything and were tortured and beaten for it. Feverish and with his "hell cuffs" cutting into his wrist bones, Air Force Lt. Al Brudno finally wrote that he regretted coming to Vietnam because the Vietnamese people had been "truly revolting for 4,000 years."[299] Although Lyndon Johnson was not popular with the POWs, they adopted the motto "All the way with LBJ" in response to the Make Your Choice program.[300] However, their defiance and subtle humor often resulted in brutal beatings, reduced food rations, and more intense torture. The pain of the "hell cuffs" was sometimes made so intolerable that some men tried to commit suicide by bashing their heads against the stone walls of their torture cells. The guards at Briarpatch also used rifle stocks to bash the heads of uncooperative prisoners. Many men were certain they were being beaten to death.

Nearly every day in the life of American POWs in Vietnam was filled with brutality, the uncertainty of survival, or the challenge of despair. Exceptional physical and moral courage had to be summoned every day. Yet despite extreme and sometimes terrifying duress, uncommon levels of courage, patriotism, and devotion to duty prevailed. Honor, loyalty, and compassionate fellowship flourished, and wise and principled leadership abounded. From torture and brutality emerged extraordinary heroism and virtue. Four men were awarded the Medal of Honor for their courage during captivity: Navy Commander. James Stockdale, Air Force Major George "Bud" Day, and posthumously Marine Captain Donald Cook, and Air Force Lieutenant Lance Sijan.

With the death of Ho Chi Minh in September 1969, the treatment of American POWs began to improve. Torture decreased significantly, but a violent beating or solitary confinement always remained a possibility each day. Though more humane, it was still a hellish environment that always remained far from the standards of the Geneva Convention.

The cruel torture suffered by American POWs during the Vietnam War attests to the inhumanity and moral bankruptcy of Communist ideology. It is unfortunate that such systematic cruelty was ignored, or went unnoticed, by the anti-war movement and so many in Congress. The moral disaster of the Vietnam War was that the peoples of South Vietnam and Cambodia were abandoned to Communist rule, resulting not only in a loss of freedom but the murder of millions.

Yet within the overall moral and political tragedy surrounding the ultimate fall of South Vietnam and Cambodia, a smaller, but important, victory was won. It was won by the moral courage of American prisoners of war who endured incredible torture and pain to maintain the honor of their country. Their extraordinary and sacrificial heroism should never be forgotten. Their proud legacy of moral courage can be shared by all who served honorably in the Vietnam War and by the American people. All honor to their names!

* * * * * * * *

A substantial part of this treatise was taken from *Honor Bound—American Prisoners of War in Southeast Asia 1961-1973* by Stuart L. Rochester and Frederick Kiley, published by the Naval Institute Press in 1999. This 620-page book is strongly recommended as a reference to anyone wishing to research the history and treatment of U.S. POWs during the Vietnam War.

Jeremiah Denton

APPENDIX 3

Missing in Action

Kham Duc was an Allied Special Forces surveillance camp about fifteen miles from the Laotian border in Quang Tin Province, South Vietnam. It was strategically located to block North Vietnamese infiltration into the Central Highlands. The small force of about 250 men there consisted of American and Australian Special Forces advisors, small contingents of U.S. Marines and South Vietnamese Army Rangers, and a company of Montagnard CIDG (Civilian Irregular Defense Group) troops. Up until May 10, 1968, it had been quite successful in its mission and had become a source of constant frustration to North Vietnamese Army (NVA) attempts to advance into the Central Highlands.

Surrounded by rugged high terrain, Kham Duc was totally inaccessible by road. It had to be supplied by USAF C-123 Provider and C-130 Hercules transports and Army CH-47 Chinook helicopters.

Following the disastrous early months of the 1968 Tet Offensive that nearly annihilated their Viet Cong allies, the NVA decided to put an end to the troublesome Allied base at Kham Duc. Turning their attention from their costly unsuccessful siege of the U.S. Marine Base at Khe Sanh, they advanced the 2nd NVA Division and the remnants of the 271st Viet Cong Regiment, a combined force of nearly 8,000 men, to assault Kham Duc.[301] This was probably part of a contingency plan for extending their Tet Offensive, but they undoubtedly believed overrunning Kham Duc would have some propaganda impact in both Saigon and the United States.

On May 10, an NVA battalion assaulted the Special Forces outpost at Ngok Tavak that blocked their way. Ngok Tavak was an old French outpost about three miles from Kham Duc, manned by eight American and three Australian Special Forces advisors and part of a U.S. Marine 105mm howitzer battery. The outpost was temporarily relieved by a small company of Chinese Nung soldiers and U.S. Marines led by Australian Captain John White. However, the outpost came under heavy infantry and artillery attack for ten hours. Out of ammunition and seeing no chance for relief, White decided to withdraw his forces several miles toward Kham Duc, where the survivors were then evacuated by helicopter. When they arrived at Kham Duc, it was already being bombarded by mortars.

Kham Duc was then reinforced by air with two U.S. Army battalions of infantry and a battery of five 105mm howitzers, a total of 1,500 men, from the

Americal and 46th Infantry divisions. Fighting was intense, but the NVA was able to seize the surrounding high ground and bring the airfield under fire. In Saigon, General Westmoreland, realizing that further reinforcement of Kham Duc was untenable and determined not to put the troops there in senseless further jeopardy, decided to evacuate all Allied personnel from the camp. He also probably realized that Hanoi stood to gain a tremendous propaganda victory should the NVA overrun and annihilate or capture such a large American force. Army Ch-47 Chinook helicopters attempting to evacuate the camp, however, were driven off by hostile fire. The task was turned over to the Air Force.

On the morning of May 11, USAF C-130s and C-123s from the 834th Air Division began landing at the small airfield and evacuating personnel as USAF tactical fighter-bombers blasted enemy positions on the surrounding hills. Many of those to be evacuated were the families of Montagnard troops. The decision was made to fly out the Montagnard troops and civilians on C-123s and the larger C-130s. Most of the rest would be evacuated by helicopter or C-123s. In the afternoon, additional U.S. fighter-bombers had to be called in to beat back a massed infantry attack on the main Kham Duc compound.

On the morning of May 12, three Allied outposts were overrun. As evacuations continued, U.S. B-52s pounded NVA positions surrounding the camp. One of the last transport aircraft to depart Kham Duc was a C-130 from the 773rd Tactical Airlift Squadron based at Clark AFB in the Philippines. Commanded by Major Bernard Bucher, it carried a USAF crew of five, an Army Special Forces Captain, a few CIDG troops, and as many as 150 CIDG dependents. It was hit by enemy fire several times as it took off and continued to take hits as it departed. A few minutes later it blew-up in mid-air, and the burning debris fell into a ravine about a mile from the camp. The scene of the disaster could not be reached, but a Forward Air Control (FAC) pilot reported that the aircraft was completely burned and that there was no chance of survivors. It was the greatest air disaster of the war at the time and the second greatest of the entire war. Seven other U.S. aircraft were lost that day including another USAF C-130 destroyed on the ground, a USAF A-1H Skyraider, two USAF O-2 Skymaster observer aircraft, a USMC CH-46 helicopter, an Army CH-47 helicopter, and an Army UH-1C helicopter.[302] Over 270 Allied soldiers and airmen were killed or reported as missing in action.[303] This included twenty-three Americans killed and another twenty-six missing in action.[304]

The very last aircraft to leave was a C-123 Provider. A three-man USAF combat control team had been inadvertently left behind near the 4,000-foot runway. One C-123 tried to land and pick them up, but came under such intense fire it had to accelerate and take-off again before the men could be located. The three airmen faced almost certain death unless they could be evacuated. A second C-123 commanded by Lt. Col. Joe M. Jackson of Newnan, Georgia, then attempted a desperate rescue. Jackson put his twin-prop C-123 Provider into a dive from 9,000 feet and in less than three minutes landed as close as possible to where the USAF combat control team was reported to be hiding under a culvert next to the runway. NVA soldiers were already overrunning the airfield. The base was in flames, and ammunition dumps continued to explode and litter the runway with debris; smoke obscured all but about 2,200 feet of runway. Jackson's aircraft was under intense fire from small arms and rockets; one 122mm rocket skidded in front of the nose of the aircraft but failed to explode. Yet while under continuous intense enemy fire, Jackson and his crew (Major Jesse Campbell, Tech Sgt. Edward Trejo, and Staff Sgt. Manson Grubbs) managed to pick up the control team and fly everyone to safety. On January 16, 1969, Jackson was awarded the Congressional Medal of Honor by President Lyndon Johnson. Ironically, Johnson also presented a Medal of Honor to Jackson's fellow Newnan native, Major Stephen W. Pless, a Marine aviator, at the same ceremony.

In August 2006, more than thirty-eight years later, the remains of eleven Marines and an Army soldier were found at what had been Ngok Tavak, the mountainous jungle outpost near Kham Duc. They were identified and returned to the United States for burial. Their status was changed from MIA (missing in action) to KIA (killed in action).

On December 15, 2008, more than forty years later, the Department of Defense announced that they had found the remains of six Americans who died in the May 12, 1968, crash of the C-130 commanded by Major Bernard Bucher. They were later buried at Arlington National Cemetery near Washington, D.C. They are, to date, the last U.S. servicemen whose status finally changed from MIA to KIA.

When the U.S. withdrew from South Vietnam in 1973, there were 2,437 American servicemen still listed as MIA. About half of these were actually considered KIA/BNR (killed in action/body not recovered). The total MIA number has now been reduced to 1,948, of which about half, perhaps at least 865, should be considered KIA/BNR. The remaining 1,083 are still unaccounted for. It is likely that most of these should be considered KIA/NBR or to have died in enemy captivity.[305]

A typical MIA case later classified as KIA/BNR occurred in the 606th Air Commando Squadron shortly after I returned to the States. One of our aircraft was blown out of the sky by a large rocket, but the crew was listed as MIA. Yet there was no chance of their survival or that any remains could be found. In 1969, I attended the burial ceremony of one of two friends who had been classified as MIA since 1967, when their A-26 was lost over Laos. The crash site in a remote mountain area was finally located and the remains of my friends were identified and returned to the States.

For several years after the war, there were thousands of reports that claimed to have seen MIA personnel in captivity. This includes 1,914 claims of firsthand live sightings. Only seventeen of these, however, have not been resolved. These seventeen and searches for missing aircraft and human remains are the current focus of American efforts to resolve MIA questions. The vast majority of the 1,914 alleged sightings have proved to be mistaken identities. Nearly a third proved to be outright fabrications. Sixteen of the unresolved cases pertain to Americans sighted in captivity. Fourteen of these were reported prior to 1976. Two were reported from 1976 to 1980, of which one was later reported to be working as a truck driver, married, with a Vietnamese family.[306] After many hearings, neither the U.S. Senate nor the U.S. House Armed Forces Committees believe that any American MIA service personnel remain in captivity.[307]

American concern with a proper accounting of MIA personnel is complicated by the well-earned distrust we came to have for Communist negotiators. They frequently used POW and MIA issues as negotiating leverage. Some have alleged that their Soviet and Chinese allies advised them to hold back release of some POWs for future negotiating leverage. But with the passage of thirty-six years since our withdrawal from South Vietnam, it is difficult to believe that any MIA personnel remain alive.

Of the 1,948 MIA remaining officially on the books, 649 are Air Force, 617 are Army, 401 are Navy, 242 are Marine Corps, and one is Coast Guard. Most of the other 38 were employees of U.S. government agencies.

Almost half of these official remaining MIA casualties, 945, occurred in South Vietnam, 524 in North Vietnam, 411 in Laos, 60 in Cambodia, and 8 in China. Sixty-eight percent of the aircraft carrier-based Navy MIAs resulted from operations over North Vietnam. Thirty-nine percent of all Air Force MIAs resulted from operations in or over Laos. In fact, Air Force operations accounted for sixty-two percent of all MIAs associated with Laos. As was pointed out in the appendix on POWs, the likelihood of surviving the brutality of captivity in Laos was extremely low, and the likelihood of finding a missing aircraft in Laos's many areas of jungle-covered mountainous terrain is also low. Seventy-eight percent of Army MIA's, as could be expected, resulted from combat operations in South Vietnam, but sixteen percent were reported as missing in Laos. Over eighty percent of Marine MIAs were associated with combat operations in South Vietnam.

Having an MIA relative or loved one is undoubtedly one of the most painful ordeals suffered by any American families during the war and still today. Unfortunately, there is little hope that any of these MIAs remain alive. Yet we should never forget them, their families, or their unseen suffering and unheralded heroism.

USAF C-123 Provider

USAF C-130 Hercules

APPENDIX 4
Glossary of Aircraft Cited in this Book[308, 309, 310]

Designations: A=Attack or Fighter-Bomber, B=Bomber, C=Cargo, E=Electronic Warfare, F=Fighter/Interceptor or Fighter-Bomber, H=Helicopter or Rescue, K=Refueler, O=Observation, R=Reconnaissance, T=Trainer, U=Utility

A-1E Skyraider   USAF single-engine prop version of the large World War II Navy carrier aircraft manufactured by Douglas. Used primarily as an attack fighter-bomber in Vietnam, it carried four 20mm cannons and 6,500 pounds of ordinance—almost as much as the four-engine WW II B-17 strategic bomber. Total aircraft losses from all causes: 271.

A-4 Skyhawk   A Navy carrier-based, single-seat, single-engine jet fighter with the primary mission of ground attack, produced by Douglas and later McDonnell Douglas. (Total) aircraft losses: 362.

A-6 Intruder   A Navy carrier-based, twin-engine jet attack aircraft. It carried a crew of two and 18,000 pounds of ordnance including air-to-air missiles. The EA-6 was an important electronic warfare version. Aircraft losses: 86

A-7 Corsair II   A Navy carrier-based, single-engine jet aircraft. It carried a crew of one, a 20mm cannon, and 20,000 pounds of ordnance. Aircraft losses: 99.

A-26 Invader/ Counterinvader   Also called the B-26K, the aircraft was an Onmark Corporation modification of the old Douglas B-26 of World War II and Korea. It was used by USAF Air Commandos primarily for night armed reconnaissance. It carried eight 50 cal. machine guns in the nose and ordnance in the bomb-bay and on eight wing stations. It was relatively slow but accurate and could stay on station for four hours. Aircraft losses: 22.

AC-47 Gunship I   See AC-47.

AC-119 Gunship III   See C-119.

AC-130 Specter   See C-130

AH-1 Cobra   See UH-1

B-52 Stratofortress   USAF eight-engine, strategic jet bomber able to carry a conventional bomb load of up to 43,000 pounds. Total aircraft losses: 31 of which 15 were during Linebacker II.

C-47 Skytrain   The C-47 twin-engine prop transport was the military equivalent of the DC-3. Frequently referred to as the "Gooney Bird" by military flyers, it had a crew of three. It could carry 26,000 pounds of cargo but had many utility uses. The **AC-47 Gunship I** modification was nicknamed both **"Spookey"** and **"Puff the Magic Dragon."** The gunships were used by Air Commando squadrons primarily for close ground support roles and were generally armed with three 7.62 mm General Electric Gatling guns, each capable of firing more than 4,000 rounds per minute. It carried a crew of eight. Twenty-one C-47s and nineteen AC-47s were lost during the war.

C-119 Flying Boxcar   The twin-prop C-119 was used extensively by the French for cargo and paratroopers during the First Indochina War and later by Allied forces in Vietnam. The **AC-119 Gunship III** modifications were used by American Air Commando squadrons. **The AC-119G "Shadow"** was used for close ground support, and the **AC-119K "Stinger"** was primarily used for truck hunting over the Ho Chi Minh Trail. Five American AC-119s were lost.

C-123 Provider   The C-123 was a twin-engine prop or turboprop cargo aircraft capable of carrying 25,000 pounds of cargo with a very short take-off and landing capability. It had many utility uses such as defoliation of jungle (using Agent Orange). Aircraft losses: 54.

C-124 Globemaster Officially named the C-124 Globemaster II, this Douglas built heavy-lift USAF cargo aircraft was powered by four large piston engines and nicknamed "Old Shakey" by its crews. It could carry more than 68,000 pounds of cargo, but at an average cruising speed of only about 220 mph, which meant long days for its normally six-man crew. There were no C-124s lost in combat.

C-130 Hercules A remarkably dependable and flexible four-engine turboprop transport aircraft manufactured by Lockheed Martin. Modified versions included the HC-130 used in coordinating air rescue and the **AC-130 Specter** gunship used for close ground support and armed reconnaissance targeting enemy trucks along the Ho Chi Minh Trail. The cargo version generally carried a crew of five and a normal payload of 36,000 pounds. **The AC-130** packed ferocious fire-power with a 40mm cannon, a 105mm cannon, and a 25mm Gatling gun. It carried a crew of 13-14. Aircraft losses: 70, of which six were AC-130 gunships.

C-141 Starlifter Primarily a USAF four-engine jet transport aircraft, the C-141 normally carried a crew of 5-6 and cargo of 63,000 pounds. Two aircraft lost.

CH-46 Sea Knight A twin-rotor, medium-lift USMC cargo helicopter, most frequently used for assault support, carrying 25 combat troops. Normal crew of four. It could carry up to three machine guns including one mounted in the rear ramp. Aircraft losses: 152.

CH-47 Chinook A large twin-rotor cargo helicopter capable of carrying 28,000 pounds of cargo, 33-35 troops, or 24 litters and 3 attendants. Crew of two pilots and a flight engineer. Aircraft losses: 152.

EB-66 Destroyer   Manufactured by Douglas, the USAF EB-66 electronic countermeasures and electronic intelligence aircraft was a B-66 modification powered by two turbojet engines. It normally carried a crew of seven and frequently accompanied fighter-bomber strikes. Fourteen aircraft lost.

EF-111 Raven   See SEAD and F-111 Aardvark

F-4 Phantom II   The McDonnell Douglas USAF, Navy, and Marine F-4 is a twin- engine jet fighter-bomber and air-to-air interceptor. The flexible F-4 was also used for reconnaissance and electronic warfare in Vietnam. It carries a crew of two. Its 16,000-pound ordnance load is twice that of the B-17 bomber of World War II. While the F-4 was primarily used as a fighter-bomber in Vietnam, USAF F-4s accounted for 70 MiG kills. The F-4G was specially modified for suppression of enemy air defenses. See SEAD and Wild Weasels. Aircraft losses: 758.

F-8 Crusader   The Vought F-8 was a single-engine jet, carrier-based Navy fighter aircraft. It was armed with four 20mm cannons, rockets, missiles, and bombs. It was credited with the best MiG kill rate of any aircraft in the war: 19 to 3. It carried a crew of one. Aircraft losses: 181.

F-105 Thunderchief   The Republic F-105 Thunderchief was a single-engine jet fighter-bomber that bore the brunt of battle over North Vietnam during Operation Rolling Thunder (1965-1968). Nicknamed "Thud" by its crews, it had a 20mm cannon in its nose and carried 14,000 pounds of ordnance. In 1965, the two-seat electronic warfare versions became operational. Designated the EF-105, with later modifications called the F-105G, these aircraft and their crews were called "Wild Weasels" and proved highly successful at suppressing enemy air defenses. The fighter-bomber versions were eventually phased out and replaced by the F-4 and F-111. Of the 833 F-105s ever built, 382 were lost in combat and another 15 from other operational causes in Vietnam.

F-111 Aardvark   The General Dynamics F-111 was the most advanced fighter-bomber of the Vietnam War. It was powered by two jet turbofan engines and carried a crew of two. It was often fitted with a 20mm Gatling cannon in its nose and carried more than 31,000 pounds of ordnance. It had terrain avoidance radar but could climb to 66,000 feet. Its maximum speed was 1,650 mph. Late in the war a modified version, the **EF-111** proved extraordinarily effective in suppression of enemy air defenses. These aircraft and crews were called **Ravens.** Eleven aircraft lost.

HC-130 Hercules   A specially modified C-130 used for special missions and coordinating air rescue searches. See C-130.

HH-3E Jolly Green   The Sikorsky HH-3E Jolly Green Giant was the standard search and rescue helicopter used during the war. It was powered by two General Electric engines. It usually had a crew of four or five and could carry fifteen litter patients, twenty-two fully equipped combat troops, or 5,000 pounds of cargo. Its armament consisted of two 7.62mm machine guns. It also carried a 240-foot high speed hoist. It was developed from the Sikorsky CH-3 transport helicopter. Fourteen aircraft lost.

HH-53 Super JG   The Sikorsky HH-53's official designation was the Super Jolly Green Giant and was specifically designed for air rescue operations. The HH-53s first arrived in September 1967 and could hoist 20,000 pounds of cargo. Ten aircraft lost

KC-135 Stratotanker   The USAF KC-135 was developed from the Boeing 707 civilian cargo and passenger aircrafts. With a range of 1,500 miles, its mission was global refueling. They were especially critical for Operation Linebacker II in December 1972 for refueling B-52s from Guam. It could carry 200,000 pounds of transfer fuel, 88,000 pounds of cargo, or up to 37 passengers. The standard crew was five. KC-135s were also used for aeromedical evacuation and carried five or more additional medical personnel. Three aircraft lost.

O-1 Bird Dog

The Cessna O-1 Bird dog was a single-propeller, fixed-wing, observation aircraft, generally carrying a crew of one or two. It was used for forward air control, artillery observation, and general reconnaissance by the USAF, U.S. Army, U.S. Marines and the South Vietnamese Army and Air Force in Vietnam. It had a maximum speed of 135 mph. A total of 469 U.S. Bird Dogs were lost during the Vietnam War.

O-2 Skymaster

The faster (200 mph) twin-engine O-2 eventually replaced the O-1 Bird Dogs. Aircraft lost: 104.

OH-23 Raven

A small bubble-nosed observation and reconnaissance helicopter sometimes used in conjunction with AH-1 and UH-1 gunship helicopters. Armed with two machine guns mounted in the door, the crew consisted of one pilot and a gunner. They were sometimes accompanied by the crew chief who could act as an additional gunner. Cruising speed was only 75 mph. This was the type helicopter flown by WO1 Hugh Thompson and his crew in opposing and curtailing the My Lai Massacre. Aircraft losses: 95.

RA-5 Vigilante

The North American RA-5 Vigilante was a twin-engine turbojet, carrier-based Navy reconnaissance aircraft. It carried a crew of two. Aircraft losses: 26.

T-10

See U-10 Super Courier

T-28 Trojan

A single-engine propeller driven trainer built by North American. In Vietnam it carried ordnance on six wing stations and was used both for training and counterinsurgency. Aircraft losses: 23.

UH-1   Iroquois

Nicknamed "Huey," the UH-1 series was the most common Army helicopter in Vietnam. Over 7,000 were in service during the war. It was most often used for troop transport (carrying 9-12 combat troops) and for direct aerial fire support. The typical armament of troop-carrying Hueys was two door-mounted machine guns. More elaborately armed versions, designated gunships, also had some combination of nose (or chin) mounted machine guns, Gatling guns, 20 mm cannons, or rocket launchers. The most elaborately armed were specially modified and equipped **AH-1 Cobra** gunships. These were faster, generally more heavily armored, and carried additional strike weapons such as grenade launchers and missiles. Total UH-1/AH-1 losses: 3,305, with 2277 crewmembers and 532 passengers killed in action.

U-10 Super Courier The U-10 is a single-engine prop, light utility aircraft used by Air Commando Squadrons. It is capable of very short take-offs and landings, and although it cruises at 160 mph, it can also fly at speeds of only 25 to 35 mph. It carries a pilot and up to five passengers. It was sometimes referred to as a T-10 when used to train South Vietnamese pilots early in the war. Twelve aircraft lost.

NOTE 1: This is not an all-inclusive list of American aircraft used during the war. Total fixed-wing (excluding helicopters) losses for all services from 1962 through 1973 were 3,720. Total helicopter losses from all services were 4,868 of the 11,827 deployed.

NOTE 2: Unless otherwise specified the aircraft losses cited are total losses from all causes.

APPENDIX 5

Military Organization and Cited Infantry Weapons[311]

**Organization Terminology for U.S. Army and Marine infantry units
(Vietnam era)
Normal Manpower Strength
Usual Rank of Leader or Commanding Officer (CO)**

UNIT	STRENGTH	USUAL RANK OF LEADER/CO
Squad	Typically about 9 men	Staff Sergeant, or Sergeant
Platoon	30-45 men in 3-4 squads	Lieutenant
Company	Typically 125-200 men in 3-4 platoons	Captain
Battalion	Typically 400-900 men in 3-5 companies	Lt. Col., or senior Major
Regiment*	Typically 2,000-3,600 men in 3 to 4 battalions. NVA full strength infantry regiments had about 2,000 men	Colonel
Brigade*	Typically about 5,000 men in several regiments or battalions.	Brigadier General or Colonel
Division*	U.S. infantry divisions were typically 15,000-20,000 men; Chinese, and Soviet Bloc infantry divisions were more typically about 10,000 men. NVA infantry divisions had only about 8,750 men at full strength, about one half the size of U.S. divisions.	Major General

*Notes: U.S. Army Infantry brigades did not have regimental components in the Vietnam War. They were generally commanded by a colonel and made up of several battalions. Army airborne, armored, and cavalry divisions are generally smaller than infantry divisions. Armored divisions have typically had about 10,000 men.

Organization Terminology for USAF and Naval Air Units
Typical Number of Aircraft in Unit
Usual Rank of Leader or Commanding Officer (CO)

	Number of Aircraft	USAF	Navy
		RANK OF CO	
Flight	Typically 3-4 aircraft	Captain, Major	Lt.,Lt. Cdr.
Squadron	Typically 12-16 aircraft	Lt. Col.	Cdr.
Group	3-4 squadrons	Col.	Captain
Wing	Several Groups or multiple Squadrons	Brig. General	Rear Admiral

Primary U.S. and Soviet Bloc Infantry Weapons
Mentioned in this Book.

AK-47 The highly esteemed standard automatic rifle of the Soviet Bloc, first developed by Mikhail Kalashnikov in 1947. Because of its ease of use, fire-power and durability, it is a favorite assault weapon around the world. It is magazine-fed and uses a 7.62mm cartridge.

B-40 A common Soviet Bloc shoulder-operated rocket launcher

M16 The standard semi-automatic and automatic, magazine-fed rifle used by the U.S. Army in Vietnam. It uses the standard 5.56mm NATO cartridge.

M60 The standard belt-fed machine gun carried by U.S. infantry units in the Vietnam War. It can be fired from the shoulder or by using its own folding bipod, or can be attached to a tripod. It was carried by one man but was most frequently used as a crew-served weapon manned by a gunner, an assistant gunner, and an ammunition carrier. It can fire 550 rounds of 7.62mm ammunition per minute.

CHAPTER NOTES

[1] Lind, Michael; *Vietnam: The Necessary War* (Touchstone/Simon & Schuster, New York, 1999) 141.

[2] Palmer, Dave Richard; *Summons of the Trumpet: U.S.—Vietnam in Perspective* (Presidio Press, San Rafael, Ca., 1978) 123.

[3] Sharp, Admiral U.S.G; *Strategy for Defeat: Vietnam in Retrospect* (Presidio Press, Novato, Ca., 1978) 184, 190-198.

[4] Palmer; 47.

[5] Sharp; 48.

[6] Nixon, Richard; *No More Vietnams* (Arbor House, New York, 1985) 32-37.

[7] Central Intelligence Agency; The 2008 World Factbook, Vietnam, North Korea, South Korea, World, United States. Published online.

[8] Johnstone, Patrick; *Operation World* (Authentic Media, Tyrone, Ga., 2001.) 675-677.

[9] Montagnard Foundation; Spartanburg, SC. Online.

[10] Sharpe; 14.

[11] Palmer; 129, 149.

[12] Courtois, Stephane et al; *The Black Book of Communism: Crimes, Terror, Repression* (Harvard University Press, Cambridge, Ma., 1999) 4, 589.

[13] Rummel, R. J; *Death By Government* (Transaction Publishers, New Brunswick, NJ, 1994) 4, 7, 8, 151, 165, 282.

[14] Nixon; 204-205, 207.

[15] John F. Kennedy, Jan. 20, 1961, as quoted in *Speeches that changed the world* (London: Smith-Davies, 2005) 142-147.

[16] Palmer; 2.

[17] Sharpe; 80.

[18] Palmer; 75, 149.

[19] Nixon; 202-205, 207.

[20] Summers, Harry G. Jr. *The Vietnam War Almanac* (Ballantine Books/Random House, New York, 1985) 111-113.

[21] Nixon; 72.

[22] Nixon; 62.

[23] Palmer; 26.

[24] Palmer; 42.

[25] Palmer; 41.

[26] Nixon; 67.

[27] Nixon; 68.

[28] Nixon; 72.

[29] Nixon; 48.

[30] Nixon; 39.
[31] Ibid.
[32] Nixon; 36.
[33] Courtois; 4, 589.
[34] Nixon; 63.
[35] Nixon; 64.
[36] Nixon; 65.
[37] My own calculation based on Johnstone; 675-677.
[38] Nixon; 35.
[39] Nixon; 66.
[40] Ibid.
[41] Summers, Harry G. Jr. Historical Atlas of the Vietnam War (Houghton-Mifflin, New York, 1995) 96.
[42] Hobson, Chris. Vietnam Air Losses: United States Air Force, Navy, and Marine Corps Fixed-Wing Losses in Southeast Asia 1961-1973. (Midland Publishing, England, 2001) 239, 268-271.
[43] Chinnery, Philip D. *Air Commando.* (St. Martin's Press, New York, 1994, 1997) 171-176.
[44] Chapter 5 was compiled from the author's own reports, flight records, notes, and letters. Brief accounts of the incident are also covered in Chinnery, 171; Hobson, 89; and Orr (See Bibliography), 201. Differences in dates reflect the twelve hour time difference between Thailand and Washington, D. C.
[45] Palmer; 47. Sharp, 48.
[46] Correll, John T. "Rolling Thunder," *Air Force Magazine*, March 2005, 62.
[47] Palmer; 76.
[48] Ibid.
[49] Palmer; 77. Sharp; 64.
[50] Sharp; 87.
[51] Correll; 63.
[52] Palmer; 123.
[53] Sharp; 80.
[54] Sharp; 2-3.
[55] Correll; 63-64.
[56] Correll; 61-62.
[57] Correll; 62.
[58] Ibid.
[59] Correll; 63.
[60] Correll; 61.
[61] Summers; Almanac. 33, 40, 44.

[62] Summers, Almanac; on page 112 has 666,000 KIA for North Vietnam, largely based on a statement by General Giap. See also citation 192.

[63] Summers; Almanac. 112-113.

[64] Palmer; 127. Sharp; 116-119.

[65] Thompson, Wayne. To Hanoi and Back: The United States Air Force and North Vietnam 1966-1973. (University Press of the Pacific, Honolulu, 2005) 31.

[66] Palmer; 15.

[67] Sharp; 49, 53, 62.

[68] Sharp; 77.

[69] Sharp; 141.

[70] Palmer; 47. Sharp; 48.

[71] Palmer; 84-89. Summers, Almanac; 38.

[72] Carland, John M; *Combat Operations—Stemming the Tide: May 1965 to October 1966.* Washington, D. C.: Center for Military History, United States Army, 2000.

[73] Palmer; 121.

[74] Summers; Almanac; 40.

[75] Sharp; 120.

[76] Palmer; 129, 149.

[77] Sharp; 188.

[78] Sharp; 177-185.

[79] Sharp; 192.

[80] Sharp; 197.

[81] Palmer; 121, Summers, Almanac 40.

[82] Palmer; 129, 149.

[83] Palmer; 148-149.

[84] Palmer; 164-165.

[85] See the official website of the Battle of Dien Bien Phu. www.dienbienphu.org/english

[86] Palmer; 167.

[87] Palmer; 168.

[88] Palmer; 186.

[89] Sharp; 218.

[90] Palmer; 183.

[91] Sharp; 214.

[92] Ibid.

[93] Palmer; 191.

[94] Palmer; 202

[95] Palmer; 202.

[96] Sharp; 214.

[97] Palmer; 202.

[98] Palmer; 203.

[99] Palmer; 164.

[100] Sharp; 232.

[101] Palmer; 204.

[102] Sharp; 141.

[103] Summers, Almanac; 47.

[104] Summers, Almanac, 48. See Wikipedia online articles on the "Chicago Seven" and "1968 Democratic Convention."

[105] Sharp; 231.

[106] Palmer; 208.

[107] Summers, Almanac; 44, 48.

[108] Sharp; 233.

[109] Summers, Almanac; 48, 55 with a slight adjustment. These are figures for the entire SVNAF, rather than just the ARVN.

[110] Spencer, Robert. *The Politically Incorrect Guide to Islam (And the Crusades).* (Regnery Publishing, Washington, 2005) 79-81.

[111] Trifkovic, Serge. *The Sword of the Prophet: Islam, History, Theology, Impact on the World.* (Regina Orthodox Press, Boston, 2002) 206.

[112] Sharp; 141, 231.

[113] Lane, Gen. Thomas A. *America On Trial: The War for Vietnam.* (Arlington House, New Rochelle, NY, 1971) 198.

[114] Lane; 200-201.

[115] Lane; 204.

[116] Lane; 205.

[117] Summers, Almanac; 48, 52.

[118] Palmer 227.

[119] Palmer; 232.

[120] Palmer; 236.

[121] Summers, Atlas; 53.

[122] Palmer; 236.

[123] Palmer; 242.

[124] Ibid.

[125] Palmer; 243.

[126] Ibid.

[127] Lane; 102.

[128] Palmer; 19, 54, 153, Nixon; 134.

[129] Summers, Almanac; 55.

[130] Palmer; 247-248.

[131] Palmer; 227, 245.

[132] Palmer; 249-250.

[133] Palmer; 252.

[134] Palmer; 250-254.

[135] Nixon; 146.

[136] Sharp; 246-247.

[137] Palmer; 253.

[138] Ibid

[139] Palmer; 252, 254.

[140] Willbanks, James H. *Abandoning Vietnam: How America Left and South Vietnam Lost Its War.* (University Press of Kansas, Lawrence, 2004, 2008) 152.

[141] Palmer; 254.

[142] Ibid.

[143] "Operation Linebacker." Online Wikipedia article. Source: Michel, Marshall L. *Clashes: Air Combat Over North Vietnam 1965-1972.* (Naval Institute Press, Annapolis, 1997) 244, 284, 288. See also:
Momyer, Gen. William W. *Airpower in Three Wars: World War II, Korea, and Vietnam.* (University Press of the Pacific, Honolulu, 1982, 2002) 33, 129, 138, 177, 199, 236-237.

[144] Ibid.

[145] Palmer; 258.

[146] The Teleproduction Group "12/72." The History of Operation Linebacker II. Online at www.teleproductiongroup.com/12_72.html. Date accessed December 5, 2008 to June 6, 2009.

[147] Ibid.

[148] Ibid.

[149] Ibid.

[150] Ibid.

[151] Ibid.

[152] "Operation Linebacker II," Online Wikipedia article at http://en.wikipedia.org/wiki/Operation_Linebacker_II. Date accessed December 5, 2008 to June 6, 2009.

[153] Palmer; 252-253. Sharp; 252-254.

[154] Nixon; 158, and Sharp; 254, have 1,300-1,600. A translation of *Victory in Vietnam* by Merle L. Pribbenow with Foreword by William J. Duiker, published by the University of Kansas Press in 2005, gives the North Vietnamese accounting at 1,624.

[155] Sharp; 254. Thompson, Sir Robert. *The Daily Telegraph,* London, September 8, 1972. Sir Robert Thompson, a retired Brigadier and expert on counterinsurgency was head of the British Advisory Mission to South Vietnam and therefore Washington. A similar NVA artillery attack on civilian refugees

was reported at An Loc during the same period, but no casualty estimates are available.

[156] Thompson; Ibid.
[157] Boyne, Walter J. "Operation Linebacker II," *Air Force Magazine;* November 1997. 57.
[158] Hobson; 96, 239.
[159] Sharp; 256.
[160] Sharp; 255.
[161] Summers, Almanac; 113.
[162] Nixon 185-6.
[163] Nixon; 191.
[164] Nixon; 75.
[165] Fanning, Louis A. *Betrayal In Vietnam.* (Arlington House, New Rochelle, NY, 1976) 17.
[166] Fanning; 18.
[167] Ibid.
[168] Summers, Almanac; 41.
[169] Summers, Almanac; 44.
[170] Palmer; 206.
[171] Based on Palmer; 202, 208.
[172] Palmer; 208-210.
[173] Summers, Almanac; 47-48.
[174] Summers, Almanac; 48. Fanning; 31.
[175] Nixon; 87.
[176] Fanning; 31.
[177] Ibid.
[178] U.S. House Committee on Internal Security, "Subversive Involvement in the Origin, Leadership, and Activities of the New Mobilization Committee to End the War in Vietnam and its Predecessor Organizations," 1970. Available online: Giorgi, LCDR Marco P, USN. Research Report: *Losing the War for U.S. Public Opinion During the Vietnam War.* Air University, Maxwell AFB, Alabama, April 2005. https://www.afresearch.org/skins/rims/q_mod_be0e99f3-fc56-4ccb-8dfe-670c0822a153/q_act_downloadpaper/q_obj_3deeff31-6780-4fe3-a54f-2e76f01093a7/display.aspx?rs=enginespage See particularly "The Communist Strategy, pages 19-23. Best accessed by Googling the author, Marco P. Giorgi. Accessed May 15, 2009 and June 17, 2009.
[179] Fanning; 32.
[180] Fanning; 35.
[181] Fanning; 37.
[182] Ibid.

[83] Fanning; 38.
[84] Fanning; 39.
[85] Fanning; 39-40.
[86] See Appendix 1 on My Lai.
[87] Nixon; 125-129.
[88] Summers; Almanac; 52.
[89] Summers, Almanac; 113.
[90] Nixon; 170-171.
[91] Ibid.
[92] The figure of 1,176,000 dead and missing is a North Vietnamese government figure released in 1995 and includes both the NVA and VC. Summers' *Vietnam War Almanac* figure of 666,000 published ten years earlier (page 112) is based on NVA Gen.Vo Nguyen Giap's statement that "they" (probably only the NVA) had lost 500,000 KIA from 1964 to 1969 alone. Since the estimate of NVA and VC dead for 1972 alone was 190,000, it makes Summer's printed estimate quite low.
[93] Nixon; 170.
[94] Nixon; 171-172.
[95] Nixon; 173, 175.
[96] Nixon; 177.
[97] Nixon; 179.
[98] Nixon; 185.
[99] Nixon; 185-186.
[100] Nixon; 187.
[101] Nixon; 191.
[102] Nixon; 191-192.
[103] Nixon; 192.
[104] Ibid.
[105] Nixon; 193-194.
[106] Nixon; 195.
[107] Nixon; 196.
[108] Nixon; 194.
[209] Nixon; 196.
[210] Nixon; 197.
[211] Nixon; 198-199.
[212] Nixon; 209-210.
[213] Nixon; 198, 203.
[214] Nixon; 199.
[215] Nixon; 167-170.
[216] Fanning; 191.

[217] This may have been a BBC paraphrase of the above quote.

[218] Fanning; 191.

[219] Nixon; 200.

[220] Fanning; 188.

[221] Fanning; 193.

[222] Schanberg, Sydney. "Indochina Without Americans: For Most a Better life." *New York Times;* April 13, 1975.

[223] Nixon; 202-205, 207. Courtois; 4. Rummel; 4, 7, 8, 151, 165, 282.

[224] Nixon; 205.

[225] Nixon; 203.

[226] Ibid.

[227] Nixon; 205.

[228] Nixon; 207.

[229] Ibid.

[230] Nixon; 205, 206.

[231] Nixon; 208.

[232] Ibid.

[233] Courtois; 4. Korea 50m

[234] Rummel; 4.

[235] Rummel; 4, 8, 80. Update on PRC, www.hawaii.edu/powerkills/NOTE2. HTM. Accessed March 15, 2009, June 12, 2009.

[236] Courtois; 546.

[237] Rummel; 8.

[238] Lind; 167-174.

[239] Winton Churchill, Nov. 16, 1934 Broadcast, London, "The Causes of War" as quoted in *Churchill Speaks: Collected Speeches in Peace and War1897-1963*; edited by Robert Rhodes James, M.P. (Chelsea House Publishers, 1980; U.K; Barnes and Noble, 1998), 586-588.

[240] Winston Churchill, Sept. 21, 1938 Press Statement, London, "Throwing a Small State to the Wolves" as quoted in *Churchill Speaks, 652.*

[241] Winston Churchill, Oct. 16, 1938 Radio Broadcast to America, London, "The Lights are Going Out" as quoted in Winston S. Churchill; *Never Give In! : The Best of Winston Churchill's Speeches* (Pimlico, a division of Random House UK, 2003), 184.

[242] From JFK's January 21, 1961 inaugural speech. See footnote 1, Chapter 1.

[243] Linn, page 246, has 50,000, but even that seems high, since the North Vietnamese estimated on 1,624 were killed in the eleven-day bombing of targets around Hanoi and Haiphong in December 1972, and U.S policy was to avoid unnecessary risk to civilian population areas.

[244] Sharp; 254. Nixon; 202-208.

[245] Tilley; John Shipley. L*incoln Takes Command: How Lincoln Got the War He Wanted.* (University of North Carolina Press, Chapel Hill, 1941) 261-267.

[246] Pancevski, Bojan. "Dresden Bombing Toll Lower than Thought." *Daily Telegraph*

[247] Wikipedia "Bombing of Tokyo" Source: U.S. Strategic Bombing Survey. Other estimates run as high as 100,000. Last accessed June 17, 2009. http://en.wikipedia.org/wiki/Bombing_of_Tokyo_in_World_War_II

[248] Tilley; 263.

[249] Nixon; 75.

[250] Summers, Harry G. Jr. *On Strategy: A Critical Analysis of the Vietnam War* (Ballantine Books, New York, 1982, 1995) 100.

[251] Summers; Almanac; 352. Palmer; 50, 62-66, 200, 202, 208.

[252] Nixon; 63-68.

[253] Sharp; 131.

[254] Nixon; 57-62.

[255] Summers, Almanac; 50.

[256] Summers, Strategy; 34-35.

[257] Summers, Strategy; 18-19, 26, 28, 31, 34-35.

[258] Summers, Almanac; 58.

[259] Nixon: 186.

[260] Summers; Almanac; 112.

[261] Angers, Trent. *The Forgotten Hero of My Lai: The Hugh Thompson Story.* (Acadian House Publishing, Lafayette, La., 1999) 12.

[262] Bilton, Michael. *Four Hours In My Lai.* (Penguin Books, New York, 1992) 75.

[263] Bilton; 75.

[264] Bilton; 283, according to the Army CID. See also Peers Report, March 14, 1970, contained in: Goldstein; Joseph et al. *The My Lai Massacre and Its Cover-up; Beyond the Reach of Law?* (Free Press/Macmillan, New York, 1976) 24, 317-345. Summary of Peers Report may be found online at www.umkc.edu/faculty/projects/trials/mylai/sumary_rpt.html

[265] Olson, James S. *My Lai: A Brief History with Documents.* (Bedford/St. Martin's, Boston, 1998) 99-102.

[266] Peers Summary Report.

[267] Goldstein; 24, 317-345.

[268] Ibid.

[269] Belknap; The Vietnam War on Trial: The My Lai Massacre and the Court-Martial of William Calley. (University Press of Kansas, Lawrence, 2002) 27-31.

[270] Belknap; 33-35.

[271] Bilton; 243.

272 Belknap; 47.

273 Bilton; 84-85.

274 Bilton; 85.

275 Bilton; 92.

276 Bilton; 94-95.

277 Bilton; 98.

278 Bilton; 99.

279 Bilton; 100-101.

280 Bilton; 101.

281 Bilton; 123.

282 Westmoreland, Gen. William C. *A Soldier Reports.* (Dell, New York, 1976, 1980) 498.

283 Bilton; 81.

284 Bilton; 169, 227.

285 Bilton; 125-126.

286 Anderson, David L., Ed. *Facing My Lai.* (University Press of Kansas, Lawrence, 1998) 126.

287 Anderson; 134.

288 Anderson; 137-138.

289 According to an August 5, 2006 Los Angeles Times news release, "Declassified Papers Show U.S. Atrocities in Vietnam went far beyond My Lai," a recently declassified file of Army CID investigations during the Vietnam War, indicated that the Army investigated 320 <u>alleged</u> war crimes—not including Son My/My Lai. These were for physical assault and sexual abuse of non-combatants and torture of enemy POWs. The number of deaths alleged was 194. Almost half (141) of the investigations were for alleged torture of enemy POWs by beating, electric shock, and simulated drowning (water-boarding, etc.). The Army found that the evidence was strong enough to formally charge 203 of the alleged perpetrators. Ultimately, 57 of them were court-martialed. Others, however, received administrative discipline. Of those who were court-martialed, 23 were convicted. Twelve of these received prison sentences of from six months to 20 years. Despite the LA Times' provocative title, the evidence is that, besides the My Lai/Son MY incidents in Quang Ngai Province in 1966, war crimes perpetrated by U.S. service personnel in Vietnam were relatively uncommon and did not exceed the experience of previous U.S. wars.

290 Nixon; 202-204. Courtois; 4, 589. Rummel; 4, 7, 8, 151, 165, 282.

291 Wikipedia http://en.wikipedia.org/wiki/Jeremiah_Denton.

292 Rochester, Stuart L Honor Bound: American Prisoners of War in Southeast Asia 1961-1973. (Naval Institute Press, Annapolis, Md., 1999) Appendix 1; 597.

293 Rochester; 146.

[294] Rochester; 597.

[295] The classified debriefing of Navy Lt. Dieter Dengler was read by all American aircraft crews flying over Laos. So far as I know, he is the only American to escape from a Pathet Lao prison and live to tell about it. He wrote a book, *Escape from Laos*, published by Presidio in 1997. He died in 2001 at the age of 62.

[296] Rochester; 413.

[297] Ibid.

[298] Rochester; 431.

[299] Rochester; 213.

[300] Ibid.

[301] This is my estimate based NVA division strength and VC regimental strength allowing for 50 percent VC attrition. Wikipedia has 5,000 to 10,000 range

[302] Hobson; 148-149.

[303] Wikipedia: http://en.wikipedia.org/wiki/Battle_of_Kham_Duc.

[304] Summers, Atlas; 144.

[305] POW/MIA Databases and Documents, Federal Research Division, Library of Congress. Vietnam-Era POW/MIA Database. Online summary at http://leweb2.loc.gov/pow/Nov0701.html.

[306] Ibid.

[307] Contact: National League of Families of American POWs and MIAs in Southeast Asia, 1605 K Street NW, Washington, D.C. 2006.

[308] Statistics on USAF, Navy, and Marine fixed wing aircraft losses are taken from Hobson; 268-271.

[309] Statistics on helicopter and Army aircraft are taken from US aircraft Losses, Southeast Asia, 1962-1973. Online at www.armchairgeneral.com.

[310] More detailed descriptions of the aircraft may be found online at Wikpedia, the Air Force Museum at Wright Patterson AFB, Ohio, the National Naval Aviation Museum at Pensacola, Florida, The Army Aviation Museum at Fort Rucker, Alabama, or under the name of the manufacturer.

[311] These descriptions come from the author's own accumulated knowledge.

SELECTED BIBLIOGRAPHY

General Vietnam War References

James R. Arnold; *Tet Offensive 1968: Turning Point in Vietnam.* (Osprey, Oxford, U.K., 1990)

Walter J. Boyne; "Operation Linebacker II," *Air Force Magazine,* November 1997.

Philip D. Chinnery; *Air Commando: Inside the Air Force Special Operations Command.* (Naval Institute Press, Annapolis, 1994; St. Martin's Paperbacks, 1997)

Carl von Clausewitz, *Principles of War,* Translated and edited by Hans W. Gatzke. (Stackpole, Harrisburg, PA, 1960)

John T. Correll; "Rolling Thunder." *Air Force Magazine,* March 2005.

Stephane Courtois, Nicolas Werth, Jean Louis Panne, Andrzej Paczkowski, Karel Bartosek, and Jean-Louis Margolin; *The Black Book of Communism: Crimes, Terror, Repression*, translated by Jonathan Murphy and Mark Kramer. (Harvard University Press, Cambridge, 1999)

Dien Bien Phu, The Official and History Site of the Battle, 1999-2000: www.dienbienphu.org/english Accessed March 15, 2009.

Louis A. Fanning; *Betrayal in Vietnam.* (Arlington House, New Rochelle, NY 1976)

Chris Hobson; *Vietnam Air Losses: United States Air Force, Navy and Marine Corp Fixed-Wing Aircraft Losses in Southeast Asia 1961-1973.* (Midland Publishing, Hinckley, England, *2001)*

Orr Kelly; *From a Dark Sky: The Story of U.S. Air Force Special Operations.* (Pocket Books/Simon and Schuster, New York, 1996)

Henry A. Kissinger, *The White House Years.* (Little, Brown, and Co., Boston, *1979)*

Henry A. Kissinger; *Years of Renewal.* (Simon and Schuster, New York, 1999)

General Thomas A. Lane; *America on Trial: The War for Vietnam.* (Arlington House, New Rochelle, NY, 1971)

Michael Lind; *Vietnam: The Necessary War—A Reinterpretation of America's Most Disastrous War.* (*Simon* and Schuster, New York, 1999)

H. R. McMaster; *Dereliction of Duty. (HarperCollins, New York,* 1997)

Robert S. McNamara; *In Retrospect: The Tragedy and Lessons of Vietnam.* (Times Book/Random House, New York, 1995)

Marshall L. Michel III; *The Eleven Days of Christmas: America's Last Vietnam Battle.* (Encounter Books, San Francisco, 2002)

General William W. Momyer; *Airpower in Three Wars: World War II, Korea, and Vietnam.* (University Press of the Pacific, Honolulu, 1982, 2002)

Lt. General Harold G. Moore and Joseph L. Galloway; *We Were Soldiers Once...And Young: Ia Drang—the Battle That Changed the War in Vietnam.* (Ballantine, New York 1992)

Lt. General Harold G. Moore and Joseph L. Galloway; *We Are Soldiers Still: A Journey Back to the Battlefields of Vietnam.* (HarperCollins, New York, 2008)

Richard Nixon; *No More Vietnams.* (Arbor House, New York, 1985)

Don Oberdorfer; *Tet! The Turning Point in the Vietnam War.* (Johns Hopkins University Press, Baltimore, 1971)

Dave Richard Palmer; *Summons of the Trumpet; U.S.—Vietnam in Perspective.* (Presidio Press, San Rafael, CA, 1978)

R. J. Rummel; *Death by Government.* (Transaction Publishers, New Brunswick, NJ, 1994)

David F. Schmitz; *The Tet Offensive: Politics, War, and Public Opinion.* (Rowan and Littlefield, Lanham, Md., 2005)

Robert D. Schulzinger; *A Time for War: The United States and Vietnam, 1941-1975.* (Oxford University Press, New York, 1997)

Admiral U.S.G. Sharp; *Strategy for Defeat: Vietnam in Retrospect.* Presidio Press, Novato, CA, 1978)

Harry G. Summers, Jr; *On Strategy: A Critical Analysis of the Vietnam War.* (Ballantine, New York, *1982)*

Harry G. Summers, Jr; *The Vietnam Almanac.* (Presidio Press/Random House, New York, *1985*)

Harry G. Summers, Jr. Historical *Atlas of the Vietnam War.* (Houghton Mifflin, Boston *1995)*

The Teleproduction Group; "12/72" Operation Linebacker II—Triumph and Tragedy at 30,000 Feet, 2003-2006: www.teleproductiongroup.com/original-programs.html Accessed December 15, 2008.

W. Scott Thompson and Donaldson B. Frizzell; editors: *The Lessons of Vietnam.* (Crane, Russak & Co., New York, 1977)

Wayne Thompson; *To Hanoi and Back; The United States Air Force and North Vietnam 1966-1973.* (University Press of the Pacific, Honolulu, 2000, 2005)

General William C. Westmoreland; *A Soldier Reports.* (Dell, New York, 1976, 1980)

James H. Willbanks; *The Tet Offensive: A Concise History.* (Columbia University press, New York, 2006)

James H. Willbanks; *Abandoning Vietnam: How America Left and South Vietnam Lost Its War.* (University Press of Kansas, Lawrence, 2004, 2008)

My Lai References

Several of the general references used for this book include excellent short summaries of the My Lai atrocity, but the subject is quite complex. The references below describe the tragic details and their consequences from several points of view. While several of these books offer excellent accounts and analysis of the massacre, cover-up, investigations, hearings, trials, and political ramifications, the general references give a more balanced account of the overall issues of the Vietnam War.

David L. Anderson, Editor; *Facing My Lai: Moving Beyond the Massacre.* University Press of Kansas, Lawrence, *1998)*

Trent Angers; *The Forgotten Hero of My Lai: The Hugh Thompson Story.* (Acadian House, Lafayette, La., 1999)

Michael R. Belknap; *The Vietnam War on Trial: The My Lai Massacre and the Court-Martial of Lieutenant Calley.* (University Press of Kansas, Lawrence, 2002)

Michael Bilton and Kevin Sim; *Four Hours in My Lai*. (Penguin, New York, 1992)

Joseph Goldstein, Burke Marshall, and Jack Schwartz; *The My Lai Massacre and Its Cover-up: Beyond the Reach of Law? 1976*. (Free Press/Macmillan, New York, 1976) Documents include the *Peers Report*.

James S. Olson and Randy Roberts; *My Lai: A Brief History with Documents*. (Bedford/St. Martin's, Boston,1998)

John Sack; *Lieutenant Calley: His Own Story*. (Viking Press, New York, 1971)

Prisoners of War References

Stuart L. Rochester and Frederick Kiley; *Honor Bound—American Prisoners of War in Southeast Asia 1961-1973*. (Naval Institute Press, Annapolis, 1999) This 620 page book is strongly recommended as a reference to anyone wishing to research the history and treatment of U.S. POWs during the Vietnam War.

John G. Hubbell, et al; P.O.W.: A Definitive History of the American Prisoner-Of-War Experience in Vietnam, 1964-1973. (Reader's Digest Press, 1976; iUniverse.com, Lincoln, NE, 1990)

Special References Pertaining to Future Potential Conflicts in the Middle East

Robert Spencer; *Islam Unveiled: Disturbing Questions about the World's Fastest-Growing Faith*. (Encounter Books, San Francisco, 2002)

Robert Spencer: *Onward Muslim Soldiers: How Jihad Still Threatens America and the West*. (Regnery, Washington, DC, 2003)

Robert Spencer; *The Politically Incorrect Guide to Islam (and the Crusades)*. (Regnery, Washington, DC, 2005)

Serge Trifkovic; *Sword of the Prophet: History, Theology, and Impact on the World*. (Regina Orthodox Press, Boston, 2004)

Serge Trifkovic; *Defeating Jihad: How the War on Terror May Yet Be Won, in Spite of Ourselves*. (Regina Orthodox Press, Boston, 2006)

ABOUT THE AUTHOR

Leonard M. (Mike) Scruggs (BS, University of Georgia; MBA Stanford University) is a combat veteran of the Vietnam War, serving as an intelligence officer and navigator in the USAF from 1961 to 1969. While serving in the 606th Air Commando Squadron as an A-26 crewmember, he was awarded the Distinguished Flying Cross, Purple Heart and Air Medal with Oak Leaf Cluster. Since his retirement as an investment executive with a major Wall Street firm in 2005, he has published more than 150 articles on American history and current political affairs. He is also the author of *The Un-Civil War: Truths Your Teacher Never Told You*. In addition, he has served as Chairman of the Board of a Classical Christian School. He is a North Carolina real estate broker living and writing in Hendersonville, North Carolina.